The Future of the Trade Unions

Books by the same author

Lord Salisbury (1975)

The Fifth Estate: Britain's Trade Unions in the Modern World (1978 and 1980)

Workers and the New Depression (1982)

The Trade Union Question in British Politics since 1945 (1993)

The Future of the Trade Unions

Robert Taylor

With an Introduction by John Monks

First published in Great Britain in 1994 by
André Deutsch Limited
106 Great Russell Street
London WC1B 3LJ

ISBN 0 233 98900 5

Cataloguing-in-Publication data available for this title
from the British Library

Printed in Great Britain by
WBC, Bridgend

CONTENTS

ACKNOWLEDGEMENTS

I would like to thank the TUC General Secretary John Monks and David Lea, the TUC's Assistant General Secretary, for commissioning me to write this book as part of the TUC's renewal programme.

Its contents are based primarily on the written and oral evidence provided by trade unions, companies and other bodies to the House of Commons Employment Select Committee in its own inquiry into the future of the trade unions in 1993–1994. I would like to acknowledge that I used the reports of that evidence published by HMSO. I have also used additional primary and secondary source material which I have found of relevance to the subject.

I have sought to reflect the views of the unions and the TUC on a wide range of issues but I was given the scope within the TUC commission to express my own views and have taken that opportunity.

I would also like to take this opportunity to thank Lord Bill McCarthy for his invaluable advice, particularly on structure. Ian Brinkley and Paul Hackett in the TUC's Economic and Social Affairs Department both provided important assistance in its completion. Christine Coates, the TUC Librarian, prepared the index in record time.

I also wish to acknowledge with appreciation the work of Sylvia Carroll of the TUC in putting the text into its final shape. Her assistance and that of Zoë Ross of André Deutsch has been invaluable.

John Cleary and Joanna Walker of André Deutsch's Production Department have shown unfailing patience in keeping me more or less to the ambitious deadlines we had set.

I would like, finally, to thank Tom Rosenthal, Chairman and Managing Director of André Deutsch for his encouragement at every stage in a venture which would not have been possible in the timescale without his total commitment.

JUNE 1994 ROBERT TAYLOR

ABBREVIATIONS

ACAS	Advisory, Conciliation and Arbitration Service
AEEU	Amalgamated Engineering and Electrical Union
ASLEF	Associated Society of Locomotive Engineers and Firemen
AUT	Association of University Teachers
BIFU	Banking, Insurance and Finance Union
CAB	Citizens Advice Bureaux
CBI	Confederation of British Industry
CIA	Chemical Industries Association
CMA	Communication Managers' Association
CPSA	Civil and Public Services Association
CSEU	Confederation of Shipbuilding and Engineering Unions
EC	European Community
EEF	Engineering Employers' Federation
EMA	Engineers and Managers Association
EOC	Equal Opportunities Commission
EU	European Union
ETUC	European Trade Union Confederation
FBU	Fire Brigades Union
GATT	General Agreement on Tariffs and Trade
GPMU	Graphical, Paper and Media Union
HSC	Health and Safety Commission
HRM	Human Resource Management
ICFTU	International Confederation of Free Trade Unions
IDS	Incomes Data Services
ILO	International Labour Organisation
IMF	International Metalworkers Federation
IRSF	Inland Revenue Staff Federation
IOD	Institute of Directors
IPM	Institute of Personnel Management
IPMS	Institution of Professionals, Managers and Specialists

LRD	Labour Research Department
MSF	Manufacturing Science Finance Union
NATFHE	National Association for Teachers in Further and Higher Education
NCU	National Communications Union
NUCPS	National Union of Civil and Public Servants
NUJ	National Union of Journalists
OECD	Organisation for Economic Cooperation and Development
PSI	Policy Studies Institute
RMT	National Union of Rail, Maritime and Transport Workers
STE	Society of Telecom Executives
TEC	Training and Enterprise Councils
TGWU	Transport and General Workers Union
TUC	Trades Union Congress
TQM	Total Quality Management
UCW	Union of Communication Workers
UCATT	Union of Construction, Allied Trades and Technicians
USDAW	Union of Shop, Distributive and Allied Workers

Introduction

The time is ripe for a resurgence of trade unionism in Britain and the TUC is gearing itself to help engender that resurgence. In 1994, we have begun a relaunch process to create a new TUC adapted to campaigning across the nation on behalf of people at work – or who would like to be at work.

Workers today need the support of trade unions as much as at any time in the past 100 years. And as I travel around the country, talking to workers and employers I find a great identification with my trade union message that the way forward for Britain lies in a combination of a strong commitment to economic success and a strong commitment to social justice. The two go together; they are not alternative strategies, as the currently dominant ideology of the government brazenly asserts.

Advanced industrial societies work best and provide the greatest opportunities for all their citizens when there is a strong democratic trade union movement working within a framework of a high level of employment and wide involvement in structural change.

Responding to New Pressures

The re-awakening of trade unionism as a central force in British public life is necessary but by no means inevitable. It will depend on our efforts to convince workers, and especially workers in the newly developing industries and services, that it is in their interests to join and play an active part in the trade union movement. Equally it is up to those of us within the unions to show employers, politicians and the community as a whole that we have a valuable and positive contribution to make to the development of public policy.

The new trade unionism will not be the same as that

of the 1960s or 1970s. Trade unions are often portrayed by our critics as unchanging, resistant to new ideas. But we can demonstrate – and Robert Taylor does this eloquently – that throughout our history we have adapted to meet the challenge of new circumstances and have done so as effectively as any organisation in public life.

In 1913 the TUC's membership was dominated by miners and cotton textile workers. After the First World War those industries went into decline and the pessimists forecast the inexorable decline and even death of trade unionism. Indeed, in Britain, union membership did decline for a time, but it bounced back as a result of the unions' achievement in organising in the new and growing industries and in the developing public sector. The motor vehicle industry, initially a sector lacking union organisation, was turned into a stronghold of union membership. Further periods of renewal were associated with the membership growth among white collar workers and women workers. The changes of the past decade have been greater than any in our history.

It has to be recalled that trade union membership is not a static pool into which membership is added and withdrawn as seen through annual figures, it is more a fast flowing river whose depth is measured once a year. For just as people move in and out of jobs, so they move in and out of the trade union movement. But those who join all do so as a matter of choice because they believe that a union can do something for them that no other organisation can. Such a commitment by so many at a time, when public policy has been hostile and when changing patterns of work make it harder for unions to reach new recruits, is to my mind an achievement which deserves far greater credit than it has been given to date.

The New Agenda

Trade unionism in Britain today is like a pruned back plant, but its roots are deep and the soil is fertile. The potential for it to grow again, albeit in a different shape, is certainly there. The strength of its roots can be seen from the membership levels and influence which we have retained. As regards the quality of the soil an astute analysis of the last Workplace Industrial Relations Survey concluded that the conditions today resemble those which led to the growth of trade unionism in the last century. That might seem a paradoxical judgement on a hundred years of progress in industrial relations, but it would certainly ring true, say, to many of the 800,000 workers who turn in desperation to the Citizens' Advice Bureaux each year because of problems with their employer.

It would also be echoed by the woman working at home for a clothing company who receives a meagre payment for turning the cloth delivered each week to her door into finished goods; a woman who has no idea about her rights, not a clue what to do if the cloth stops arriving or the payment is reduced or if she develops a long term injury as a result of the repetitive work. It would not seem far fetched either to a freelance accountant previously well paid by a multinational company looking forward to a secure career in management, but now shaken out as a result of the last review. She has to make do with odd temporary jobs, never sure how long they will last, stuck with a personal pension of dubious worth and facing the prospect of insecurity all the way through to retirement, and all the time she has to pay a mortgage and meet other commitments taken on when the prospects looked so much better.

It is workers like these, insecure, ill-informed about their rights, victims of the new flexibility, who need someone to turn to, someone informed about rights, able to speak for them, to advise and, if necessary, to go to court on their behalf. Such a role for unions has been widely acknowledged. But as Robert Taylor shows, it is the collective role of trade unions that differentiates them from the insurance company and the firms of solicitors. Unions have a wider vision, a desire not just to fight for individuals but to play a part improving society as a whole for the benefit of people at work and their families.

Unions will continue to be relevant as the nature of work changes in the future. Workers on individual contracts, the self-employed, people moving between jobs, people working in small firms – all of them will still benefit from union services, like advice on contract terms, pensions and employment rights. Unions can also monitor performance related pay systems and see that they're fair and don't discriminate. And unions will still represent individuals when problems arise.

Unions have been aware of the implications of the changing gender balance in the workforce. Long before John Major announced Opportunity 2000, unions had been bringing issues like childcare, maternity leave and equal pay to the bargaining table. The facts show that unions have a strong sword of justice effect, narrowing differentials based on gender and race. Over the past decade unions have radically changed their priorities and structures to address the needs of women workers.

Within the TUC we have recognised the scale of the challenge facing unions in Britain today. We have acknowledged that our old ways of working are not necessarily the best way of providing the support which our unions and their members need if they are to take advantage of the potential which is there for a resurgence of trade unionism. We are determined to focus our resources on the key issues, such as jobs, the rights of people at work, and developing a trade union response to new management styles, characterised as human resource management. We also want to provide better services for unions in areas like health and safety, equal rights, and pension protection. It is through a better targeting of our activities that we believe we can play our part in turning the potential for the resurgence of trade unionism into a reality.

The Failures of Public Policy

In the 1980s many people took seriously the government's claims that an economic miracle was being achieved, equivalent to that which took place in West Germany in the 1950s. Now the evidence to support those claims has been shown up to be no more than a mirage, based on an unsustainable boom built on North Sea oil revenues and an unsustainable fiscal policy based on financial deregulation and the receipts of public asset sales being used to finance current expenditures. The net result however is that Britain is now further down the European league table than it was in 1980.

The recession of the early 1990s has revealed the reality of a barren landscape left behind by the destruction of much of our manufacturing industry and an unemployment level so high that it became fashionable to argue that the concept of 'full employment' – for so long one of the central principles of economic policy – should be removed from the political dictionary.

Throughout the 1980s trade unions laboured under an exceedingly heavy burden. The continuous barrage of anti-union legislation made it harder for unions to undertake their job of protecting their members interests at work. The burdens imposed by the 1993 Act – demanding, for instance, far more stringent requirements on the collection of trade union subscriptions deducted direct from the members' pay packets – are as great as any placed on unions during the 1980s. All this legislation was intended to limit trade union power as an essential ingredient of a strategy to improve economic performance. Judged by the present condition of the British economy that policy has failed.

At the same time, the deregulation model prized by the British government is now under heavy criticism in the United States from where it originated. The US Labour Secretary, Robert Reich, has remarked memorably of deregulation: 'When they talk of flexibility, look out for your wallet' – a sentiment I have no doubt many British workers would endorse.

Social Partnership and Reciprocal Responsibility

We are now reaching for a new balance of rights and responsibilities, in society as a whole, whether these concern the running of companies or the public agencies, rights as consumers and rights as citizens. There is such a thing as society. Both history and international comparisons in the present day demonstrate the close correlation between strong trade union organisation and the possibility of a gradual reduction in inequality and the elimination of poverty and of deprivation. These lessons need to be learnt once again in Britain, where growing inequality is drawing Britain up a cul-de-sac.

The concept of social partnership of workers, employers and governments co-operating for the common good is a central feature of the European way of doing things.

To take a current example which is both practical and symbolic – the Directive on Information and Consultation. The more we deal with multinational companies the more we realise that they cannot be subject to public influence or made accountable by the law and practice of any one country. They can – and do – allocate resources between countries and continents to meet their own financial goals.

The current Conservative government may opt out as much as they like, but this stance is increasingly untenable and one way or another, be it through the obligation on multinational companies to establish workers councils for Europe as a whole or through British workers demanding parity with their European colleagues, those standards will arrive here.

This debate has a much wider significance for the future

of British trade unionism. The process of thinking through how we would apply this European Directive will inevitably spotlight all the major decisions which we will need to take with a view to introducing a broader scheme of statutory representation in Britain.

For example, the Directive comprises a most ingenious mixture of two ingredients: the statutory back-up and the scope for agreed action within a broad framework. In particular, the Directive states that a Special Negotiating Body of employee representatives would have the right to agree virtually any machinery with the employer and only if agreement is not reached would the necessarily precise requirements of the statutory fall-back procedure become applicable. It is, of course, at that point and only at that point, that there would be an obligation to observe statutory rules governing candidates, constituencies and so on.

The general approach to social dialogue at European level contains many useful lessons for Britain. It demonstrates that an industrial relations system can be rooted in the search for consensus. It means institutions that are designed to generate agreement rather that resolve conflict. This requires a cultural change on the part of British employers. In particular it means that employers must recognise the legitimate demands of their employees for collective representation. Furthermore, companies must recognise that they have social obligations – it is not only shareholders who have a stake in a company's success. The European Elections in June 1994 have shown that the British people believe in the Social Chapter as an integral part of the European Union.

Full Employment and Sustainable Growth

Central to all our futures is convincing the nation as a whole that full employment is an attainable, if not an easy, goal.

It will involve a combination of competitive success and innovation in our productive industries.

It will require difficult choices by government, employers and trade unions to ensure that we create secure jobs and achieve sustainable, non-inflationary growth.

It will require difficult choices to develop a bargaining agenda that puts training and equal opportunities at the top of the list.

Above all it must be recognised that work is not simply the

price that we pay for our leisure. Work is of value because it gives people a sense of achievement, self-respect and independence. Determined efforts to raise the quality of working life and create full employment are likely to lead to a more stable and secure society.

Reaching this goal requires social partnership and a shared commitment to full employment at both national and international level. The trade union movement is ready to play its part and highly capable of doing so.

About this Book

Robert Taylor's book owes its origins to the inquiry by the House of Commons Employment Select Committee into the Future of Trade Unions. The TUC and many individual unions undertook a great deal of work to prepare both written and oral evidence for the Committee. Employers and other organisations also provided evidence.

These various submissions form much of the raw material for this book but Robert Taylor has not relied solely on this one source. As one would expect from a journalist of his quality he has sought out other material to supplement or, in some cases, counter some of that presented to the Committee. The result is a thorough and highly readable account of where unions fit into working life in Britain today and how we can expect their role to develop in the near future. I hope it will provide a basis for debate among our friends and critics alike.

John Monks
General Secretary
TUC

CHAPTER ONE

The Relevance of the Trade Unions

Over recent years it has become fashionable in many quarters to write off Britain's trade unions, to deride them as obsolete institutions out of touch with the new realities and incapable of change. Some critics have even suggested that they have completed the historical mission that many of them began in the last century. Not so. On the contrary, most of them are still very much alive as they seek in different ways to adapt to the severe challenges that confront them through intensive global competitiveness and the adverse social consequences of an increasingly deregulated and polarised labour market.

In today's world of individual employment contracts, performance-related pay schemes, Human Resource and Total Quality Management and all the other ingredients of the so-called 'new' workplace, trade unions are often wrongly regarded as anachronistic obstacles to the success of the market economy. As collective voluntary organisations that represent employees in the workplace, it is argued, trade unions no longer serve a useful purpose.

The British government certainly appears to hold this opinion very strongly. 'Unions were and remain in secular decline,' the Department of Employment explained to the Commons Employment Committee. 'Unions have apparently failed to adjust to the restructuring of the economy over the last fifteen years.' 'Unions remain important participants in the labour market,' it conceded, but went on to assert, 'all signs, however, point to their long term decline. The main reason for this is their inability to adapt to rapidly changing conditions in the labour market and the economy more generally where competitive pressures have become more intense.'[1]

'There is a new recognition of the role and importance of

the individual employee,' argued the government's February 1992 document, People, Jobs and Opportunity.

> Traditional patterns of industrial relations based on collective bargaining and collective agreements seem increasingly inappropriate and are in decline. Many employers are replacing outdated personnel policies with new policies for human resource management, which put the emphasis on developing the talents and capacities of each individual employee. Many are also looking to communicate directly with their employees rather than through the medium of a trade union or formal works council.

In the government's view the need is to 'energise the country's workforce by opening up choice and opportunity and responding to the growing expectations and aspirations of individuals.'[2] In this vision of the future, it remains unclear whether any role at all – let alone an independent one – can be found for the trade unions to perform.

As Employment Secretary David Hunt asserted in a speech to the Industrial Society in March 1994:

> We have seen a cultural shift in this country. People have become more individualistic. They are less inclined to belong to mass organisations like trade unions. They do not identify with such bodies. The union members of the future will be motivated by pragmatic considerations when joining a union, not by some spurious notion of class solidarity. Value for money will be uppermost in their minds. Unions clearly need to sell themselves to individuals more effectively. The sales pitch will need to focus more and more on the value of membership to each individual.[3]

The belief that employees are self-regarding individuals, who have less need than in the past to organise themselves collectively to defend or promote their interests in the workplace, is also held strongly by the Institute of Directors. As that right-wing business organisation argued:

> Looking at some of Britain's most competitive and successful companies, it is striking to note that their success is built upon the way in which they are able to encourage and motivate their employees as individuals. Employees in competitive, successful companies are not numbers or ciphers but individuals, fully informed and increasingly involved as partners in small teams of workers. In addition, technological changes are ensuring more and more companies will organise in this fashion. More

> and more successful businesses are 'people' businesses, reliant entirely for their success on a highly skilled and committed workforce of individually motivated employees.[4]

'The trend towards individualised employee relations is the most substantial and significant workplace development of the past decade,' wrote Philip Bassett and Alan Cave in their 1993 Fabian Society pamphlet. 'Individualism is the key element in modern employee relations. It is the heart of modern trade unionism. Unions need to try to determine what individual employees want, to examine their current products to find out whether they meet that need – and if they do not, to re-engineer themselves to provide new products which will appeal more strongly to the individual employee market.'[5]

The Confederation of British Industry (CBI) has taken a similar view. In 1991 in a study on employee involvement, it proclaimed:

> A feature of the past decade has been that many organisations have adopted simpler organisational structures. In many cases this has created new relationships between managers and workers – smoothing the way for each employee to become more autonomous and self-sufficient and reorientating the manager's role towards that of facilitator from problem chaser. This greater autonomy for the individual has been manifested through quality circles, flexible work groups, action teams, joint problem-solving groups, total quality programmes and others. Flowing from this have been changes too in reward patterns; reflecting improvements in productivity, quality, flexibility, skills levels and individual performance.[6]

The concept of worker individualism is not new to the trade unions. Nearly thirty years ago a survey of manual workers in Luton suggested they joined trade unions not because they wanted to change the world or challenge the authority of employers but to improve their own terms and conditions of employment as a way to increase their prosperity. It was Dr John Goldthorpe and his colleagues who coined the telling phrase 'instrumental collectivism' to explain that phenomenon. As they wrote: 'Neither as a way to greater worker participation in the affairs of the enterprise nor as a political force is unionism greatly valued. Rather, one would say, the significance that unionism has for workers is very largely confined to issues arising from their employment which are economic in nature and which are local in their origins and scope.'[7]

But it is possible to go much further back to the origins of organised labour to find workers have always regarded being collectively organised through trade unions as a means and not an end in itself. Those formidable Fabians, Beatrice and Sidney Webb, defined a trade union as 'a continuous association of wage-earners for the purpose of maintaining or improving the conditions of their working lives.'[8] Their description has never really been bettered and it holds as much relevance today as it did nearly a hundred years ago when they wrote their classic account of trade unionism. A crucial connection exists between the worker as an individual in association with others in the workplace and his or her wider role in the social networks of class, family and community.

The recent emphasis on worker individualism is wrong because it fails to recognise an employee in any organisation is part of an interdependent workforce. Very few people enjoy an unfettered freedom at work that the concept of the individual worker seems to presume. The workplace performance of every employee depends in varying degrees on the efforts of other employees. Working is an interactive process of social association. Indeed, new techniques of Human Resource Management – well exemplified by the Japanese multinational companies operating in Britain – are concerned with the worker as part of a team in a collective organisation of work. Effort and performance are determined by group and not individual worker involvement. The concept of the worker as an individual is actually hostile to the consensual needs of the new workplace. It produces a false antithesis. Outside the obvious confines of small companies where managers and workers can be in daily personal contact with one another, it remains difficult to envisage the successful growth of an enterprise that pursued the ideology of individualism to its logical conclusion. Inevitably, most companies make use of some form of representative institution to ensure stability and harmony in their workplaces. There is little scope in a modern office or plant for free-ranging individuals of the kind to be found in neo-liberal economic models. In fact, it is no exaggeration to suggest that the concept of a 'new individualism' amounts to little more than an ideological deception that masks, behind its façade of reassuring language, the all too depressingly familiar inequities that still so often persist between an employer and employees.

The Unequal Relationship at Work

It has always been recognised as self-evident that the worker as an individual in the workplace suffers from having an unequal power relationship vis-à-vis his or her employer. Only when workers decide for themselves to combine together collectively can they establish enough unified strength to provide themselves with a strong and credible workplace voice to counter the often arbitrary demands being made upon them by their employer. As USDAW, the Shopworkers union, has explained: 'Trade unions came into existence in the last century to provide a counterbalance for workers against the unfettered power of their employers.'[9] 'Trade unionism – the great British invention – grew out of the day to day experience of working people in the world's first industrial society,' explained the TUC. 'From the nineteenth century onwards, trade unions developed because working people could not rely on employers to look after their welfare, working conditions and wages unprompted.'[10]

It is true that the trade unions have always provided a wide range of services to their members as individuals. In Britain, before the creation of the national welfare state, trade unions were crucial institutions for working people in the role of voluntary friendly societies that offered social benefits to their members. But what they also provided their members with was representation, without which the assertion of their individual rights before an employer would have proved quite useless. The support of a large and permanent independent organisation was of vital importance to the worker who had no power at all to stand up for his or her workplace rights against a determined employer, backed up whenever necessary by the normally anti-union common law tradition and a hostile or more often indifferent state.

That insight is as true today as it was in the nineteenth century. Many trade unions may have often been too slow in their responses to external change in servicing the particular new needs of their existing or potential members but an unbalanced emphasis on catering for so-called worker individualism would narrow rather than widen the popular appeal that the trade unions will need to make in the future if they want to stem their current decline and start to grow again. The relevance of trade unionism for employees in Britain is much more fundamental than the provision of individual benefits. An over-concentration on the trade union as a servicing agent, a kind of Automobile Association of the workplace, might suggest that employees no longer need to belong to a representative and autonomous organisation that can speak up for them on a wide range of workplace issues. It tends to presuppose a relatively high level of substantive employee participation already exists in today's workplaces, through the various forms of employer initiated and imposed consultation and communication arrangements, as a substitute for trade unions, but that is erroneous. It also gives the misleading impression of an assertive, self-confident and affluent workforce at ease with itself, exists in most of Britain's workplaces, in what Professor Kenneth Galbraith has called 'the culture of contentment'. Nothing could be further from reality. There was and there still remains a clear and urgent need for workers to practise freedom of association – what the International Labour Organisation has described as their 'inalienable right'. The TUC has explained:

> Employee representation is needed because the individual contract of employment is not concluded between two equal parties. An individual worker, with only his or her skills and experience to offer, is in a weaker position in the labour market than a company. That is most self-evidently true when considering large, often multinational companies with huge resources. Although they may not see it that way, employers in small companies are also in a position of advantage over individual employees. This is emphasised in times of high unemployment when a replacement workforce is easily available. Collective representation goes some way – but only a limited way – to create a balance between the resources of the employer and those of the workforce.[11]

The chronically insecure condition in which workers find themselves in today's labour market suggests trade unions ought to be much more in demand in the workplace to carry out their fundamental purposes as protectors of people at work than possibly at any time since before the First World War. Only through the collective strength trade unions provide can workers really have any hope of protecting their individual interests in the workplace.

As USDAW explained:

> We do not dispute there are some employees with skills and talents that are sufficient to allow them to reach satisfactory

> arrangements over their terms and conditions and security of employment. They can be found in the highly skilled occupations in technologically advanced industries, in some professional occupations and in arts, entertainment and sport. But they are small in numbers by comparison with the working population and their experience is a minority one. Most people have a different experience of work. Recent opinion polls show people feel increasingly insecure in their jobs. Their fear flows directly from the experience of high levels of unemployment over the last fourteen years coupled with the fact that many of those who lose their jobs are out of work for so long. Inevitably this has produced a significant shift in the culture of employment.
>
> Workpeople at every level feel a growing insecurity not only about their long-term employment prospects but also about their rights at work. Employers are increasingly adopting a 'take it or leave it' attitude to their employees. Workers feel deeply constrained in their ability to challenge unjust and unfair treatment at work. These developments have in no way contributed to the partnership and cooperation which should be the mark of a confident and innovative economy.[12]

USDAW argued 'these developments have made trade unions more necessary than ever . . . Our organisations have a vital contribution to make to ensure that fairness and equity are done and seen to be done in the workplace. Trade unions in the current climate are attempting to provide a balance on a wholly unequal playing field.'

The National Union of Civil and Public Servants (NUCPS) also emphasised the importance of the collective in its evidence to the Commons Employment Committee. 'We think of trade unions as essentially collective organisations, in the sense that what is distinctive about us is our ability to improve the lot of members through collective representation,' it said. 'The whole point about trade unionism is that the individual worker will always be weak, confronted by the power of employers – and nowhere is this more so now than in Britain, with its traditional insistence on treating the employment contract as if it were some kind of commercial contract entered into by equal parties, together with the systematic weakening of trade union powers in recent years. We offer workers the possibility of combining together and achieving collectively what they could never achieve separately.'[13]

The insecure labour market

The primary feature of today's labour market is its fundamental lack of certainty. A great fear for the future exists among employees in the workplace. This instinctive feeling is no longer confined to unskilled manual workers or to the fringes of the labour market among the ranks of the million long-term unemployed who have been without a job for more than twelve months. It also radiates through the complex layers of occupational hierarchy that make up Britain's diverse and polarised workforce. Anxiety can be found among the vulnerable ranks of senior management facing the threat of compulsory redundancy in companies such as British Telecom and the country's leading financial institutions as much as it can among the clerical and manual employees across both the private and public sectors. 'Down-sizing' is hitting white-collar employment not just among the shrinking ranks of what remains of the old industrial working class. As Professor Edward Littwack has observed, 'the central problem of our days [is the] completely unprecedented personal economic insecurity of working people, from industrial workers and white-collar clerks to medium-high managers.'[14]

'Such has been the urgency to drive down payroll costs that redundancy and early retirement exercises have been opened to all comers and hardly any volunteer has been turned away,' ACAS Chairman John Hougham has pointed out. 'And when volunteers have dried up, then there has been recourse to enforced redundancy. For a whole range of people who expected to see their careers out in the same organisation and who had been enjoying a high degree of job security, insecurity is a new factor with which they have had to come to terms.'[15] 'There are millions of people in this country who need the kind of help a trade union can give,' argued TUC General Secretary John Monks at the 1993 Congress. 'There is exploitation, vulnerability, low pay, poor conditions. The lowest tenth of manual workers earned only 64 per cent of average income in 1991 compared with 68 per cent in 1886. In some ways it is no exaggeration to say we are slipping back behind standards that were acceptable in Victorian times.' He emphasised the new labour market insecurities that make trade unionism still so relevant. Reminiscing about the days when he was at school in Manchester in the 1960s, he pointed out that in that period, for the vast majority of young people, society offered 'a reasonably steady job where we could function as a valuable worker and as a useful citizen with a stake in the community.' 'Jump forward with me now to the class of 1993,' said Mr Monks. 'What prospects do they have of landing any job, let alone a secure, steady job? Their chances are poor. Large private companies are shedding jobs. The public sector is following suit. Deregulation, privatisation and weak employment laws are helping reduce jobs and casualising much of what is left. What is on offer today – fixed term contracts, contract working, part-time working. All too often that is not a matter of choice but it is forced down people's throats. It is as true now for the white-collar professional as it is for the manual worker, and it is as true in the south as it is in the north. They are not steady jobs. They are here today, gone tomorrow jobs with no security, no pension, no sick pay and no paid holidays.'[16]

Trade union leaders are not the only ones who have expressed public concern about the emergence in Britain of a more polarised and segmented labour market and the re-assertion by management of its unilateral right to manage. As Mr Geoffrey Armstrong, Director-General of the Institute of Personnel Management (IPM), told its annual Harrogate conference in October 1993:

> While encouraging flexibility in matching the needs of organisations with those of their employees and prospective employees, we must stand out against abuse. The creation of a permanently casualised industrial peasantry, with little protection and no stake in the future, cannot be in the interests of organisations or society. Maybe the 'steady job' has gone, but to ensure trust is maintained with their workers, employers need to make sure they give them 'security where they can', 'treat them consistently in a principled manner', and equip them 'with the generic skills and employability which will enable them to find alternatives if we can no longer employ them.[17]

The National Association of Citizens Advice Bureaux (CAB) has provided graphic evidence of the human consequences of the 'new' flexible labour market. The CAB argued the recession had made 'a devastating impact' on the employment experience of its clients. It reported that there had been a dramatic increase in the number of people coming to its bureaux with employment problems. In 1987 – 1988 641,912 people came, 8.9% of total enquiries; by 1992 – 1993 the number had risen to 882,257, 11.4% of total enquiries. This amounted to a 31 per cent growth in five years in the volume of employment problems brought by workers to the Citizens Advice Bureaux. 'Numbers of employees are faced with an impossible choice – accepting a severe deterioration in their working conditions or losing their job. With unemployment standing at over three million, the implications of this dilemma are obvious,' said the Association. It suggested that the vulnerability of workers had been 'compounded by the absence of adequate employment protection.'[18]

> Since 1979 the qualifying period for gaining the right to claim unfair dismissal has increased from six months to two years. This means that a large proportion of employees are unable to enforce their statutory rights and are severely restricted in opposing unilateral changes in their terms and conditions of employment. The extent and significance of this vulnerability is demonstrated by some employers' increasingly systematic exploitation of existing employment legislation. Advice Bureaux clients have been routinely dismissed where there is no suggestion that they have failed to perform their jobs adequately. Clients are losing their livelihoods and incurring all the problems that entails, purely because their employers want to prevent them from attaining employment protection. The threat of redundancy represents one further element in the vulnerability of employees. Uncertainty over selection criteria combined with a lack of knowledge about employment rights and obligations, mean that even employees who are protected against unfair dismissal cannot feel confident about their job security.

The Association found, in numerous reports from its local bureaux, that unilateral changes by employers in the terms and conditions of their workers were widespread. It also revealed many examples of imposed pay cuts being made on workers without any explanation being given by their employer. The Association expressed particular concern about the exploitation of young people after the repeal in 1989 of both the Factories Act and Shops Act that had provided at least some statutory minimum protection for the most vulnerable of workers. A CAB in West London reported a seventeen-year-old client who had been employed by a car dealer for two months. His contract stated Saturday work was paid at time-and-a-half but his employer informed him he intended to change this to ordinary pay. A CAB in Avon reported a nineteen-year-old client who was employed at a gardening centre. He worked from 8am to 5pm, six days a week, at an hourly rate of £2.00. He had no written contract. His hours were gradually increased to seventy per week without overtime pay. When he protested, he was sacked. Another CAB in Somerset reported a seventeen-year-old client who worked part-time for a local fast-food restaurant. He was dismissed because he objected to the introduction of compulsory Saturday working. His sister, who also worked at the restaurant, was then made full-time and expected to work for fifty hours a week with no overtime pay.

The Association discovered many workers were being employed without having any written employment contract. Its report also highlighted an increasing number of cases where workers were being pressurised to become self-employed so the employer could avoid a legal obligation to pay their tax and national insurance contributions. The growth in the use of compulsory competitive tendering was highlighted as a particular example of how workers' terms and conditions of employment were being eroded. Unfair dismissal cases now make up a large part of the Citizen Advice Bureaux dossiers of employment problems. 'The practice of dismissing employees who have no employment protection is not a new experience for CAB clients,' acknowledged the report. 'What is new is the increasingly systematic way in which some employers are exploiting that lack of protection. The crudest form of this systematic exploitation is the practice of dismissing employees just before they qualify for protection against unfair dismissal.'

The CAB report indicated hundreds of thousands of workers and their employers do not 'fully appreciate their rights or obligations.' It recommended that all workers, when they start a job or when they are dismissed by their employer or have 'significant changes made to their employment conditions', should have the right by law to have a general written introduction to their employment rights.

A further disturbing survey was published in March 1994 by the National Association of Citizens Advice Bureaux on gender and racial workplace discrimination, despite the existence of laws on the statute book designed to prevent or at least discourage such behaviour. This provided further evidence of the depths of insecurity in the deregulated labour market. Sexual harassment at work is 'one of the most common forms of discrimination experienced by CAB clients. Many of the problems experienced by CAB clients are the result of legislation and policies which have general discriminatory effects – such as inadequate rights for pregnant workers and qualifying conditions for essential employment rights which discriminate against part-time workers,' said the report. 'However many CAB clients experience discrimination which is rooted in the policies, practices and attitudes of particular employers.'[19]

Such subjective impressions have been confirmed by the facts. The Advisory, Conciliation and Arbitration Service (ACAS) has reported over recent years an enormous increase in the number of cases concerned with abuses of individual and collective employment rights and protections that have been brought before industrial tribunals. Over 75,000 individual conciliation cases were dealt with in 1993 alone – a 14 per cent increase on the previous year – and there were nearly half a million requests for help from employers and employees. Complaints of unfair dismissal totalled 46,000 – up 12 per cent on the 1992 figure – while the number of cases covering complaints of sex discrimination soared. ACAS also received more than 1,200 requests for conciliation in collective disputes in 1993, with as many as 163 cases being referred to arbitration or mediation for resolution. 'Relationships between individuals and groups in the workplace will be under strain – perhaps even greater than has existed in the past decade,' ACAS Chairman Mr John Hougham has predicted. 'This pressure may not manifest itself in a wave of industrial action but the harmful stress it causes will nonetheless be detrimental to the effectiveness of organisations.'[20]

The Rise of the Divided Workforce

The British labour market is not just deregulated; it is also increasingly segmented. The growth of part-time employment (defined as workers employed for less than thirty hours a week) has strengthened the deep sense of worker insecurity. In 1981, 4.5 million people were in such jobs, 21 per cent of the employed labour force; by 1993 the number had risen to 5.8 million, making up 28 per cent of the employed labour force. This figure is perhaps an exaggeration because it includes those doing a second job, who grew by 37 per cent between 1984 and 1992, from 690,000 to 949,000. But it has been estimated – from the evidence of the official Labour Force Survey statistics – that

5.2 million people were working in part-time occupations in the spring of 1993. Only around 22 per cent were trade union members, and most of them were employed in the public sector.

Part-time workers have no legally enforceable employment protections like those who are employed in full-time jobs. The TUC has estimated as many as 6.3 million workers in the winter of 1992 – 1993 had no claim to legal employment protection rights; 57 per cent of them were women. The TUC explained: 'These are, in practice, minimum estimates. There will be many unorganised workers who have a claim in principle but are unable to exercise it in practice. This will include workers afraid of losing their job or otherwise being victimised; those who are unaware of their rights and those who do not feel they have the time, knowledge or resources to pursue a claim.'[21]

The retail distribution sector which employs 2.5 million people, just under 10 per cent of the employed workforce, is particularly vulnerable to this kind of employee insecurity. USDAW spelt out the problem in its Commons Employment Committee evidence: 'Full-time working is being replaced by flexible hours working at the behest of the industry's employers. As such, the current drive towards flexibility is geared toward and driven by their demands,' it said.

The union pointed to:

> Cuts in normal weekly hours and pay by employers as staff have become part-time employees. Gateway Foodmarkets Ltd, with 25,000 employees, has been reducing full-time working from thirty-nine hours a week to sixteen hour weeks, with some staff asked to work two separate shifts in the same day. The Burton group has cut the hours of the majority of its full-time staff from thirty-nine to fifteen with swingeing cuts in pay.
>
> Flexible or core time working has been introduced at some retailers. British Home Stores, for example, made a third of its full-time workforce redundant in February 1993, replacing them with employees on flexible hours contracts.
>
> Zero hour contracts were introduced at the Burton group in January 1993. They are also operating at the Storehouse group and Kingfisher company. This requires an employee to be constantly on standby without any guarantee of work being on offer. The contract is only in force when the worker is actually working and there are no minimum or maximum hours.
>
> Even with trade union representation, employees in retailing find their working lives unstable, insecure, low paid and undervalued. Without trade unions all the evidence suggests

> that their experience would be even more impoverished than it is at the moment. With the expected developments of further deregulation and the extension of flexibility across all the major retailing employers, the outlook is grim. These developments force trade unions into a role which is eventually defensive and not one we would choose.[22]

Thirty per cent of the labour force fail to qualify for any of the existing main employment protection rights because they have worked for the current employer for less than two years or because they work under sixteen hours a week. A substantial number of those affected are women. The TUC believes the proportion in this position will increase over the 1990s. As it explained: 'This is not only because the government has reduced the scope of employment protection but also because of the growing insecurity of employment and the expansion in forms of employment (part-time work and second jobs) which do not qualify for protection. These trends will have been reinforced by the decline in trade union membership in the 1980s. Fewer people in unions means fewer workers able to enforce whatever rights they might have had.'[23]

It is not just trade unions and Citizens Advice Bureaux who believe the emergence and encouragement of a more 'deregulated and flexible' labour market has weakened the position of employees, making them anxious and insecure. The most significant and comprehensive evidence to sustain the view that fear of the future has grown more widespread in the British workplace was provided in the government's own commissioned Workplace Industrial Relations Survey (WIRS), carried out in 1990 and published at the end of 1992. This discovered the overwhelming majority of non-union employers had not introduced new forms of work organisation to boost productivity and improve their competitiveness. On the contrary, the survey suggested many of them are taking unscrupulous advantage of labour's strategic weakness to preside over a return to the kind of degrading and exploitative master-servant relations much of Britain suffered from during the last century.

As Dr Neil Millward of the independent Policy Studies Institute (PSI) argued:

> British industry and commerce appear to be moving towards the situation in which non-managerial employees are treated as a 'factor of production.' The country is approaching the

> position where few employees have any mechanism through which they can contribute to the operation of their workplace in a broader context than that of their own jobs. There is no sign that the shrinkage in the extent of trade union representation is being offset by a growth in other methods of representing non-managerial employees, interests or views. There has been no spontaneous emergence of an alternative model of employee representation that could channel and attenuate conflicts between employers and employees. Nor is there much of the legal regulation that is so extensive in other developed economies to provide a basic floor of employment rights and minimum labour standards. The recent growth in inequality in wages and earnings which has been widely observed to be greater in Britain than in almost all other developed economies is being matched by a widening in the inequalities of influence and access to key decisions about work and employment. Many would welcome this as a sign that Britain is moving towards the type of unregulated labour market that economic success requires. Others would see it as a reversion towards the type of economy that gave rise to the birth of trade unionism in the last century.[24]

The WIRS survey indicated just how vital trade unionism still remains in Britain. Its findings revealed 'repeatedly how much worse off are employees who do not enjoy the protection of collective bargaining. They are, on average, less favoured than their unionised brothers and sisters in terms of pay, health and safety, labour turnover, contractual security, compulsory redundancy, grievance procedures, consultation, communication and employee representation.'

As Professor William Brown has concluded: 'Faced with this sort of evidence, future British governments will have to be very confident that there are countervailing advantages accruing to employees from the discouragement of collective bargaining if they are to continue to have it as a main policy objective. It is quite possible that the sort of arguments that have convinced British governments for a century or more to foster orderly collective bargaining will be revived.'[25]

Along with the insecurity of the labour market has come a rapid redistribution of income and wealth away from the poor and those earning average incomes to the very rich. Mr Howard Davies, the Director-General of the Confederation of British Industry (CBI), recognised this in a speech he made in March 1994 to the Manchester University Business School. Up until the end of the 1970s he pointed out, the dispersion of net incomes in the United Kingdom had been narrowing for a considerable time, but during the 1980s the trend was reversed. In that decade, while the average income for the population as a whole increased by 36 per cent, the real incomes of the top tenth of the population climbed by 62 per cent whereas the real incomes of the bottom tenth fell by 14 per cent. Mr Davies said this had ushered in a new kind of poverty to Britain. The total number of non-pensioner families on incomes below the income support level doubled in the 1980s from just under 3 million to just over 4 million. These were made up of single parents, the unemployed, long-term sick and disabled workers.

The Commission on Social Justice, created by the Labour party, reported in a 1993 publication on 'the new map of injustice'. It pointed out that almost two thirds of the population now have an income that is below the average. 'The inequalities in wealth have grown enormously. Now the top one per cent of the population owns 18 per cent of all the wealth and the top 10 per cent half the nation's wealth. Half the population account for only 8 per cent of the wealth. Rising unemployment, tax cuts for the rich and regressive changes in the welfare benefit system have all conspired to widen social inequalities in the workplace.'[26] This has been most indefensibly revealed by the pay bonanza enjoyed by top executives in recent years. Between 1977 and 1992 the salaries of the most senior directors of the *Financial Times'* top 100 companies increased by 133 per cent compared with an average increase in earnings of only 48 per cent. The staggering salary rises actually underestimated the massive accumulation because they excluded perks such as share options, which have proved particularly lucrative. The growth in the wealth and income of executives persisted throughout the recession despite the cutbacks required from most of their employees.

The evidence contained in the 1990 WIRS survey suggests nothing credible has emerged to replace the voluntary collective bargaining system through recognised trade unions. In the words of Dr Millward, 'Broadly speaking no alternative models of employee representation – let alone a single alternative model – had emerged as a substitute for trade union representation.'[27] Despite much fashionable talk about Human Resource Management as another possible approach to trade union management-based industrial relations, very few companies have bothered to introduce any of its techniques. Indeed, the WIRS survey discovered most progress had been made in the introduction of HRM techniques not in non-union but in unionised companies, where they have become a 'complement' not a substitute for existing collective bargaining arrangements. Non-union firms are not really interested in innovative ideas for employee involvement and participation but instead seek to exert a unilateral authority in their relations with their employees without recourse to any form of joint consultation. The 1990 WIRS survey suggested 'the overall reduction in the number of workplaces with joint consultation committees from 34 per cent in 1984 to 29 per cent in 1990, is explained by the changing composition of the workplaces rather than general abandonment. The significant point, however, is there has been no increase in joint consultation which might have been expected if British management had been seeking to substitute joint consultation for collective bargaining. In non-union workplaces, the incidence of joint consultative committees is down from 19 to 16 per cent over the decade. British management, it seems, has not been anxious to encourage forms of collective activity, be they union or non-union.'[27] Only a minority of non-union companies have introduced grievance-raising procedures or health and safety arrangements. Moreover, establishments where trade unions are not recognised dismissed two-and-a-half times as many workers employed per 1,000 as did those where trade unions are recognised. Compulsory redundancies were reported in 46 per cent of the workplaces without recognised unions that had seen workforce cutbacks compared with 17 per cent where unions were recognised. Private sector workplaces were less than half as likely to have any form of health and safety representation if they were not unionised than if they were. The quit rate averaged 11 per cent where trade unions were recognised and 20 per cent where there were no recognised unions.

The startling evidence in the WIRS survey suggests that employers are trying to silence the voice of their employees both collectively and individually. As Professor Keith Sisson has argued, 'freed from the pressure of unions, managements in the small and medium-sized workplaces especially are more likely to follow the "traditional" approach of a Grunwick than the HRM of an IBM or Marks and Spencer.'[28]

Further evidence of current social instabilities was also

found in the government-commissioned Employment in Britain survey, published in June 1993. 'Only about one third of employees in British industry felt that they had any substantial degree of influence over decisions that could result in changes to their work,' it reported.[29] 'Nearly half of all employees thought they should have more say in decisions affecting their everyday working lives.' The study – based on a sample of 3,855 of workers aged between twenty and sixty between May and August 1992 with a 70 per cent response rate – is the most comprehensive of its kind. 'Overall there is no evidence of a significant trend towards increased employee satisfaction with their level of involvement in decisions about organisational change,' it noted. In many ways the survey had some positive results, not least in the high levels of in-house training it discovered and the surprising fact that just over half of the employees made use of new technologies in their jobs. There were also signs that 'the expansion of the service sector and the rise in skill levels across the broader range of industries have provided jobs that are more satisfying in the sense of meeting better people's concern about the quality of work.' But the survey also pointed out that the 'process of upskilling' had been 'associated with a sharp increase in the pressures at work, it found there has been an intensification of work effort, employees have been required to assume greater responsibility in their work and quality standards have become more demanding. This is related to a marked increase in the degree of tension experienced during the work process itself and to higher levels of work stress.'[30]

Back to the Future?

The combination of workplace insecurity and evidence of a squeeze on living standards has made conditions in the labour market ripe for a trade union revival among millions of workers who are in need of representative support as well as protection. Britain is particularly susceptible to such feelings in a time of rapid technological change and economic weakness. Employers do not have to adopt basic recognised fair standards of labour practice, thanks to the lack of legal regulation of the employment relationship. The rapid decline of multi-employer bargaining with the weakening of employer associations in recent years has also made it easier for employers to avoid any need to behave in a civilised manner towards their workers if they do not wish to do so. Professor Keith Sisson at Warwick University provided another persuasive explanation for the way in which many companies are dealing with their employees:

> The pressure of a number of mutually reinforcing considerations in corporate governance push British managers towards short-termism in their approach. They include the relative lack of education and training of British managers; the dominance of the finance function and its modes of thinking; business strategies and structures which put the emphasis on 'numbers-driven' rather than 'issue-driven' planning; patterns of financing which seem almost designed to restrict investment; and the ease with which companies are subject to takeover by predator conglomerates concerned primarily with financial engineering rather than with making things or providing services.[31]

But none of this means that Britain's employers have launched or are about to launch a fierce and coherent anti-trade union offensive in the workplace against the presence or threat of organised labour. Unlike in the United States, here trade unions do not have to face companies that are involved in hysterical 'search and destroy' campaigns against any signs of an emerging collective organisation inside their plants.

Indeed, the Employment in Britain survey found 'in general the position of the trade unions in companies was not seen as an issue of major controversy.' It pointed out:

> . . . overall, only 9 per cent of employees felt that their employers were trying to discourage trade union membership. The figure was somewhat higher for those that were in establishments where there were no unions (15 per cent) and particularly for men in such establishments (18 per cent). More workers felt that their employers had a policy of encouraging employees to belong to unions (14 per cent) and the figure rose to 50 per cent among those who were employed in unionised establishments. For the greater part, however, employer attitudes towards trade unions were thought largely to be passive; 33 per cent believed employers simply accepted the fact that people became union members, while 45 per cent felt that it was not an issue at their workplace.'[32]

A separate study carried out by the Labour Research Department in 1993 confirmed those findings. It found in a sample of 144 establishments that workers in only 7 per cent of them believed they worked for anti-union employers while 49 per cent said their employers welcomed workers joining trade unions.[33]

Trade Unions are Popular Again

If the deterioration in workplace conditions ought to encourage a resurgence of trade unionism, no deep and lingering hostility towards trade unions appears to exist any longer among the general public. Indeed, in Britain in the 1990s, trade unions arouse widespread popular sympathy, not fear or contempt among people at large. In the turbulent years of industrial conflict during the 1970s and early 1980s trade unions were believed to have grown far too powerful, but this hostile feeling has almost disappeared as their perceived influence and power has declined steeply. Today trade unions enjoy a relatively favourable image in the eyes of public opinion. Eight out of ten people polled in September 1993 said they believed trade unions were necessary to protect workers' interests, while the same substantial proportion also agreed with the view that business works better when management takes notice of the views of its employees and trade unions. A Gallup survey taken at the same time found 71 per cent of those polled thought trade unions were a 'good thing' and only 18 per cent thought them a 'bad thing'. That favourable rating for the trade unions equalled the previous all-time high recorded by Gallup in 1954 and 1987. A MORI survey carried out for the GMB union in January 1993 showed similar popular sympathy. Three out of four people polled thought trade unions were essential to protect workers' interests and 59 per cent said they were good at their job. There is also little public concern about any alleged strength the trade unions might be able to wield nowadays. For the first time in more than twenty years, in September 1993, more people (27 per cent) believed the trade unions were not powerful enough than believed they were too powerful (17 per cent). Less than a quarter of the people polled believed trade unions had too much power and nearly two thirds thought bad management was more to blame than the trade unions for the country's economic problems. Nearly 60 per cent of people believed trade unions did a good job for their members.

The 1993 Gallup survey also discovered that as many as 55 per cent of the people believed the balance of power in industry had tilted much too far in the direction of management, compared with a mere 5 per cent who said the trade unions still had the advantage. While 42 per cent believed the laws regulating the trade unions were 'about right', 27 per cent said they had gone too far. The 1990 British Social Attitudes Survey data found considerable support amongst employees for recognised trade unions in their workplaces. Only 4 per cent thought their union wielded too much power there, while around half believed it enjoyed about the right amount and 37 per cent said they had too little power. Whatever the public image of trade unions might be, their role in the workplace was looked upon favourably by most workers. The same survey also discovered 53 per cent of union members believed that trade unions were necessary to protect employees' interests while only 27 per cent of non-unionists accepted that notion.

Not all the public poll findings make such welcome reading for trade union officials. The September 1993 Gallup survey discovered 46 per cent of voters believed the views of trade union leaders did not represent those of the ordinary member and only 22 per cent actually thought they were becoming more representative, despite the fact that since 1984 trade unions have been required by law to elect their executive committees and leaders by secret ballot vote. The January 1993 MORI survey for the GMB still found a quarter of respondents who tended to agree and 9 per cent who strongly agreed that 'most trade unions are controlled by extremists and militants'. As many as 24 per cent still agreed with the statement that 'trade unions have too much power in Britain today'.

To a large extent, however, public attitudes towards trade unions are conditioned by the level of inflation in the economy and the incidence of strikes in the labour market. 'The more trade unions are needed to combat the eroding impact of inflation upon employee's living standards and the more they employ strikes and other forms of industrial action to maintain or to enhance these standards, the less popular they become,' P K Edwards and Professor George Bain have argued.[35] On the other hand, they also discovered that 'the more prices rise and the more unions push up wages through strikes and other means, the more employees tend to join them.' This apparent contradiction suggests that workers in their own workplace tend to rate their own trade union more favourably than they do trade unions in general. But Edwards and Bain concluded, the recent revival of public support for trade unions in the early 1990s was due to a decline in both the inflation rate and the number of strikes rather than from 'inherent qualities of the unions' and therefore suggested trade union weakness rather than strength as the reason for their improved public image.

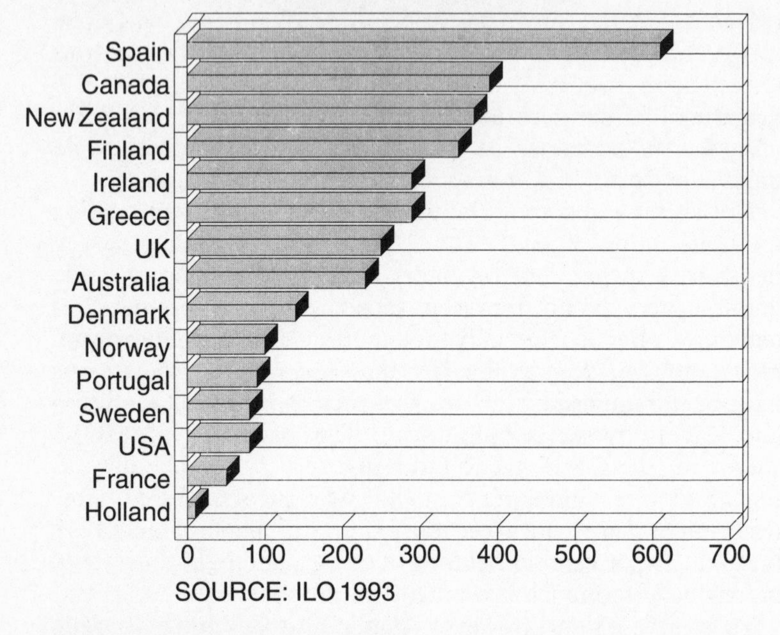

Whatever Happened to Strikes?

The sharp decline in industrial conflict since the middle of the 1980s has undoubtedly helped to improve the public image of the trade unions. In the early 1990s – as the statistics indicate – the incidence of striking and other forms of disruption fell to levels not recorded since reliable labour statistics in Britain were first collected in 1891. Government ministers have drawn much comfort from the emergence of a strike-free Britain, suggesting their industrial relations strategies provide the main explanation for the arrival of workplace peace. Their claim is unjustified. As international comparative figures indicate, Britain's strike statistics were never as appalling as tabloid newspapers liked to suggest in the 1960s and 1970s. Indeed, the decline of industrial conflict is not a trend confined to this country. It occurred across most of the western industrialised world during the 1980s and the early 1990s. Britain still remains about halfway down the strike league table of OECD countries, just as it did ten years ago. But over the 1988 – 1992 period the United Kingdom lost an annual average of 100 days per thousand employees as a result of strikes, amounting to one tenth of a working day a year per employee or less than one working hour a year. This was 75 per cent lower than the estimate of 400 days per thousand employees for the previous five-year period. Only Denmark among other OECD countries experienced a more drastic reduction in working days lost because of strikes.

A detailed industrial breakdown of British strike statistics for 1992 indicates that the coal industry had the highest number of working days lost per thousand employees, totalling 120,000, followed by the utilities with 94,000 lost working days per thousand and the public services with 85,000. Over a longer time span it is clear that the limited number of sectors which used to be strike-prone, such as the docks and the car industry, are now virtually free of industrial disruption which has become relatively more common in the public sector. In the United Kingdom the strike rate in the services sector is now more than double the figure in private manufacturing.

Reasons for Joining Trade Unions

Why do people join trade unions? It is not perhaps surprising that mutual protection and the desire for higher wages and better conditions still remain the main reasons given by workers for belonging to a trade union. These have been at 'the bedrock of trade unionism since its birth' and they have not changed. In the 1989 Social Attitudes Survey, as many as 93 per cent believed the primary reason for becoming a trade unionist was 'to protect me if problems come up', followed by 80 per cent who sought 'higher pay and better working conditions'. Seventy one per cent suggested receiving member's benefits was a reason to join a trade union, while 67 per cent said they believed in trade unions on principle and 55 per cent that they had joined because most of their work colleagues were also members.[36]

While many people at work might see the value of belonging to a trade union, it does not follow that they either belong to one themselves or wish to join. Nowadays trade unions have to operate in a highly competitive labour market and they must convince workers by their deeds that union membership is in their interests. As Mr Geoffrey Armstrong, the IPM's Director

General told the Commons Employment Committee: 'Employees need to be sold on the value of belonging to a trade union in a way that perhaps twenty or thirty years ago would not have been the case in many of the organisations in which most of us worked. It would have been automatic that the majority of employees at all levels, certainly all of the blue collar levels, would have been members of unions. That is no longer the case. The unions are having to demonstrate to those people there is some additional value in belonging to trade unions.'[37]

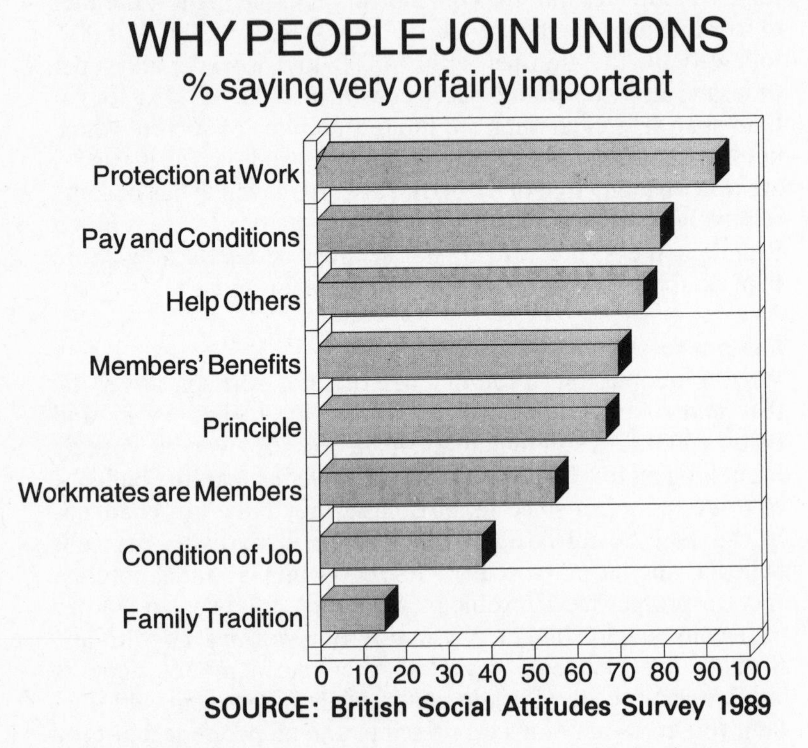

But he did not suggest that this meant the trade unions were finished. 'We do not see the days of trade unions as being numbered,' he insisted. 'We do see there having been a very fundamental shift from the old ways of trade unionism and we see the trade unions looking for new ways of contributing value. The fact that there are over seven million members of trade unions would indicate there is a sizeable interest in retaining membership.' Mr Armstrong went on to point out that he did 'not see trade unions as just sitting still and letting the decline continue.'

Moreover, he also argued 'there will always be the need for people to take a second opinion and for somebody to explain things that perhaps have not been explained by the employer. There will always, in many establishments, be a need for a protector, an insurance policy. It is more than just a provider of a few fringe benefits.' In Mr Armstrong's opinion trade unions are still necessary. 'I think you are going to find there is a very solid core of companies, of types of employment, where trade unions will continue to have appeal. I think too there are many areas where employees might say, "We trust our bosses. We believe that our managers have our interests at heart but we do believe we need somebody to bargain our pay and conditions on our behalf. We need somebody to protect our interests in the pension scheme because it is a very sizeable investment in our future."'

Mr Howard Davies, the CBI's Director-General, has also insisted many of his organisation's member companies have no wish to roll back the trade unions. 'There are still quite a large number of our members who, particularly in present circumstances, find they have a perfectly satisfactory relationship with the trade unions and one that they do not wish at this stage to disturb,' he explained. 'On average, at the present time, our members believe their relationship with trade unions representing their workforces are generally quite good and their ability within existing structures to discuss the future of the business and gain understanding and cooperation from trade unions in taking required decisions on investment and restructuring is positive. I would regard the position as broadly stable.'[38]

However, Mr Davies added it was difficult to say how the position of trade unions would develop in the future. 'It probably depends as much on the way that trade unions evolve and manage their relationship with employers as it does on the way that employers behave,' he said. In its written evidence, the CBI suggested there was 'no evidence that employers had been 'generally forcing the pace' in de-recognising trade unions. 'More commonly it reflects a shared wish in the workplace for dealings on a different basis,' it argued. 'An essential prerequisite of recognition is that people should want to exercise their right to join (which is fully protected by law). And the fact is that fewer employees wish to be union members.' The CBI asserted 'Union membership has fallen far more sharply than recognition in the private sector. This does not suggest that employers are generally moving ahead of workforce wishes in this area.' It quoted the 1990 workplace survey observation: 'Management antipathy cannot be the major reason for over a third of private sector workplaces having no union members.' The CBI added that 'few employers set their face against recognition.'[39]

The Engineering Employers Federation (EEF), in its written evidence to the Commons Employment Committee, did not reveal any marked hostility to trade unions either. 'The EEF believes that, provided trade unions continue to operate within the law and do not seek a confrontational role, they can continue to develop constructive relationships with employers,' it argued. 'The EEF believes formal procedures for the resolution of individual or collective grievances are of assistance in maintaining orderly industrial relations.'[40] 'The trade union movement has a significant role to play in the economic development of the country,' Mr Ronald Taylor, Director-General of the Association of British Chambers of Commerce commented on the TUC relaunch in March 1994. 'We look forward to a continuing constructive relationship between chambers of commerce and trade unions across the country.'[41]

Mr John Hougham, the ACAS Chairman, is also convinced that the trade unions are not going to fade away. 'There is a great deal of talk about the need for unions to redefine their role and to increase the support and service they offer individual members,' he told a conference in January 1994. 'To paraphrase Mark Twain, however, the death of collective bargaining has been greatly exaggerated. Change there may be but there is every sign that collective bargaining will continue to be a major factor in employer/employee relationships in the foreseeable future.'[42]

Conclusion

Trade unions are having to operate in a relatively hostile atmosphere and adapting to change will not be easy for them. But they have never been able to take anything for granted in the past. They have always had to struggle, often in the face of economic adversity, an indifferent or hostile state, an unsympathetic legal system and a flexible and deregulated labour market. Today, however, the trade unions have enormous opportunities open to them for staging a comeback, with a ground-swell of generalised sympathy for them among many workers who are not trade unionists in a divided labour market which is often an affront to a sense of fairness as well as an obstacle to economic workplace efficiency.

NOTES

1 Department of Employment written evidence, HMSO p 6.
2 People, Jobs and Opportunity, Department of Employment Cmnd 1810 HMSO 1992, p 39.
3 D Hunt, March 1994 Industrial Society Speech.
4 Institute of Directors written evidence, p 14.
5 P Bassett and A Cave, All for One, Fabian Society September 1993, p 27.
6 Employee Involvement, Confederation of British Industry 1991
7 J Goldthorpe et al. *The Affluent Worker In The Class Structure?,* Cambridge University Press 1969, p 26.
8 S and B Webb, *The History of Trade Unionism*, Longmans 1920 edition, p 1
9 USDAW written evidence, p 75.
10 TUC written evidence, p 1.
11 ibid, p 4.
12 USDAW written evidence, p 75.
13 NUCPS written evidence, p 176.
14 *London Review of Books* Vol 16 No 7, 7 April 1994, p 6.
15 J Hougham, ACAS Chairman, April 1994 speech.
16 TUC 1993 Congress Report, p 364.
17 IPM Conference speech 1993.
18 Job Security, CAB Report March 1993.
19 Unequal Opportunities, CAB Report March 1994.
20 J Hougham, ACAS Chairman, January 1994 speech, p 11.
21 TUC written evidence, p 12.
22 USDAW written evidence, p 80.
23 TUC, Full Employment submission to Commons Employment Committee, October 1993, p 11.
24 N Millward, The New Industrial Relations? Policy Studies Institute 1994, p 133.
25 W Brown, The Contraction of Collective Bargaining in Britain, Journal of British Industrial Relations June 1993, p 198.
26 The Justice Gap, Institute for Public Policy Research 1993, pp 45 – 46.
27 N Millward et al, Workplace Relations In Transition, Dartmouth 1992, p 350.
28 K Sisson, In Search of HRM, British Journal of Industrial Relations, Vol No 2, p 207.
29 D Gallie and M White, Commitment and The Skills Revolution, Policy Studies Institute 1993, p 29.
30 ibid, p 41.
31 K Sisson, p 207.
32 D Gallie and M White, p 42–43.
33 Labour Research Department

Bargaining Report June 1993, pp 12–13.

34 J Monks, British Journal of Industrial Relations, June 1993, p 230.

35 P K Edwards and G Bain, Why Are Trade Unions Becoming MorePopular?BJIR,November 1988.

36 Social Attitudes Survey 1989, Dartmouth, p 22

37 G Armstrong oral evidence, p 402.

38 H Davies, oral evidence, p 402.

39 CBI written evidence, p 321.

40 EEF written evidence, p 379.

41 TUC, Messages of Support for the Relaunch March 1994.

42 J Hougham April 1994 speech.

CHAPTER TWO

Trade Unions in a Hostile Climate

Since the beginning of the 1980s the trade unions have been going through one of the most traumatic periods in their history. Trade union density as a proportion of the employed workforce has dropped sharply since 1979, from an historic high watermark of 55 per cent to around 31 per cent by 1993. Total trade union membership in Britain has fallen by more than a quarter from 13.3 million in 1979 to 9.0 million in 1993, a net decline of around a third. In 1993 the workforce in employment totalled 25 million. Trade union density has contracted for fourteen consecutive years with the sharpest drops taking place in the recessions of 1981–1982 and 1990–1991. But even during the short-lived recovery of the mid-decade organised labour continued to fall, suggesting the decline was as much due to structural changes in the labour market as it was to the ups and downs of the business cycle.

In ten years the number of establishments employing twenty-five or more employees who recorded that they had trade union members among their own workers dropped from 73 per cent to 64 per cent. In the manufacturing sector, trade union density declined from 58 per cent to 48 per cent between 1984 and 1990, while overall in private industry and services the fall was from 42 per cent to only 35 per cent. Trade union recognition by employers during the 1980s declined from 64 per cent to 53 per cent, with a significant drop of almost a third in the private manufacturing sector from 65 per cent to 44 per cent. More serious was the evidence of a contraction in collective bargaining. The 1990 WIRS survey estimated less than 8.4 million out of an employed workforce of 22 million in 1990 had their pay directly determined by collective bargaining, a mere 38 per cent of the total. By 1990 54 per cent of employees in plants with over twenty-five employed had their wages partly determined by collective bargaining, compared with a figure of

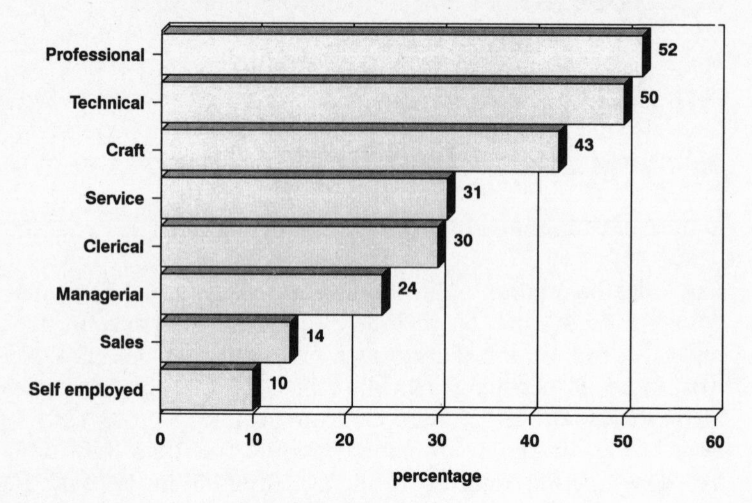

source: Dept of Employment 1992 (1991 statistics)

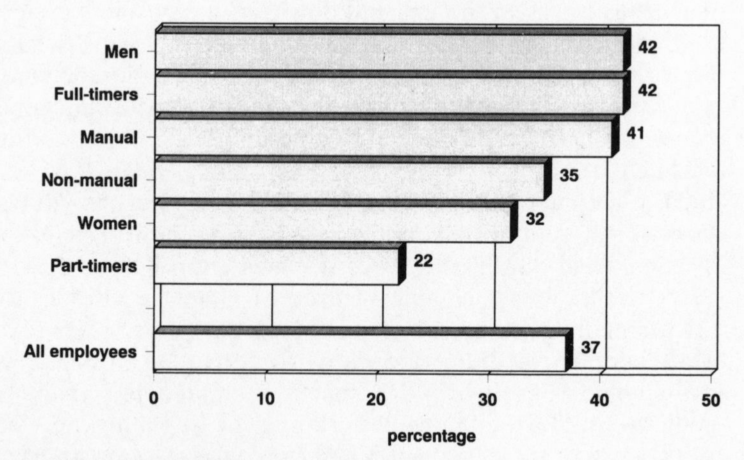

source: Dept of Employment 1992 (1991 statistics)

71 per cent only six years earlier. The 1990 WIRS survey described the decline in collective bargaining as being 'stark, substantial and incontrovertible'.[1] Trade union membership has fallen faster than recognition, suggesting that management hostility to trade unions could not provide the main explanation for their decline. It is perhaps not surprising that these startling figures have done much to puncture the complacent view of the mid-1980s that tended to stress continuity rather than change as the most noticeable feature of the British industrial relations scene.

Further research carried out since the 1990 WIRS survey has provided conflicting evidence on the incidence of trade unionism. The 1992 Employment in Britain survey stressed there had been greater workplace stability over the previous five years. It found 43 per cent of employees in its sample were trade unionists and 59 per cent said trade unions were present in the organisations in which they worked. Overall, two thirds of the sample reported 'there had been no change in the importance to them of being a trade union member', though 'women were more likely to have come to consider trade union membership more important while men were more likely to have changed in the direction of feeling that the unions had become less important to them.'[2]

Employers have reasserted greater control in the workplace over the past few years, with a resulting decline in the countervailing strength of the shop-floor. The 1990 WIRS survey found there had been a growth in the later 1980s in what it called 'complete management flexibility'. Three quarters of workplaces with union recognition gave management complete flexibility, extending to 90 per cent in the trading sector workplaces. Fewer than a fifth of workplaces in the survey were found to have any form of joint consultation, though team briefings had risen to 44 per cent of the trading sector compared with 30 per cent in 1984.

Putting Trade Union Decline in Perspective

Such findings have come as a shock to many trade union activists but they are not as negative as they look. Considerable stability and continuity remain, particularly in the workplaces of big plants in the larger manufacturing companies which still account for a substantial share of Britain's exports. TUC General Secretary John Monks points out that forty-seven of the top fifty biggest companies have collective agreements for some, if not all of their employees.

A number of salient points need emphasis that are often overlooked in the debate over trade union decline. As the independent research organisation Incomes Data Services (IDS) has pointed out, the 1990 WIRS survey found 'no evidence of an overall decline in either union membership, or recognition, or collective bargaining in workplaces employing over 200 employees – the larger workplaces',[3] though it was true that over the previous fourteen years the number of such workplaces fell because of closures across manufacturing industry and a growth in the creation of much smaller establishments. Nor was there found to be much decline in workplace trade union organisation where collective bargaining was already well-established. The actual number of factories with joint steward committees rose by a third to more than half between 1984 and 1990. This is not the first time that Britain's trade unions have experienced a period of dramatic decline. During the inter-war depression with its mass unemployment and deflation, the number of workers in trade unions fell by almost half from 8,000,000 to under 4,500,000 between 1920 and 1933.

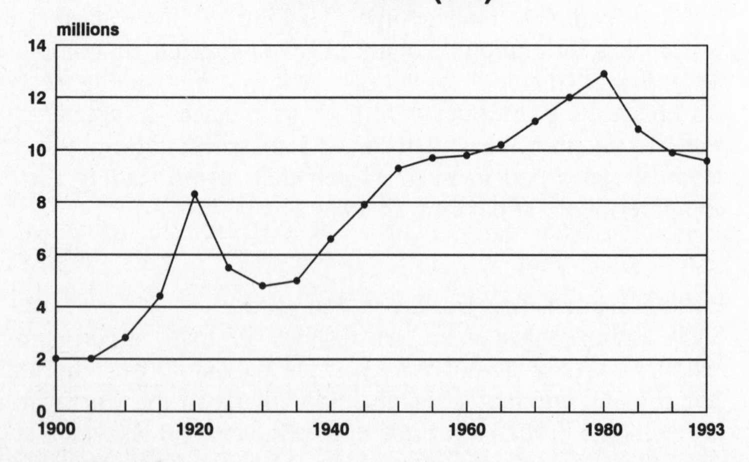

Moreover, the actual drop in the numerical strength of British trade unionism looks less dramatic when placed in an international perspective. The contraction in the size of the organised labour force during the past sixteen years was not confined to this country. Over most of the western industrialised world since the end of the 1970s a significant fall has taken place in the number of workers belonging to a trade union. During the 1970s there had been a net growth of 17,000,000 in the numbers of workers unionised in the OECD countries but this was followed in the 1980s by a net decline of 5,000,000. In the United States only around 16 per cent of workers were estimated to be organised in trade unions by 1993, with a mere 11 per cent of the labour force in the private sector of the labour market. In France the proportion of trade unionists in the workforce was down to under 10 per cent, after a fall of more than 40 per cent in the numbers unionised during the 1980s. A dramatic contraction in the size of trade union membership also took place during the 1980s in Holland – down from 35 per cent in 1980 to 22 per cent in 1993. Only in the Scandinavian countries, most notably Sweden, did organised labour demonstrate an impressive resilience.

Structural Change Means Union Decline?

The contraction in the size of Britain's unionised workforce – as elsewhere in western economies – is explained in part by the enormous shift that has taken place since the late 1970s in the occupational structure of the labour market. The Department of Employment's own figures reveal the proportion of workers in British manufacturing industry fell from 31 per cent in 1979 to only 20 per cent by 1993, while the employed number in the services sector climbed from 58 per cent to 67 per cent during the same period. In the recession of the early 1980s 2,000,000 manufacturing jobs disappeared from the labour market and a further 1,000,000 have gone in the second recession between 1990 and 1993. It is estimated trade union membership in the manufacturing sector has declined from 7,000,000 to under 5,000,000. In private services – the main area for potential employment growth during the 1980s – the proportion of workers unionised in 1990 was only 27 per cent. The evidence also suggested trade unions have found it difficult to recruit new members and secure recognition for collective bargaining in private companies in expanding areas of the economy. The decline of membership with the contraction of the heavily unionised smokestack industries has not therefore been offset by any dramatic expansion on so-called green field sites. The 1990 WIRS survey discovered that only 30 per cent of newly established workplaces recognised trade unions in the late 1980s. The 1993 Warwick University study of large companies confirmed this trend. It found 'the single most important factor behind changing patterns of union recognition amongst large companies appears to be management decisions at new sites where recognition was noticeably less common than at existing sites.' It concluded: 'In the prevailing industrial relations climate the exercise of management choice in the direction of trade union recognition is perhaps not unexpected. Nonetheless, given high levels of site openings (and closures) the medium-term implications of these findings are profound.'[4]

Public sector trade unionism has so far proved to be more resilient although the numbers employed in the public sector in Britain have also declined since the early 1980s. In 1981 there were 7.1 million; by 1993 the figure had dropped to 5.6 million, a decline of nearly a quarter. But an estimated 72 per cent of workers employed in the public sector continue to remain in trade unions. In some industries, such as the Post Office, up to 85 per cent of workers are unionised and have their pay and conditions negotiated by collective bargaining at national level. As the chart indicates, trade unionism also remains strong on the railways and in the recently privatised utilities.

Occupational and social change in the labour market has also led to an important shift in the composition of the unionised workforce. The most numerous unionised group of workers in Britain today are teachers and health service professionals. Fifty two per cent of them are organised. Half the employees defined as technical workers are also inside trade unions and 43 per cent of those in craft skills. In contrast only 31 per cent of service workers are organised, 30 per cent of clerical staff, 24 per cent of those in managerial grades and 14 per cent in sales jobs. These figures – from 1992 – suggest that trade unionists are likely nowadays to be better educated, more qualified, and in relatively higher paid jobs than those in the lower end of the market. As many as 47 per cent of members are middle-class, covering A, B and C1 social categories. If Britain is

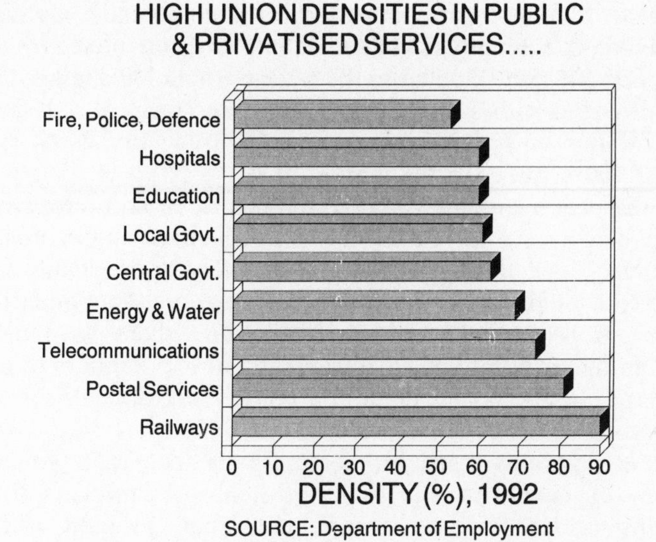

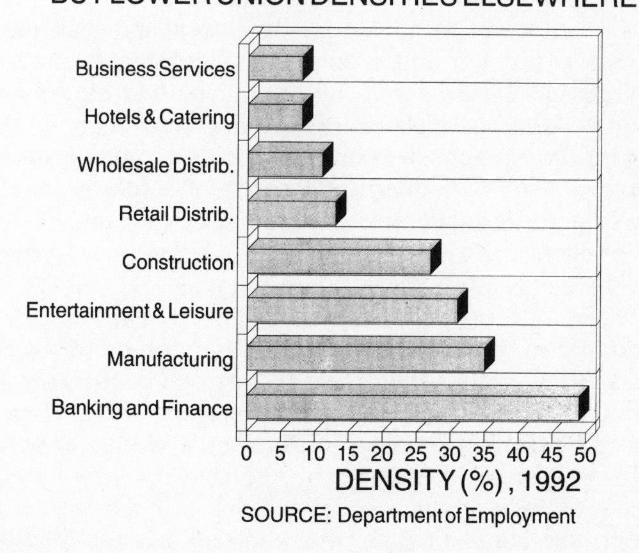

growing into a two thirds/one third society it seems likely – on the present evidence – that the unionised segment of the workforce is going to be coming from the ranks of the relatively more secure, and better paid. Such a trend has worrying features. It could mean many unions will come under pressure from their own members in a segmented labour market to make sure they are protected from the ravages of global competition and provided with a range of individualised services, but leaving millions unrepresented outside the trade unions to face the arbitrary forces of the market place.

If the economic and social conditions in Britain have been more or less similar to those of many other industrialised countries since the end of the 1970s, this has certainly not been true of the legal and political climate within which the trade unions have had to function. Here there have been substantial changes that have transformed the contours of our industrial relations and made life much more difficult for the trade unions to operate effectively.

John Edmonds, General Secretary of the GMB general union, explained to a conference held by Professor John Dunlop's commission on management-labour relations in the United States in March 1994 just how drastic the transformation of the British industrial relations system had been over the past fifteen years. 'A revolution has swept away all the old certainties and left most employees and many employers bemused and unsure about the future,' he told his American audience. 'The optimists believe we now have a great opportunity to try out new ideas and that Britain could become the laboratory where a modern philosophy of employee relations is developed. Most people observe a country so stunned by the pace of change it has lost the energy to build a new system to meet the needs of an advanced economy.'[5]

The role of public policy in Britain remains of crucial importance in understanding the rise and decline of the trade unions. In the past they grew and prospered because they were able to establish institutional supports both from the state and quiescent employers. As John Purcell has written: 'If this support is withdrawn by the state or employers the strength of trade unions recedes and the secondary institutions of collective bargaining'; in the words of the one-time TUC General Secretary, Vic Feather, 'it takes two to tango'. In the years since 1979 many of the institutional supports for the trade unions have either been pulled away or deliberately weakened by state action. 'We are seeing the progressive collapse of the system of industrial relations created over the past hundred years to bring order and stability to industrial relations.'[6]

More of the Same? Future Labour Market Trends

Accurate predictions about the future trend of trade union density in Britain are difficult to make. But it seems most unlikely that, even if a sustained upturn in the business cycle and a growth in tital employment does occur over the rest of the 1990s, the size of the organised workforce will return to anything like the levels it reached during its years of apparent dominance during the 1960s and 1970s.

The CBI has argued future economic recovery will not 'provide conditions conducive to union expansion' if the experience of the mid-1980s was an indicator to what could happen:

> Firstly, most of the new opportunities (at that time) arose in areas of activity which have traditionally proved unfruitful recruiting grounds for trade unions: self-employment; part-time work in smaller enterprises and private sector services. Few larger enterprises, with their traditionally higher levels of union density, increased their recruitment. Secondly, many of the new jobs were taken by women who have generally been less inclined to join unions. Recent labour market developments pointed to a continuation of these trends. Many parts of the trading sector with relatively high trade union density are continuing to shed labour: coal; steel; the railways; the utilities; post and parts of telecommunications amongst them. Contracting out, market testing and the general need for more cost-effective service provision may be reflected in real reductions in public sector employment overall.[7]

The CBI went on to argue future employment growth through to 2000 'will tend to be concentrated in smaller establishments, mainly in the service sector, while larger firms surveyed have indicated they will continue to look first to non-traditional sources to solve any emergent labour shortages, including not only women but older workers too; again a group who are relatively less inclined to be organised.'

Department of Employment labour market projections up to 2006 point to employment continuing to fall in many sectors in the labour market where trade unionism has been traditionally strong. The numbers employed in skilled and less skilled manual jobs will decline while the number of managerial, professional and associated occupations will increase. The Institute for Employment Research at Warwick University has estimated more than a million jobs will be lost in primary and manufacturing industries between 1990 and 2000, an 18.4 per cent decline from 5.4 million to 4.4 million. It has also forecast a 24.1 per cent fall in the numbers employed in the utilities – gas, water and electricity – from 294,000 to 223,000 over the period; a virtual elimination of employment in mining; and a one per cent drop in total employment in transport and communications.

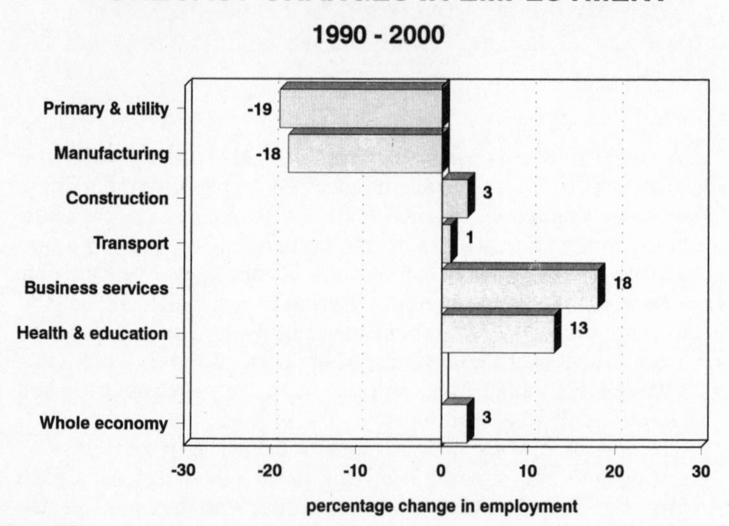

source: IER

The sectors of net job growth will be in construction with a 2.7 per cent overall increase, but this will mask a 7.3 per cent fall in employees and a 17.5 per cent increase in the number of self-employed in the industry. Business services (including banking and insurance) are expected to grow by 13.2 per cent from 3.1 million to 3.5 million, while there will be small 1.8 per cent growth in distribution employment; with a 16.9 per cent expansion of jobs in hotels and catering. In 'miscellaneous' services that cover a multiplicity of different occupations from research and development to cultural and recreational activities, a 24.7 per cent net jobs growth is forecast. The public health and education services are also expected to provide more job opportunities, with a 16.7 per cent growth from 3.2 million to 3.8 million, while public administration is forecast to increase employment slightly by 6.5 per cent from 1.9 million to 2.0 million.

The most significant change in the labour market over the next few years will be the growth in female employment. The Institute for Employment Research has suggested a 7 per cent net increase will occur during the 1990s in the number of women in the workforce, a rise of 823,000. The largest net job gains for women look set to come in senior managerial and professional occupations as a clear sign of the success of equal opportunity strategies in the higher echelons of companies. This will amount to a 43 per cent improvement or an extra 208,000 jobs, taking the proportion of senior women managers and administrators in the workforce from 24 per cent in 1990 to 29 per cent by 2000. Women can also expect to enjoy a 21 per cent increase in jobs for them in the professional associate and technical employment category, a rise of 215,000. Although the overall number employed in clerical occupations looks likely to show little change during the whole of the 1990s, an 160,000 jobs growth is expected in that area of the labour market for women. A 9 per cent net increase is also predicted in the level of female employment in the personal and protective service sector of the workforce.

However, job prospects for women are mixed. As R A Wilson from the Institute of Employment Studies at Warwick University has pointed out: 'Before celebrating the removal of barriers to women's employment it is important to consider the quality aspect. Much of the increase in employment that is expected will be part-time. To some extent this reflects personal choice and part-time working is growing amongst most occupations. However a large proportion of such jobs is likely to be of relatively low status with poor levels of pay.'[8]

The increasing importance of women in Britain's labour market and the implication of this trend for the trade unions has not yet been fully appreciated by most men who tend to dominate trade union internal structures, even where women make up a majority of the membership. But trade unions will have to adapt themselves quickly to this important gender shift in the workforce and begin to reassess their whole attitude to their female members by giving them a much higher bargaining priority and involving them far more in their own organisations. If trade unions want to grow again they will have to focus on the problem of how to attract far more women into the unionised sector of the labour market than at present but this will not be easy to achieve. Women more than men have dependent children to care for. An estimated 1.3 million one-parent families exist in Britain but as many as 94 per cent of them are headed by single lone mothers. The high divorce rate has also made women particularly vulnerable. More households than ever are dependent for their well-being on the employment prospects for women.

By contrast the overall level of male employment looks likely to remain the same in 2006 as it was in 1990 but with a marked shift towards skilled occupations. Significant falls are expected in the number of jobs available to plant and machine operatives and drivers (down by 11 per cent or 218,000) and among less skilled elementary occupations (down 19 per cent or 197,000). Employment in those two male categories looks set to drop from 21.7 per cent of the total employed workforce in 1990 to 18.9 per cent by the end of the decade. A 5 per cent decline is predicted in the level of craft and skilled manual employment, with a loss of around 165,000 jobs, and male clerical and secretarial jobs are expected to decline by 11 per cent or 117,000. The number of male professionals, however, is forecast to rise over the same period by as much as 18 per cent or 296,000, with most of that increase accounted for by science and engineering professional occupations. Male employment for managers and administrators looks set to rise by around 8 per cent or 350,000 people.

Goodbye to Fordism?

The most important structural change that has affected the level of trade union strength in the workplace during the 1980s has been the decline of the large scale enterprise where at least since the 1940s workers were mainly represented by trade unions. In his evidence to the Commons Employment Committee, Mr Peter Wickens, Personnel Director at Nissan UK Ltd, explained that those 'highly centralised' companies with their 'rigid hierarchies and power' were based on a 'control philosophy' of so-called 'scientific management', with a rigid demarcation of jobs broken down into requiring the simplest of tasks from the worker who was allowed little discretion and needed limited skill. Large, indirect departments for finance, personnel and engineering removed authority from the frontline managers and supervisors. 'The paradox was that while trade unions abhorred many of these practices, it was these very conditions that led to their growth and success, often built on a mutual view that there was an inherent conflict of interests between employers and employees and their unions,' explained Mr Wickens.[9]

Over recent years, that once familiar hierarchical structure of the enterprise has changed fundamentally and as a result it has altered the way companies behave towards their employees. Mr Wickens laid particular emphasis on the importance of internationalisation in a company's resources and markets. He wrote:

> Domestic natural resources are no longer a source of competitive advantage. In fact Japan has demonstrated that a lack of natural resources can be an advantage, allowing it to purchase the cheapest and best on the international market. Multi-market companies are able to operate in those countries which best suit them and are easily able to transfer funds and technology. All are now exposed to the cost structure of the most efficient and with the development of global markets, high profitability based on a unique technology or product is but short lived. We have moved from a producer-led to a customer-led market place and rapid reaction is now seen as one of the critical competitive factors.

Mr Wickens also pointed to the importance of technological innovation in speeding up the pace of change in the workplace. As he explained: 'Product life cycles have collapsed from ten to twelve years to, at the extreme, a few months. In some businesses, particularly consumer electronics, whoever generates new technology most rapidly is in the pole position to conquer the market place.'

The CBI has developed its own analysis of managerial development over recent years. It argued:

> The 1980s saw determined efforts in two directions: first, to generate a more flexible, involved workforce capable of meeting the challenges of an increasingly competitive and international market-place; second, to devolve functions not just to company level but to the establishment and below.
>
> Long-standing – but inefficient and demotivating – demarcation boundaries were tackled; flatter organisations were

> developed with fewer management layers, and businesses became better focused with non-core elements being contracted out to specialists.
>
> Typical developments included the amalgamation of maintenance and production work, multi-skilling and teamworking. The latest recession has seen many managers revisiting the same territory. The pace of change has accelerated again.[10]

The CBI has drawn attention to the growing use of more flexible forms of labour by companies who want to cut their costs and be better positioned through lean production methods to meet the ups and downs of the business cycle. This has meant a huge growth in temporary staff, contract labour and, in particular, the use of part-time workers, who are being used 'much more widely to cover the peaks and troughs in the workload.' It also suggested employer flexibility in labour utilisation was 'associated with the passing of more authority down the line.' As the CBI maintained: 'Local managers can build more constructive relationships when they clearly have the scope to take key decisions. And increasingly, employees are seeing their local managers are the ones who do this.' The CBI believed these developments would continue to erode the position of trade unions. There is – it said – 'the tendency for people at work to seek protection in collective strength', maybe in 'secular rather than cyclical decline.' 'Higher skill levels, higher manning and the associated need to secure the full and free commitment and enthusiasm of individuals at work – both personally and as team members – point to a new relationship,' the CBI suggested.

The Institute of Personnel Management (IPM) also drew attention to workplace restructuring in its 1993 policy document: Managing People – The Changing Frontiers. It argued that the global competitive pressures experienced by advanced economies are having a profound effect on work organisation.

> The vision which emerges when the changes of the past decade are extrapolated is one of scaled-down 'leaner and fitter' organisations, in both private and public sectors, new organisational structures made up of autonomous units, many more small businesses and a rise in self-employment, a shift of emphasis from collectivity to individualism, increasingly sophisticated information and communication systems and production technology and a business climate which is customer-driven, quality focused and fiercely competitive. It is against this

background that the management of people needs to be considered.

The old approaches of jobs for life, negotiations on every change, motivation through piecework and overtime 'to get the job done' are on the decline. But the new frontiers are only beginning to be pushed forward and properly explored. Changes abound but many employees express great scepticism: 'We hear what is said but nothing has changed.'[11]

Britain's Anti-Union Union Laws

Any analysis of the current state of trade unionism can become gloomily over-deterministic. Current economic and social trends may well point to a continuing retreat in the long march of organised labour but this is by no means certain. The outcome will depend on the political and legal environment within which trade unions have to operate in the future.

Over the past fifteen years, seven separate pieces of legislation have been passed by Parliament, designed to weaken the trade unions and undermine collective bargaining in Britain. The following provides a brief guide to their main provisions. Each by itself might not seem harmful but taken together they represent a massive and detailed intrusion by the state into the functioning of trade unions as voluntary institutions. The only saving grace is that sensible employers have been keen to avoid making any direct use of all the legislation in their dealings with organised labour despite some threats to do so.

1980 Employment Act

- Picketing was to be limited to strikers in lawful strikes at their own place of work.
- Secondary action by strikes was made lawful only if it was concerned with contracts of employment, limited to the first supplier or customer of the goods and services of the employer in dispute and where the principal reason for the action was to prevent the supply of goods and services during the period of the dispute.
- Legal remedies were provided for workers to use against their trade unions if they were 'unreasonably excluded or expelled' from the union on the grounds of refusing to join a closed shop. This right was extended to cover not

just employees with genuine religious convictions against closed shops but also to those who object 'on grounds of conscience or often deeply held personal conviction.'

- New closed shops were to be deemed lawful only where there was a majority support from employees for them in secret legally mandatory ballots where 80 per cent of those entitled to vote did so.

- The burden of proof was lifted from an employer that he had acted reasonably in dismissing an employee in a case of unfair dismissal. A worker had to be employed for two years to be able to bring an unfair dismissal case before an industrial tribunal and not six months as it had been under the 1975 Employment Protection Act.

- The trade union recognition provisions of the 1975 Employment Protection Act were repealed.

- So was Schedule 11 of the same Act which had enabled unilateral action by employees to secure pay rises from their employers to bring them up to the general level of recognised terms and conditions with other employees in the area.

- Financial aid was to be provided for trade unions that wanted money to assist in the holding of strike ballots and elections of union officials as well as union rule changes.

1982 Employment Act

- The key change – by far the most important of any after 1979 – was the repeal of section 14 of the 1974 Trade Union and Labour Relations Act that removed the legal immunity from trade unions for action in tort. This enabled, for the first time since 1906, the suing of a trade union in a court for punitive damages in an unlawful dispute. The trade union was made liable for any unlawful actions that had been authorised or endorsed by its specific trade union officials.

- Legal immunities were removed from trade unions where actions were taken that were not 'in contemplation or furtherance of a trade dispute'. A new and much narrower definition of a trade dispute was introduced to outlaw solidarity action by workers at home or abroad, as well as sympathy strikes or inter-union disputes.

- Further moves were made to limit the closed shop. All closed shops had to be balloted if they had not been in existence for five years and an 85 per cent majority of those voting needed to confirm their lawful existence. An employee could bring a joint claim against both the employer and the trade union for unfair dismissal in a closed shop where the legal requirements had not been met.
- Trade union-only commercial contracts were declared illegal.
- Trade unions and others organising industrial action lost their legal immunities where they tried to force an employer to sign union labour only contracts.

1984 Trade Union Act
This measure was motivated by the government's declared wish 'to return the unions to their members'. But it involved the most intrusive involvement by the state in the internal affairs of trade unions in the western world. It involved:

- The holding of secret ballots for the direct election of trade union executives at least once every five years, where practicable by post but otherwise among their members in the workplace.
- A secret ballot had to be held before a trade union could call its members out on strike. If this was not done the union lost its immunity from civil action in the courts. A majority had to agree to the proposed strike and the ballot had to be held no more than four weeks before the stoppage began.
- A secret ballot had to be held by the trade unions on holding political funds to ensure members approved of the use of trade union finances for political purposes.

There was a brief hiatus in the 'step-by-step' strategy until the passage of the 1986 Wages Act. This decreed:

- The abolition of the Truck Acts so manual workers had in future all to be paid in cash.

- The removal of young workers under the age of twenty-one from the provisions of the Wages Councils designed to protect low-paid employees from exploitation.

1988 Employment Act
This brought further restrictive moves against trade unions. These involved:

- The abolition of all remaining legal protections for the post-entry closed shop. No strike was to be lawful that tried to enforce a closed shop.

- Trade unionists in a lawful strike who crossed picket-lines to work could not be disciplined by their own trade union even if the majority of the employees concerned supported the strike.

- No trade unionist could be called out on strike without the holding of a secret ballot.

- All trade unionists had the right to a postal ballot in all union elections and pre-strike ballots.

- The Commission for the Rights of Trade Union Members was created with the stated purpose of helping trade union members with legal advice and financial support.

1989 Employment Act
- Most laws discriminating between men and women in employment were repealed.

- The abolition of the Training Commission and its functions were returned to the Department of Employment.

1990 Employment Act
- The abolition of the pre-entry closed shop was carried through by making it unlawful for an employer to refuse employment to a worker over the question of trade union membership.

- Trade union officials were required to repudiate or

take responsibility for unofficial strikes.

- Legal immunities were removed from trade unions in any industrial action taken to support people dismissed selectively for taking part in an unofficial strike.
- All remaining forms of secondary action in disputes were made unlawful.

1993 Trade Union Reform and Employment Rights Act

- The check-off system (the automatic deduction of trade union membership dues by an employer from employees) was made unlawful unless each trade union member gave his or her written authorisation every three years.
- Workers were given the right to join the trade union of their choice, which undermined the TUC's 1939 Bridlington agreement that regulated which trade unions workers could join.
- All trade union pre-strike ballots were made postal, subject to independent scrutiny, with at least seven day's notice to be given by the trade union after the ballot result to enable the employer to prepare for it. As a result of a High Court ruling in February 1994 – sustained in the Court of Appeal – against the college lecturer's union NATFHE a trade union was required, if asked to provide an employer with the names and addresses of all its members involved in a strike ballot.
- Everybody who used public services had the right to seek an injunction against a trade union to prevent the disruption of those services by unlawful industrial action.
- Everybody who worked more than eight hours a day for an employer was entitled to receive a clear written statement of terms and conditions of employment.
- The terms of reference of ACAS were changed so it no longer had to promote and encourage collective bargaining.
- The abolition of all Wages Councils and the end to any minimum wage fixing for workers.
- Industrial tribunals had their jurisdiction extended to

cover breaches of employment contracts.

- All women to enjoy a fourteen week continuous maternity leave with protection for pregnant women from unfair dismissal.

- Employers were allowed to offer trade unionists financial inducements to leave their unions. This was the result of an extraordinary decision to introduce an amendment in the House of Lords stage of the measure after a High Court judgement against Associated Newspapers for paying higher wages to journalists in return for the de-recognition of their union. No other legal provision since 1979 against the trade unions has been more controversial. Such a move would even be deemed legally impermissible in the United States where labour law works mostly against the trade union interest.

- Protection under the law for workers who faced victimisation and dismissal in health and safety cases where they sought to protect themselves and other workers from imminent danger.

Anti-Union Employers Using the Law

A number of trade unions gave graphic examples to the Commons Employment Committee of the way in which some employers have been using their new legal powers both in the systematic erosion of employee rights as well as campaigns for trade union de-recognition.

The TGWU compiled a 'dossier of disgrace' in July 1993 which catalogued a range of employment right abuses that have been inflicted on its members in recent years.[12] These included a number of notorious cases

- Ninety part-time women foodworkers were dismissed by Middlebrook Mushrooms near Selby in Yorkshire for refusing to accept a pay cut. Tearing up agreements with the TGWU, the employer tried to impose longer hours on the women instead, who earned £93 a week. When the women introduced an overtime ban, they were fired and casual workers were recruited to do their work for less pay.

- Nineteen shop stewards at Tilbury docks were fired by their employer after a strike in 1989. Two years later they won their case for unfair dismissal before an industrial tribunal. The chairman of that tribunal said the employer had planned 'a purge of all shop stewards at Tilbury to ensure that in the future there would be no organised resistance to the new regime.' The workers concerned had to wait a further three years to secure victory before an industrial tribunal when the employer admitted they had been dismissed unlawfully.
- Sandra Hook, a TGWU member, worked as a cashier at William Hill, rising to become a manager. But as the mother of two young children she was sacked when she refused to sign a new contract for evening work.

There have been a number of clear examples of companies that have made use of the new restrictive laws to push trade unions and collective bargaining out of their establishments.

In February 1994 Caterpillar UK, the subsidiary of the large American multinational, de-recognised MSF and GMB (APEX) who had represented their staff employees. As part of its annual salary and conditions negotiations, the company offered the workers concerned a 2 per cent pay rise and each a one-off payment of £500, along with health and legal benefits, in return for giving up collective bargaining and moving to individual contracts of employment with future pay based on individual performance. Caterpillar conducted an internal staff ballot without the consent of the trade unions in which they secured substantial majorities for their offer. The company's action brought swift condemnation from Mr Marcello Malentacchi, General Secretary of the International Metalworkers' Federation (IMF), who declared this was 'the first time since World War II that a multinational from a democratic country has so crudely sought to bribe its employees to give up their rights to union membership and surrender their rights to have their pay and conditions settled by collective bargaining.'[13] Both MSF and the GMB (APEX) doubted whether the company could sustain its position.

As they explained in a joint response: 'The only justification Caterpillar offer for these actions is to improve employee involvement. In essence Caterpillar is seeking to bypass the unions. The question is what corporate benefit the company expects to gain from this strategy. Whilst they may gain acceptance for their initiative, will they necessarily gain consent? We believe that the application of modern manufacturing methods, without genuine consent through independent trade union representation of the workforce, will in the medium- to long-term result in failure.'[14]

A particularly blatant case of trade union de-recognition came after the merger in November 1992 of Reed International with the Dutch publishing company Elsevier to create one of the world's largest publishing and information groups. Within forty-eight hours of the shareholders approving the merger, the new company gave formal written notification in their British publishing operations that it intended to withdraw recognition from the GPMU and the National Union of Journalists (NUJ). It also announced that as from 31 March 1993 its employees would no longer be covered by collective agreements but would each have to sign individual contracts. A substantial campaign was launched by the two unions against the company's action both at a national level and across the European Union.

Another notorious case of de-recognition highlighted by the GPMU has been at the Bristol printing company, J W Arrowsmith. Here 121 workers were dismissed in April 1993 when they refused to abandon a work-to-rule and overtime ban in support of a pay claim after the breakdown of national negotiations. Locked out, they were offered new contracts that involved a two year pay freeze, lower shift and overtime rates and in return acceptance of trade union de-recognition. The workers were given fourteen days to sign up. Only three did so. Unfair dismissal claims against Arrowsmith failed and the company began recruiting a replacement workforce.

The GPMU also gave examples of de-recognition of their agreements with the Newspaper Society, covering provincial newspapers in England and Wales, which culminated in 1991 with the employers' unilateral decision to terminate their national collective agreement with the trade union. This led to an acceleration of de-recognition at company level and the imposition of lower wages and inferior conditions on GPMU members. As the union explained in its written evidence to the Commons Employment Committee: 'Many examples can be shown where a combination of changes through technology, the use of current legislation, the introduction of individual contracts and the general employment situation, has enabled employers in the newspaper industry and in areas of publishing where the same groups are involved, to impose individual contracts. The legislation has been used at the same time to reduce wages and conditions of employment without any discussion with either the individual employee or the unions, who as part of this whole process will have been derecognised.'[15]

The GPMU went on to explain how individual contracts were being introduced:

> When individual contracts are imposed, workers may be made lucrative offers 'they cannot refuse'. Pay rises of over £1,000, promotions, company cars are all used to bribe individuals to sign away their union rights. Often, employers have been prepared to underwrite all existing employees' union-negotiated terms and conditions in return for a free hand to change these terms for those who follow. For the employers all this is a cheap way to pay for creating a union free environment, where they have the freedom to treat employees differently in future.
>
> A growing number of employers are not even bothering to offer bribes. They issue employees with new contracts and warn them of the consequences of not signing. Promised promotions are blocked. Individuals refusing to sign union-busting contracts are refused pay rises – and told that they will never get a pay rise again unless they sign. Staff may even be told that if they do not sign, they will be deemed to have dismissed themselves. Under present law, employers are legally perfectly free to behave in this way.

The AEEU engineering union also found itself in 1993 having to deal with a particularly harsh case that achieved national notoriety. The management of the Timex corporation's circuit board production plant in Dundee decided to dismiss its entire workforce and replace it with another when they refused to accept new employment contracts involving a rotation of lay-offs, a twelve month pay freeze, a 10 per cent cut in the value of their fringe benefits and the introduction of a profit-sharing scheme. The workers, who were mainly women with long years of service with the company, had been on strike and had decided to go back to work but 'under protest'. This was not enough for the company, who locked them out and then dismissed them along with seventeen workers who had defied the strike and gone to work. Timex said it had taken such drastic action because it feared individual workers – with the help of their union, the AEEU – could have taken the company to court to seek compensation for having new terms and conditions imposed upon them. 'Nowhere else in Europe are decent men and women being sacked for taking legitimate and legal industrial action,' said Mr Jimmy Airlie, the AEEU's executive officer for Scotland.[16]

The AEEU nationally made strenuous efforts to achieve a compromise settlement with Timex but the company refused to enter into any discussions until the end of ninety days from the date of the mass dismissals. This is the minimum period required under the law before a company can rehire selectively from among dismissed employees without facing an unfair dismissal charge from those who are not rehired. The company failed to secure the injunctions it sought in court against the strikers who were picketing the Dundee plant entrance. The AEEU took every precaution – with legal advice – to stay within the law, repudiating strike leaders on occasion and opposing mass demonstrations.

In early June 1993 the dispute reached its dénouement when the dismissed workers repudiated a deal agreed after negotiation between the company and the AEEU which would have involved the reinstatement of all of them or redundancy payments for those who did not want to return to work. Three months later Timex announced it was closing down the Dundee plant. Eventually the dismissed workers reached belated agreement on redundancy terms but it turned out to be a Pyrrhic victory.

BIFU, the banking union, also provided evidence to the Commons Employment Committee of the perilous legal position trade unions now find themselves in when they are dealing with a resolute employer. 'The present situation encourages bad employment practices and denies individuals the right to be represented – the right to have their voices heard or their grievances considered – either through collective bargaining or in individual cases, leaving them in a position of considerable weakness under existing employment law.'[17]

BIFU gave a number of examples from its own experience:

- When the majority of staff of the North of England Building Society voted overwhelmingly in favour of a transfer of engagements of their staff association to BIFU which occurred in July 1990, their employers immediately withdrew recognition from the union. With the formation of a new staff organisation within the Society management steadfastly refused to recognise BIFU who represented some 70 per cent of its workforce and in spite of a subsequent ballot of employees in which the majority again confirmed their wish to be represented by BIFU. It was only after two years of vigorous campaigning and many attempts at conciliation through ACAS that the Society finally accepted the wishes of the majority of staff and signed a recognition and procedure agreement with BIFU in September 1992.
- Barclays Bank had withdrawn recognition from 400 BIFU members who were transferred to a new subsidiary of Barclays de Zoete Wedd in 1985. The union complained to an industrial tribunal that this was a breach of the 1981 Transfer of Undertakings (Protection of Employment) Regulations but the bank had arranged the transfer to avoid the impact of the regulations and the Employment Appeal Tribunal ruled in the bank's favour.
- In October 1991 staff of Royal Bank Insurance Services Ltd. and Royal Bank Insurance Consultants Ltd. for whom BIFU was recognised were placed under the control of the Insurance Division of the bank and union recognition was withdrawn without any prior consultation, despite BIFU having over 60 per cent membership amongst those staff.

As BIFU argued: 'Such resistance in the face of a clear preference for collective representation produces unnecessary conflict and does the employer no credit at all. BIFU is particularly concerned, therefore, that even when faced with an overwhelming case for recognition for collective bargaining purposes there is no legal mechanism or industrial relations procedure in the United Kingdom to support collective bargaining and prevent potentially damaging disputes over recognition.'

The union recognised that the roots of the law's weakness go much deeper than the accumulated anti-union legislation of the Thatcher – Major years since 1979. As BIFU has explained:

> The basis for the employment relationship between an employee and an employer remains the contract of employment. In law this contract is assumed to be agreed by mutual consent between two equal parties. Although the outcome of collective agreements between employers and trade unions may be incorporated into individual contracts of employment, these collective agreements themselves remain largely unenforceable and individual contracts can be varied unilaterally by an employer with relative ease. The only legal remedy available to the individual employee in these circumstances is to give up one's job and claim constructive dismissal or to pursue a civil action where the loss is quantifiable. These remedies are especially difficult to pursue in times of high unemployment, and many employers exploit the relatively weak legal and economic position of employees, often ruthlessly, to reduce unilaterally their previously agreed terms and conditions.

BIFU pointed to its own recent experience of adverse changes imposed on their members in pay, pensions, holiday entitlement, housing loans, sick pay and sickness benefit. It argued:

> The collective strength of the union is the most effective means of preventing such unilateral changes. When there is no legal minimum wage and where legal protection for the individual against dismissal and redundancy is also limited to those with relatively long service who work full-time hours, it is inevitable that workers of all occupations and in all industries and professions will turn to trade unions to protect and represent them. One particular example of great significance during the current recession is the union's ability to protect members faced with redundancy, often carried out by employers in the most cursory and arbitrary fashion, and to obtain benefits for those made redundant which are well in excess of the maximum legal entitlement or where they have no legal entitlement at all.

Conclusion

Britain's trade unions have to operate in a cold climate. Even if there was a change of government and a more sympathetic political attitude towards them, with the passage of legislation that would ease the legal troubles that trade unions face today in carrying out their work, the structural changes in the labour market would still make it difficult for them. There can be no return to the way it was in the 1960s and 1970s. The world has moved on. Perhaps between a half to three quarters of the decline in trade union density since 1979 can be blamed on the dramatic contraction of a large part of the manufacturing sector where trade unions were once strong. The growth of smaller, service companies operating in small units whose workers, for a number of reasons, are hard to organise in trade unions. Certainly the fall in support for trade unions in other western economies suggests the trouble is not confined to Britain. However, there are no good reasons why trade unions should not be able to reshape themselves to meet the challenge of the new workplaces. Public opinion is sympathetic to them. There is little indication of ideological hostility among most employers to the existence of trade unionism. Workers do feel insecure of their position. Perhaps too many trade unions in Britain have grown too inert for their own good. Going back on the recruitment campaign trail in larger numbers might produce a much more positive response from workers than the trade unions expect.

NOTES

1 N Millward et al, Workplace Industrial Relations, Dartmouth 1992, p 352.
2 D Gallie and M White, Commitment and The Skills Revolution, PSI 1993, pp 41 – 42.
3 Incomes Data Services Report, December 1992, p 100.
4 P Marginson
5 J Edmonds speech, Washington DC, April 1994.
6 J Purcell, The End of Institutional Industrial Relations, Political Quarterly, Vol 64 No 1 1993, p 10.
7 CBI written evidence, pp 317–318.
8 Labour Market Structures and Prospects for Women, Equal Opportunities Commission 1994, p 27.
9 P Wickens, Nissan written evidence, pp 2–4.
10 CBI written evidence, p 320.
11 Managing People: The Changing Frontiers, Institute of Personnel Management, 1993 evidence, p 396.
12 TGWU written evidence, Dossier of Disgrace, July 1993.
13 International Metalworkers Federation press release.
14 GMB/MSF document on Caterpillar, March 1994.
15 GPMU written evidence, p 91.
16 *Financial Times*, 4 March 1993, p 8.
17 BIFU written evidence pp 81–82.
18 Incomes Data Services, December 1992, p 10.
19 ACAS annual report 1992, p 18.
20 Department of Employment written evidence, p 4.

CHAPTER THREE

Revitalising the Trade Unions

Britain's trade unions are going through a period of rapid change as they try to adapt to the conflicting pressures imposed upon their own organisations by an increasingly fragmented labour market. First and foremost, they are concerned with the problems of recruitment in the new workplaces and among millions of employees who do not belong to a trade union. 'Working people should be queuing up to join trade unions,' the GMB's John Edmonds argued. He accepted the fear of dismissal can be a deterrent for many who see the value of becoming trade unionists, but he also suggested other workers are not in trade unions because they have simply never been asked. Even when they have, they have often felt that a trade union is not for them. 'Trade unions are still associated with the traditional industries and services – coal mines, railways, big factories, council offices and the civil service,' he explained. 'When a young man or woman starts work in a shop, or an hotel, or in any of a thousand private service jobs they do not expect to find a trade union.'[1]

Jobs have moved from the traditional industries and trade unions have found it difficult to follow workers into their new occupations. Many of them seem content to stay in their traditional core areas and have no coherent recruitment strategy to break out onto the new terrain. Organising can be a painful and laborious process often with no quick results. In the late 1980s the TUC launched a 'Union Yes' campaign, initially in the Trafford industrial park area of Manchester and London's Docklands. Through a combination of public events, meetings, training in recruitment techniques and specific recruitment activities, the campaigns tried to bring trade unions together on a non-competitive basis to increase membership. The campaign was not a great success but fresh inter-union efforts have also been made at the local level in the Bristol area and in the north west of England. 'The unions themselves have undertaken intensive recruitment campaigns aimed at various target groups such as women, part-time workers, new industrial estates and new enterprises,' explained the TUC in its evidence.

> Such activities have included factory gate leafleting, direct approaches to employers for recruitment rights, responding to enquiries and the use of advertising to promote trade unionism. Determined efforts are being made to recruit in those areas where employment growth is likely as the economy recovers. However, the fact is that union recruitment is a two-way process involving a recruiter and recruit. If, for a variety of reasons, the recruit is unwilling to join, frightened to join or too apathetic to join, no amount of recruitment activity will succeed. While it cannot be disputed that there are a significant number of unorganised work people and workplaces and that various sectors are less well-organised than others, the causes of non-unionism are more closely related to labour market structure and employer attitudes than union recruitment strategies.[2]

The problems of trade union growth or even membership consolidation are considerable. In its evidence to the Commons Employment Committee the TUC pointed out that the hostile climate within which trade unions have to operate has exacerbated the difficulties of organisation by forcing them to devote 'limited resources to defend the jobs of existing members and dealing with redundancies rather than focusing on new recruitment strategies.'

This chapter will examine what trade unions are doing to recruit new members, look at the limited resources with which they have to develop new strategies and examine the different forms of trade union structure that are making a range of targeted appeals to particular segments of the labour market.

Women in Trade Unions

The biggest potential area for trade union growth lies among female workers. As many as 38 per cent of trade unionists in Britain in 1994 were women. However only a third of all women in employment are organised in a trade union or staff association although women now make up 49.2 per cent of the labour force. A growing number of trade unions are now giving high priority to female recruitment and trying to integrate them into their structures. But there is a great deal still to be done. In 1994 the Labour Research Department carried out a survey of the ten largest unions representing 5.7 million members. It found none of them had a level of female representation on their executive committees in proportion to their membership. Three unions – the GMB, MSF and USDAW – came closest to that ratio. In the TGWU only 5.4 per cent of national executive council members are women though 18.4 per cent of the membership are female. Just five unions provide reserved seats for women on their national executives. In 1993, 28 per cent of delegates to the Trades Union Congress were women.

The lack of women in the ranks of full-time union officialdom is even starker. Only four of the leaders of the sixty-eight TUC affiliated trade unions are women – Liz Symons, of the FDA, civil service union; Judy McKnight of the Probation Officers; Alison Gray of the Writers' Guild and Helen McGrath of NUKFAT, the Knitwear and Footwear Union. The LRD also discovered that only 20 per cent of UNISON's senior national officers are women, women make up 68 per cent of the union's rank and file.

Women Members in the Biggest Ten TUC Unions 1991

Union	*Total Membership 000s*	*Female Membership 000s*	%
UNISON	1,487	955	64
TGWU	1,037	190	18
AEEU	884	63	7
GMB	831	306	37
MSF	552	144	26
USDAW	316	189	60
GPMU	270	48	18
UCW	175	45	26
NUT	162	121	75
UCATT	157	1	1
Total of above	5,871	2,062	35
All Affiliates	7,647	2,678	35

Most of the larger unions have launched recruitment strategies designed to attract women into their ranks. The TGWU has given a high priority to this objective since 1987 when it started its 'Link-up' campaign using a range of innovative methods such as women-only recruitment campaigns, advice work in alliance with community groups, and serious efforts to make local trade union work more welcoming for women to participate in. UNISON claims to have an estimated one third of all women trade union members and it is making a particular effort to reflect this gender balance within its structure and activities. The union's declared objective is to ensure fair representation by having women members involved in the union's decision-making process proportionate to their members in the union by the end of the century. In its bargaining agenda, UNISON is committed to the cause of its part-time low paid women workers. It can point to a number of successes in equal pay for work of equal value cases; the removal of gender discrimination in the electricity supply industry; the negotiation of improvements in occupational pensions schemes for part-time members; and its efforts to secure childcare facilities for its women members through the introduction of childcare allowances, vouchers, workplace nurseries and out of school care. Combating sexual harassment in the workplace has also been given a high priority by UNISON.

The GMB is also a union that is taking a keen interest in women's issues. An estimated 37 per cent of its members are female with one in three of them working in part-time employment. The union has made a deliberate effort to increase female representation in its organisation. Ten seats on its executive council have been reserved for women since 1987. A further fifteen were elected by the members as a whole to that body in 1991. USDAW explained that 'in many respects equal opportunities are the cornerstone of our existence as a trade union.'[3] It said it had made some progress in negotiating agreements that provide over 75 per cent of its members with cancer screening provisions at work. BIFU, the bank staff union, appointed its first equality officer in 1991. It has established a helpline for advice and counselling to members suffering from sexual harassment in the workplace.

Trade Unions and Young Workers

The trade unions are also finding it hard to recruit young workers under the age of twenty-five into their ranks. The 1990 WIRS workplace survey found only 22 per cent in that age group were unionised. There has been a surprising lack of consistent interest – let alone concern – among the unions over their inability to make a popular and successful appeal to that vital segment of the labour force. It is not as if there are no issues on which to secure strong support for trade unionism among young workers. The anxieties of high youth unemployment and the insecure, low paid jobs on offer for many young people, particularly since the mid-1980s ought to have provided trade union recruiters with convincing arguments to win backing among the young in the workplace.

Certainly 24-year-old James Sorah, member of the RMT rail union and winner of the 1993 TUC Youth Award, did not believe there was any intrinsic resistance to trade union membership among the young people he knew. 'Most of them are very willing to sign up to become members,' he told the Commons Employment Committee. 'They appreciate the protection that they get from trade unions because a lot of them have worked in jobs where they did not have the opportunity to join a trade union. They have been messed about by bad employers and they appreciate the protection we give them.' From his own experience Mr Sorah suggested trade unions 'bend over backwards to help young people. To say they are fuddy-duddy organisations is an absolute nonsense.' But he went on to point out they were run by 'middle-aged men and women'. 'I should like to see a bigger effort made to encourage younger people to become active in the union,' he added. 'Actually to come to the branch meetings and partake. I should like to see a higher profile brought to youth conferences: there are many unions that do not do that.' He also suggested fewer and fewer young people were joining trade unions because they did not 'have the opportunity to work in trade unionised companies because there has been a growth in casualisation and in part-time working and in companies which are just not interested in the welfare of their employees.'[4]

Few trade unions have so far made a systematic attempt to win wider support among the crucial age group of the under 25's. Only five of them (MSF, TGWU, GMB, AEEU and CPSA) have established any formal youth structure or youth committees while six hold either annual or biennial youth conferences. A TUC survey in 1991 found a mere eight out of twenty-two unions surveyed offered a range of services specifically aimed at young people while twelve produced recruitment materials to attract young members. As it explained: 'If we were to judge the movement's youth work simply by the state of development of its internal processes then it is clear that the situation leaves considerable room for improvement.' There was little sign of any progress on the issue in the trade unions in a TUC follow-up survey in 1994 for its youth conference.[5]

Despite such disappointing evidence the TUC itself has made some efforts to focus attention on young workers. It has produced a Youth Charter that is a declaration of rights that should be held by young people between the ages of sixteen and twenty-five, as well as laying down trade union objectives for them. These recommend that every trade union should 'aim to ensure' that young members' views are represented by young people themselves within the union who should be given every encouragement and opportunity to participate in its activities. The Youth Charter also recommends that trade unions should provide equal opportunities for their young members to participate in its affairs. The TUC would like every trade union executive to consider establishing youth advisory committees at different levels of their structures.

The TUC itself has been promoting a programme designed to ensure young people in schools gain accurate information about the work of trade unions before they leave school to join the labour market. Traditionally trade union officials have been suspicious of youth movements, mainly because of their fear that they would be subverted by political extremism. But the experience of many mainland European trade union movements, particularly in Scandinavia, suggests such grounds for opposition are misplaced if trade unions ensure their youth activities are linked more closely to educational training programmes for young activists.

Trade Unions and Black Workers

Trade unions have not been particularly active in integrating black workers into their organisations either although blacks are more likely to be unionised than their white colleagues, mainly because they tend to have jobs in more organised sectors of the labour market such as transport, engineering and the public services. Mr Bill Morris, the TGWU's General Secretary, is black and he was elected in a ballot vote of his union's entire membership, but he remains very much an exception. In September 1994 the TUC will elect three black trade unionists (one of them a woman) onto the General Council. This was a symbolic recognition by the trade unions after the successful lobbying for black self-representation particularly through the TUC's black workers' conference. In recent years union leaders have been embarrassed by the lack of progress being made to provide black trade unionists with more opportunities to participate inside their structures. The change in the TUC will not allow the black representatives to be elected by black workers alone. They will be elected by all the trade unions at Congress and not be accountable to the black workers' conference.

Two recent independent studies indicate the unions have much to do to meet the needs of black workers. In 1992 the Commission for Racial Equality looked at the role of ethnic minority members in local branches of three unions – the CPSA, the NUCPS and the TGWU. It found that, for all their good intentions, the race issue in the workplace was not receiving the attention it needed. As with other questions, the gap between the trade union nationally and its presence at ground level remains considerable. As the study explained: 'The distribution of nationally-produced recruitment literature to all branches was shown to be a continuing problem. Union policies on tackling discrimination and promoting equality of opportunity as well as other more general information, were often not known of by members. Indeed, information on a range of policy initiatives, as well as practical advice on matters such as handling race-related grievances, encouraging black members to take part in union activities etc. often did not reach the constituency it was aimed at, let alone individual lay members.'[6]

The CRE also found that there could be resistance to dealing with racial questions on the shopfloor among local union officials. 'The practice of sending information only to the branch secretary or branch organiser meant that if these officers did not have a particular commitment to tackling racial discrimination, then the information would not be passed on,' it observed. 'The heavy and increasing work load of branch officials, particularly in those branches where there is not a great deal of member participation, makes even smaller the chances that such materials will get passed on to the relevant members.'

A 1991 survey of the involvement of black workers in ten TUC affiliated unions provided further evidence that trade unions are still not doing enough in this controversial area. It concluded that the overall picture was 'patchy'. As the survey noted: 'Of particular concern has been the degree to which developments aimed at improving the representation of black workers have not always given them sufficient access to decision-making in the union or adequate resources and opportunities to give them a feeling that their voice can be raised and heard in a manner that is acceptable to them.' Much of the survey made for dismal reading. It suggested unions themselves were not following equal opportunities for black workers in their structures. 'Monitoring of union employees was too often restricted to counting up, often on the fingers of one hand, the number of black employees at head office,' it noted. 'There was little evidence of racial issues being placed on union bargaining agendas. Nor did unions appear to keep a close eye on allegations of racial harassment in the workplace.'[7]

Examining the position of black workers in a wide range of unions, the study observed that, 'Even a cursory glance at the composition of union conferences, their regional or national executive bodies, their TUC delegations or their full-time officer post holders, shows an under-representation of ethnic minority members.'

The CRE study's conclusion was sensible enough – that equality of opportunity in the trade unions for blacks and women needs the creation of new structures and monitoring to check the effectiveness of its introduction. Just sending out worthy printed material to the members was seen as not enough. The report was keen to see more emphasis on overcoming the hurdles in unions to black worker recruitment. It maintained that the lack of direct union black representation in the workplace led to a low level of black recruitment. 'The perceived or alleged overt racism of local workplace stewards and some branch officials had an obviously negative effect,' it noted.[8]

Trade Unions and the Excluded

Trade unions have found it very difficult in the past to create a popular appeal among workers once they become unemployed. Some are trying to retain members who have no job, those who have retired or those who work at home. In February 1993 the Labour Research Department carried out a survey of eighteen TUC affiliated unions, each with more than 100,000 members, to discover how they maintained contact with those members who were unemployed. Most said they allowed the jobless to stay in the union for free or at a reduced subscription rate. Only two (the CPSA and the NCU) were found to have rules restricting membership only to those in work. However, the vast majority of trade unions do not pay any benefits to their unemployed members at all. Only the GMB and USDAW did so. The GPMU pays its jobless members £10 a week for ten weeks in the year if they have paid more than one annual subscription, while USDAW's jobless receive a modest £2.40 a week for thirteen weeks though they have to go on paying a normal subscription rate of £1.10 a week. The LRD survey found that, in practice, very few unions are able to retain their unemployed as members. The TGWU has around 25,000 of its members at any one time 'on remission' who pay 20p a week but it finds it much harder than the craft unions to hold them in their ranks. In the GMB 65,000 members pay a reduced fee of 5p a week but this includes retirees as well. The LRD survey found that MSF has the best record in retaining the unemployed mainly because they do not have to pay membership dues and are informed by post by the union that their rights are unaffected by the fact that they are out of work. The NCU introduced a 'portable membership' approach in June 1989 to enable members made redundant by British Telecom to move eventually to work in the other telecommunication companies without loss of union benefit entitlement. However most trade unions have not given much attention to this problem, even though the experience of unemployment is widespread across the labour market.

However, trade unions are seeking to keep in much closer contact with their retired members. The TGWU – very much under the powerful influence of its former General Secretary, Jack Jones – has established a retired members' association. The union told the Labour Research Department that 'as a result of the link, retired members have greatly assisted in union recruitment drives in various regions and in providing much needed support for union campaigns in defence of the National Health Service and in opposition to the deregulation of public transport.'[9] The LRD found fifteen out of forty-one unions it surveyed in 1993 had retired members' groups and only two – the Prison Officers' Association and Communication Managers Association – had no arrangements at all for their retired members. A number of them, including the GMB, the MSF and BIFU, entitle their retired members to receive whatever union benefits they need.

Trade Unions and their Financial Resources

Trade union activities – recruitment included – are limited by the size of their resources. Here finance is crucial. The demands placed on trade unions require the provision of a growing range of sophisticated and professional services in both collective bargaining, other workplace questions and on activities outside the workplace. None of this comes cheap. Hardly any of Britain's trade unions are wealthy bodies with substantial investments and accumulated assets. Traditionally the members have paid relatively low financial subscriptions compared with their counterparts in other western countries. In 1992 the average annual subscription rate totalled only £57.99, which was less than 0.5 per cent of a worker's total average earnings in real terms. But in the face of falling memberships, many trade unions have been compelled to raise their subscription levels, while their total income has also grown by securing an increased proportion from other sources.

In fact in 1992 the trade unions made an aggregate surplus of £21.9 million of income over expenditure. Their total gross income was £623 million and gross expenditure £576 million. The total assets of the trade unions were valued at £838 million, of which £290 million was in property and £290 million in investments. It has been estimated that the fifteen largest unions drew as much as 90 per cent of their operating income from subscriptions. These varied from a low figure of only £28.83 a year for members of the NAS/UWT teachers' union, to £100.69 for the National Graphical Association (now part of the GPMU), with an average annual subscription for the larger unions of £54.85.

During the 1980s, as Professor Paul Willman and colleagues

at the London Business School revealed, many trade unions grew much more efficient in the administration of their own finances despite membership recruitment and retention problems. They managed to increase their real incomes and reversed the fall in their net worth that had taken place during the 1970s, the decade of alleged mighty union power. Fewer members are now paying more to their unions and the asset base of the unions has been able to cover both any income shortfall and provide a surplus for reinvestment. One of the main reasons for this improvement in the state of union finances was the increasing centralisation of their resources with the decline in branch activities and the closure of local union offices. But Willman and his colleagues have questioned whether trade unions can maintain their present, relatively healthy financial position. 'While unions are becoming more sophisticated in their financial management, it seems unlikely that the pattern of 1992 can continue indefinitely,' they wrote. 'Some unions may be able to raise income through mergers or the sale of fixed assets but such income can only mitigate the effects of membership decline. Furthermore, if membership continues to decline and competition for membership becomes sharper, the capacity to raise real subscription levels must be brought into question, not least for those unions trying to recruit part-time and private service sector employees on relatively low earnings.'[10]

The administrative cost burdens on many unions look set to increase substantially after the government's 1993 decision to phase out state funding for trade union training programmes and for the running of the mandatory postal ballots for union elections and pre-strike balloting by 1 April 1996. This will force unions to allocate a larger portion of their financial resources to meet the shortfall.

The financial independence of trade unions is perilous because they have grown so reliant on the active cooperation of employers for the collection of their subscription fees from members through the so-called check-off system direct from the pay packets of workers. A 1993 survey carried out by the Labour Research Department found that in eighteen out of the top twenty unions 82 per cent of their members (4.9 million) had their subscriptions paid in that way, compared with a mere 8 per cent of members who paid through direct debit from their bank accounts, although that figure is rising.

The rest is collected by union activists in more decentralised unions. Some employers – most noticeably British Rail, British Coal and the Conservative dominated Wandsworth Council in London – withdrew check-off facilities in 1993. Some unions – notably the NUT teachers union – have launched a campaign to encourage a shift by members to direct debit and the proportion having their subscriptions paid through that system rose from 17 to 29 per cent between 1991 and 1993.

The London Business School study concluded that trade unions cannot fund their day-to-day operations indefinitely any longer from their own resources without the provision of massive subscription increases or an exhaustion of their assets. As a result they have grown 'employer-dependent' in order to survive. It admitted that 'to some extent such dependence was an indication of negotiating successes, given the structure of British unions.'

As the study explained:

> Lay involvement, the key to cost control and perhaps to a wider range of union objectives, depends on employer support. But too much employer support may threaten their independence and in fact usurp the union's role unless the employer is simultaneously dependent on the union. Employer dependence for trade union facilities to encourage lay participation is a sine qua non for effective union organisation but that dependence on the employer for revenue and recruitment may be dangerous [because over time it could] encourage passive joining decisions and reduce the recruitment effort made by the unions.[11]

The 1993 – 1994 trade union check-off campaigns – required by the 1993 Trade Union Reform and Employment Rights Act – found very few employers who were prepared to abolish the system. On the contrary, many of them cooperated enthusiastically in helping the trade unions to ensure the check-off stayed in place, at least for a further three years. A survey of 144 well-organised workplaces carried out by the Labour Research Department in the summer of 1993 found none had faced any move by an employer to eradicate check off.

Freedom of Trade Union Choice

Workers in Britain have been legally entitled since 1993 to join the trade union of their choice. This has profound consequences for the trade unions. It has already led to the end of the TUC's famous 1939 Bridlington principles which sought to govern inter-union relations. Their main feature had been the ruling that no member or ex-member of a trade union could be accepted into the membership of another without an inquiry into his or her position in the former union. That union was required to reply within fourteen days, stating whether the applicant had resigned, whether they were free of arrears, whether they had been fined or penalised by the union under its rules and finally whether there was any reason why the application should not be accepted. The reason for the introduction of the Bridlington rules was to try and ensure greater workplace stability through inter-union cooperation rather than rivalry. The multi-union character of so many workplaces had encouraged sectionalist attitudes and bitter inter-union feuding over members. From 1939 until 1993 TUC Dispute Committees sought to defend and administer the Bridlington Principles in the interests of shopfloor peace and for the most part it proved to be highly successful.

Today sectionalism does not seem to be much of a problem though the 1993–94 conflict in the construction industry between UCATT, the TGWU and the AEEU suggests inter-union wrangling over recruitment has not entirely disappeared from the scene. The TUC has sought to re-establish some form of stability through the establishment of new rules aimed at trying to prevent one union from seeking to recruit members off another under the threat of facing financial sanctions. Whether these new TUC rules will work in practice remains unclear but Congress House wants at least to coordinate inter-union relations while acknowledging the provisions of the new legislation have to be accepted.

The Importance of Trade Union Democracy

Trade unions are much more democratic bodies than they used to be. The voting systems for their leaders and executives must now be carried out by postal ballot and they are covered by a wide range of intrusive regulations to ensure they are fair and free. Contrary to government expectations, the arrival of the mandatory ballot has not so far produced any dramatic changes of political power within most trade unions. On the other hand, it does seem to have brought members, activists and leaders into much closer rapport than before. As a study of union elections held between 1984 and 1990 concluded:

> Workplace organisation provided a ready-made structure for

> ballot administration and where it was absent, ballots provided an occasion for its construction. Lay and professional representatives discharged their tasks with efficiency; there were specific cases of maladministration but the only accusation as to extensive ballot rigging failed to supply any conclusive evidence. Activists performed a supportive administrative role, provided information as to candidates and mobilised participation. Thus despite the expressed intention of the 1983 Green Paper – Democracy and the Trade Unions – activists were enfranchised in a novel way within union political processes, strengthening their relationship with members.[12]

The change in 1988 from workplace to postal ballots may have begun to affect the membership participation rate in elections but there is little evidence to suggest this has led to the triumph of so-called individualistic over collectivist values among employees. A study by Templeton College, the Oxford Management Centre concluded:

> [the] constitutional reforms initiated by the legislation enhanced the opportunities within unions for electoral competition but this did not automatically generate factional political systems. In some cases factions have developed following the amalgamation of unions with different political traditions although this process may be inhibited but not prevented by the increasing prevalence of sectional constituencies. Factionalism increases the range of views that are articulated within a union and potentially at least, this could subvert the capacity for collective action; but ballots can also provide a mechanism through which policy disputes can be legitimately resolved, thus enhancing cohesion.[12]

However, they also suggested 'the legislation has singularly failed to initiate a transformation in the political complexion of union leadership or a reorientation of union policy in a "moderate" direction nor was this outcome ever likely.'

Union Mergers and Amalgamations

The most dramatic change in recent years in the trade unions has come through the quickening pace of mergers and amalgamations. In 1978 there were 112 trade unions affiliated to the TUC; by 1994 the total was down to only sixty-nine. A number of further mergers are probable over the next few years including one between the NCU and UCW in the communication industry and among unions inside the civil service. It is even possible that two of the giants, the TGWU and the GMB, might come together in a new union. By the end of the century the total number of unions looks set to be a good deal smaller. The degree of union concentration has also been considerable. In 1993 five unions accounted for 62 per cent of the TUC's total membership. These were UNISON (1,486,984 members), the TGWU (1,036,996), AEEU (898,542), the GMB (799,101) and the MSF (552,000). The days have long gone when critics of the unions used to lament there were too many of them and their inflexible structures and regulations were barriers to workplace innovation.

In its supplementary evidence to the Commons Employment Committee the TUC listed four factors that have become influential in encouraging the trade union merger process: the need to secure the trade union's financial base; enhancing the range of services that trade unions could provide their members; enabling the newly merged union to extend its influence; and improving the competence of union organisation. 'The financial factors driving mergers include the savings associated with economies of scale through the more efficient use of personnel and capital resources; the release of assets; a sounder financial base; a route out of financial difficulties for an individual union,' said the TUC. 'Certain services within the union can more easily be provided and delivered with a larger membership and financial base. This can include research facilities, employment of experts (eg covering health and safety, legal issues, management techniques etc.) and the provision of trade union education.'[13]

The TUC added that the hostile industrial relations environment of the 1980s had exacerbated the problems for the trade unions in their organisational activities as they had been forced to devote 'limited resources to defend the jobs of existing members and dealing with redundancies rather than focusing on new recruitment strategy.'

The Rise of the Super Union: UNISON

UNISON is Britain's newest mega trade union with an estimated 1.4 million members who are employed in the country's public and private services. It is the third biggest trade union in western Europe after the German mega unions IG Metall and the public service union OTV. The union's budgeted expenditure for 1993 – 1994 amounts to £105 million, a quarter of the total amount of the money that is spent annually by all TUC affiliated unions. Its membership is extremely diverse and covers low paid part-time workers earning less than £100 a week to executives on salaries of over £50,000 a year. But on balance the majority of UNISON members are at the bottom end of the labour market with as many as 54 per cent of the rank and file earning under the Council of Europe definition of the low paid.

UNISON, led by Mr Alan Jinkinson, former General Secretary for NALGO, was founded on 1 July 1993. It is the result of an amalgamation between three trade unions – the Confederation of Health Service Employees' (COHSE), the National and Local Government Officers Association (NALGO), and the National Union of Public Employees (NUPE). A ballot of the members of all those unions was held in December 1992 and it produced overwhelming majorities in support of the creation of the new union.

The result on a 33 per cent turnout was as follows:

	YES	NO
COHSE	57,789 [93.9%]	3,737 [6.07%]
NALGO	227,429 [73.2%]	83,375 [26.8%]
NUPE	166,007 [93.7%]	11,131 [6.3%]

'The ballot success heralds a new era in British trade unionism,' declared Mr Rodney Bickerstaffe, former NUPE General Secretary and now UNISON's Associate General Secretary. 'A union for our time,' said Mr Jinkinson of the new union. 'It was created not from weakness but strength.'[14]

Nearly two thirds of UNISON'S members are women, most of whom are working in the public caring services. The union accounts for an estimated one third of all women trade union members in Britain. It has nearly half of all local government workers in its ranks and over a third of those employed in the electricity, water and gas industries. As the union explained:

> The organisational arrangements and objectives of the union have been deliberately designed to reflect the members' varying work responsibilities, employment patterns, backgrounds and personal circumstances. A commitment to equal opportunities and fair representation lies at the heart of UNISON's organisation and is embedded in its constitution. Care must be taken to ensure that women, lower paid members and those from disadvantaged groups (disabled, gays and lesbians) are fully represented in the internal democratic and internal decision-making structures.[15]

UNISON's declared objective therefore is to ensure fair representation in its internal structures. It wants to have women members represented in its decision-making process in proportion to their numbers in the union by the end of the century. Until mid-1995 an interim national executive will continue, made up of the existing three union executives. All funds and assets are to be merged and a new sliding scale of contributions based on salary levels has been introduced.

One of the main reasons for the giant merger between the three mainly public service unions was to achieve the advantages of scale through the eventual consolidation of resources, skills and supports better to benefit the members. 'The new union will be able to eliminate duplication of effort and better focus its activities on behalf of its unified membership,' UNISON argued in its written evidence to the Commons Employment Committee. 'This is especially important for members in smaller services or groups; they can be better organised and provided with improved services.'

A second reason for UNISON's creation was to make it easier to adapt to the changing climate in the public services caused by the emergence of new patterns of ownership, the application of new management techniques, the arrival of more private contractors with compulsive competitive tendering, changes in technology and the growing awareness of the importance of training at work.

UNISON has emphasised from the start that its members are committed to the provision of 'quality services' to the public. The union says it has 'a direct interest in maintaining and improving services to the public and the pursuit of that object is strengthened by amalgamation.' As the union's written evidence explains; 'UNISON sees itself as one of the major bodies concerned to ensure appropriate investment, training and quality assurance in the services where its members work, whether in the public or private sectors. It expects to be involved in debates about and actively supports high quality, efficient and user-friendly services across a wide sphere of activity.'[16]

The union may oppose privatisation of public services and new methods of working involving private contracts but as UNISON explained, when changes occur in the workplace it 'is committed to sharing responsibility for securing transition, managing change and working pragmatically in the interests of the members and the service. Employers are often grateful that unions provide the machinery for a consultative process, especially in large organisations.'

The trade unions that make up UNISON were opposed on principle to the gas, electricity and water industries being privatised but they argued that they had 'worked hard to assist in the peaceful creation of the new enterprises and to safeguard the terms and conditions of members and quality of service to the public.' UNISON has invested significant resources in training to familiarise workplace representatives with the private sector and company dynamics,' it said. 'Individual members have received advice from the union on personal contracts and other new working arrangements. UNISON sees itself as an indispensable part of the management of change at work and provides the machinery for consultation with staff where the law or good sense requires it.'

The union emphasises the 'wide-ranging and attractive' package of services it can provide for its members. It points to the development of its education and training programme, its activities in the health and safety area, the provision of comprehensive free legal support and professional publications to keep members abreast of its activities. UNISON has its own credit card, Unity First Mastercard – organised with the Bank of Scotland – and applications have exceeded 50,000 since it was launched. The union also has its own travel agency and owns two hotels and three convalescent centres. It also provides financial assistance for members suffering hardship through the provision of grants and loans. As much as £547,500 was spent in such a way between October 1991 and September 1992. The union also has a range of benefits for accident, death and incapacity, although these do not add up to substantial sums of money.

Two of UNISON's inherited membership services are particularly important for members. UIA (Insurance) Ltd. provides householders' insurance at competitive premiums for around 100,000 UNISON members. Its funds are more than £40 million and annual premium income is around £14 million. Motor insurance is provided by the brokers Frizzell. UNISON also has an arrangement with the Britannia Building Society to provide cheaper mortgages for members at advantageous discounts.

The union remains committed to national bargaining and

'the fairness and stability which it brings in industrial relations.' However, the union has also been 'adapting its structure and bargaining arrangements to meet the growing flexibility and casualisation of the labour market.' It is, in particular, committed to the protection of their most vulnerable members – part-time low paid women workers and others in atypical employments.

GMB: Innovation in General Unionism

The GMB is at present Britain's fourth largest trade union representing around 800,000 blue-collar and white-collar members across private industry and both the public and private services. As the union explained to the Commons Employment Committee they 'work on the factory floor and in offices, in shops and in hospitals, in depots and on vehicles, in classrooms and in canteens, on oil rigs and on building sites, indoors and in the open air.'

An estimated 38 per cent of the GMB's members are women of whom one in three are in part-time employment. By contrast, as many as 95 per cent of the union's male members work in full-time employment. An estimated one in ten of GMB members are under the age of twenty-five and 2 per cent belong to black or other ethnic groups. The annual membership turnover is between 15 and 20 per cent so the GMB needs to recruit 150,000 new members every year just to stand still. It remains very much a manual trade union with five out of six of its members manual workers, but the GMB believes this will change rapidly in the future with women and white-collar workers becoming important recruitment targets.

Over the past ten years the union has been involved in a series of important mergers. In 1982 the Boilermakers Society amalgamated with the General and Municipal Workers. This was followed seven years later by APEX the white-collar union and the Greater London Staff Association mergers. In 1991 the Tailor and Garment Workers Union merged with the GMB, followed in September 1993 by the Furniture, Timber and Allied Trades Union (FTAT).

Since 1979 the balance of the GMB's membership has shifted from private sector manufacturing into private service employment while public service membership and that in the privatised utilities has dropped leaving their relative strength in the GMB almost unchanged.

The GMB's Changing Membership by Industry Since 1979
% of Total GMB Members

	1979	1992
Metals and Engineering	33	12
Clothing and Textiles	10	9
Public Services	20	23
Privatised Industries	7	9
Food, Drink and Distribution	8	15

In 1990 the GMB drew up a new 'mission' statement that is inscribed in its rule book. It declared its avowed purpose was 'to improve the quality of life for all members and their families, widening horizons and bringing new opportunities into reach.' 'We aim to enhance the lives of GMB members and ensure that their achievements spearhead the advance of working people in Britain and the world,' it added. But the union also made it clear that it sought to 'work in partnership with the more far-sighted employers, negotiating constructive and beneficial agreements which help to achieve' its purpose. 'We will work to widen the understanding of employers whose horizons and objectives are more limited. The GMB will be a friend to humanity but an enemy to exploitation, discrimination and injustice.' A new emphasis was placed on the need for recruitment.

The GMB has restructured itself internally around eight sections covering its main areas of membership and these enjoy a considerable degree of autonomy. They are run by section national committees made up of elected lay representatives and meet periodically through the year with an annual section national conference. This enables the union to retain a sharp industrial focus and it marks a clear change of focus away from the GMB's traditional strength among the regional secretaries.

The union's General Secretary Mr John Edmonds has spearheaded a fundamental reappraisal of the GMB's strategy. In his opinion, the collective bargaining agenda lies at the heart of trade union activity and this needs to be developed not in reacting sceptically to management initiatives but in developing one of its own. This is not an agenda that is antagonistic to employers. On the contrary, its aim is 'to achieve as close a match as possible between the priorities which the union pursues in negotiations with employers and what GMB members want from work.'[17] As the union explained: 'Surveys conducted for the GMB and for other organisations suggest that a bargaining agenda which is narrowly pay-related could not achieve the kind of match which we need to serve our members well. Pay will always remain a vitally important issue to working people and their unions. But job security, the opportunity to develop your abilities, flexible work arrangements and jobs that allow workers to use their initiative and earn promotion all count highly with working people.'[18]

MSF: Agenda for the Next Century

The Manufacturing Science and Finance union (MSF) was formed in 1988 through the merger of the Association of Scientific Technical and Managerial Staffs (ASTMS) and the Technical Administrative and Supervisory Staff union (TASS). It represents an estimated 552,000 skilled and professional people who are employed in a wide variety of industries and services with nearly half of them working in manufacturing as engineers, scientists, researchers, technologists, managers, and in craft skills. Around 27 per cent of the union's members are women and they account for about half of all MSF's new recruits. By the end of the century MSF estimates as many as 40 per cent of its members will be women. If trade unionism in Britain is to revive again in the future, it will do so in trade unions like MSF who have staked out an area for recruitment in the growth areas of the labour market.

Its leaders are very conscious of the need for change. They produced in May 1994 a fascinating strategy document, MSF into the 21st Century, that spelt out the way ahead. What encourages its General Secretary Roger Lyons are signs that MSF is well placed to take advantage of the future occupational trends in the labour market. Forecasts from the Institute for Employment Research at Warwick University suggest there will be a 27 per cent growth in the number of science and engineering professionals between 1990 and 2000; an increase over the same period of 18 per cent for corporate managers and administrators; a 14 per cent expansion in health professionals and a 26 per cent rise in the number of other professionals.

The union claims it has found no evidence that white-collar employees see trade unionism as a 'growing irrelevance'. Early in 1993 it commissioned a profile survey of its own membership.

Its findings reveal the changing characteristics of Britain's trade unionists. MSF members are noticeably affluent workers with 40 per cent of them earning more than £25,000 a year and 16 per cent more than £35,000 compared with a national average of 7 per cent at this figure. The bulk of members were classified in social class C1 but 27 per cent were ABs. As many as 90 per cent were owner-occupiers, with 17 per cent owning their homes outright. Just under half MSF members were over the age of thirty-five and 39 per cent more than forty-five years old. As many as 78 per cent had some formal educational qualification with 18 per cent holding university BA or BSC degrees and 3 per cent doctorates. They enjoy a comfortable lifestyle with 34 per cent taking two holidays a year and a further 18 per cent three or more holidays. Forty five per cent of MSF members own a home computer; 93 per cent have a car; 72 per cent possess a credit or charge card; 70 per cent contribute to a company pension scheme.

The survey made it very clear that MSF members have 'bread and butter' reasons for wanting to belong to the trade union. The union insists people join MSF 'to redress the imbalance of power between employer and employee.' That primary role cannot be ignored. 'Whether it is national bargaining in a multi-union workplace or individual representation in a company that refuses to recognise a union for collective bargaining, MSF's job is to provide collective support and assistance to members and to effectively represent their interests in the wider trade union and political environment. Although change is altering the old patterns of industrial relations and bargaining, the essential role of trade unions remains and will remain unchanged,' argued the union strategy document.[19]

But MSF leaders have also recognised increasingly that the union will have to become much more of a service provider to cater to the needs and demands of its members as individual workers. 'Our structures still reflect the assumption that the collectively-organised workplace is the norm; this is no longer the case,' argued MSF. 'Members as well as potential members, particularly now that the latter have a free choice as to which union to join with the abolition of the old Bridlington procedures, are looking to MSF as a service provider as well as a means of organising workers collectively.'

As the union's strategy document went on to explain: 'This is especially the case with the trend in some sectors and companies towards "individualisation" of employment relationships. An individual employee on a personal contract will need support in a different way; for example, advice on contract terms, working conditions and pensions and individual representation.'

This will involve a much more professional approach from its full-time officials who will become less active as collective bargainers and more active as servicing agents catering to the needs and demands of individual members. 'We should be adapting our services to these new circumstances and marketing them in new ways. We also need to define more clearly what are the services members are entitled to: this could include different levels of service for different levels of subscription. We need to make sure our staff resources are used effectively as providing service to individuals is more time-consuming than collective bargaining for a large workplace group.'

The quality of service a trade union provides has to be emphasised in the new competitive labour market. 'Providing quality service means that it has to be available when members need it and in a way that is easily accessible to them rather than convenient to us,' explained the MSF document.

The union leaders also accept they will have to refocus the union if it is to stem membership decline and ensure financial viability through the development of a 'recruitment culture' that will concentrate around the need to retain and renew individual membership. The union has lost members heavily in recent years in manufacturing and with a strong presence in the defence equipment companies it could suffer further membership decline in the future. But MSF has also made a number of important gains in areas of real potential such as the voluntary sector, financial services and health service. These have included: the staff of the Wildlife Trust Partnership; the staff association for ceramic research workers; the Hospital Physicists Association and the National Union of Scalemakers. Sole recognition agreements have been signed with the Stonham Housing Association (1,300 staff) and Glenfiddich bottling plant in Paisley.

The union believes there is enormous potential for further mergers with smaller unions faced with financial difficulties and devolved bargaining structures but this will require a more strategic approach.

Mr Lyons is a strong believer in trade union corporate campaigning, using modern techniques of communication to present the case for trade unionism and to mobilise wider public opinion. He has been much influenced by his personal experience in organising trade unionism among staff in California's Silicon valley. In 1994 MSF enjoyed an unexpected success at the Zurich Insurance Company that could become a model for future trade union efforts to thwart derecognition efforts by employers. Early in 1993 the Swiss-based company acquired Municipal Mutual Insurance. At once it announced – without any consultation with its workforce in the United Kingdom – that it was de-recognising MSF, although the company recognised trade unions in every other EC country where it operates. The union responded with a campaign of resistance to the move which focused on lobbying Zurich's British customers, especially local authorities, raising the issue in Parliament both in the United Kingdom, Switzerland and the European Parliament, and publicising their case through the trade press. The company eventually caved in.

'The development of effective campaigning techniques will grow in importance,' argued MSF. 'In the past the term "campaign" was generally used to describe a press release and some leaflets. A proper campaign, by contrast, has to be well thought-out, targeted at a particular objective and well resourced and monitored. Companies can be just as sensitive to pressure on their public image as they are to industrial action.'[20]

Zurich was a clear victory for the union but MSF has suffered a number of other setbacks in its battles against the threats of de-recognition. In January 1991 Cable and Wireless, for example, de-recognised the union for both collective bargaining and individual representation. Meetings with the company and lobbying at parliamentary level in the EU failed to bring a change of heart. In December 1992, Hilliers, an engineering company in Reading, dismissed members for taking part in official industrial action in protest against its decision to cut wages and conditions unilaterally. The company refused to negotiate, de-recognised MSF and the AEEU and replaced the dismissed workforce with a new one to maintain production. Union action through ACAS and representation at industrial tribunals failed to convince the company to rescind its decision. At the British American Tobacco company MSF was de-recognised in the spring of 1993 when the company told the union's seventy members were to have their contracts transferred to another part of the firm where there would no longer be recognition for collective bargaining purposes. The company then broke a three year pay deal agreed with the union and imposed worsened terms and conditions on the workforce in return for a one-off cash payment. The union tried unsuccessfully to use local and national procedures as well as the services of ACAS to remedy the problem.

The RCN: Bucking the Membership Trends

The 300,000 strong Royal College of Nursing (RCN) may not be a TUC affiliated trade union but it is now the sixth largest trade union in Britain and the world's largest professional union of nurses. Its members represent 80 per cent of all qualified nurses, midwives and health visitors in the country, more than two thirds of all qualified nurses and students working inside the National Health Service. In its evidence to the Commons Employment Committee the RCN argued that the reason for its current success stemmed from an ability to perform three distinctive functions.

> The RCN does not offer a one-dimensional form of trade unionism. It exists to provide representational services (individual and collective), professional services (to members, to the medical profession and to health care organisations) and educational services. The RCN will long argue the advantages of collective bargaining for nurses but will equally seek to work with colleagues across professions, employment sectors and in government, to secure the highest professional and educational standards for nursing. The RCN will remain a source of help, advice and advocacy. It appeals to a much wider audience than traditional trade unionism and does not rest on one dimension, i.e. recognition and bargaining – although this is of vital importance.[21]

The RCN insists the 'three dimensions' of its activities are 'mutually dependent'. 'Debates about professional practice, standards and quality inform many representational discussions (whether individual discussions or through, say, the Pay Review Body evidence); in turn both these discussions are fed and informed by debates about educational needs, structures and outcomes.' The RCN does appear to have moulded its diverse activities into a coherent whole which has enhanced its appeal among nurses, judging by its membership growth in recent years. It is also acutely sensitive of the need to keep in close contact with the general public to ensure it enjoys an instinctive sympathy. The RCN rejects – through its own rule book – the use of any form of industrial disruption to further the cause of nurses. It believes 'the right to strike is a right of citizenship which it chooses voluntarily to relinquish because of the primacy of patient need.'

The RCN told the Commons Employment Committee:

> By rejecting militancy in favour of broader political campaigning the RCN has certainly been free to develop a wide range of activities to achieve objectives on behalf of the members, the profession and society. Thus a strong relationship with the public is sustained. This pact with the public and a commitment to give the highest quality care is strengthened and magnified through the unity offered by the professional body.

Ms Christine Hancock, the RCN's General Secretary, told MPs: 'I think we would see and most of our members would see strike action as a failure in good relationships and not necessary in a mature society. But certainly internationally it is not common for nurses' associations to have been as successful as we are without taking industrial action.'[22]

The RCN has developed a local servicing function to deal with individual disciplinary and grievance representation procedures. 'Without the advice and assistance of the RCN many more nurses would be vulnerable to unfair action or the failure of the true facts of a case to be presented and properly considered,' the union explained. 'Investment of resources and time on any individual case can be very considerable. The expertise of RCN officers and stewards in nursing issues is crucial to the significant success of the RCN in dealing with such cases. This success is a powerful recruiting platform in attracting other nurses into RCN membership.'

Ms Hancock told MPs that the union provided the members with indemnity insurance and employed twenty lawyers with two thirds of them dealing with personal injury cases. When asked what the case was for the future of trade unions she replied: 'I believe very strongly that the case is to have the ability to represent, support and help individual employees in problems and difficulties they may have at work but also to represent collectively groups of staff, groups of workers who have a shared interest best articulated through a trade union.' With as many as seventy-five different groups covering a variety of nursing specialities, the RCN can provide an expertise at local level for nurses that more general unions cannot.

The Growth of Professional Trade Unions

The RCN is not alone in seeking to combine a trade union function with that of a professional body. In written evidence to the Commons Employment Committee, David Triesman, General Secretary of the Association of University Teachers (AUT) argued that while his union would continue to pursue 'the traditional trade union activities of acting to protect members' interests,' it also believed it needed 'to protect academic excellence and the wider interests of the profession'. 'Activities designed to protect the individual and collective interests of its members can – and should – be concurrent and complementary parts of the association's role,' Mr Triesman added.

He would like university teachers to have 'formal rights as a key stake holder in quality maintenance and in establishing and sustaining professional ethics. This would put academics on a par with, for example, the medical profession, in terms of responsibility and status,' he added. 'In substance this is not new. Our rules have sought to uphold academic values since our foundation in 1919. What is new are the additional resources and visibility given by the association to this side of our work.' Mr Triesman suggested the role of the trade union as an association dedicated to professionalism should not be restricted to white-collar staff. 'There is scope for such a role for the blue and "pink" collar trades also, for example in different aspects of training and maintaining standards of output and service,' he argued. 'The issue is one of acceptance that trade unions, as the bodies representing the workforce in any profession, have a vital and legitimate role in discussions on the future of that profession.' Mr Triesman noted that many pre-eminently professional bodies such as the Law Society and the British Medical Association had themselves adopted more traditional union roles with 'the tightening and hardening of management practice across most of the economy.' 'Just as some unions are developing a more professional role, some professional bodies are developing a quasi-union stance. It is wrong to suggest an antithesis. Both roles are needed by any organisation of employees (whatever its titular description) to represent fully members' interests in the highly complex and challenging environment of working life in the nineties.'[23]

Mr Triesman stressed the 'potential for cooperation' that lay in seeking between employers and employees an indentification of their common interests. 'In spheres of work where a mature professional group provides the service – as is plainly the case in education – the cooperation which relies on professional engagement is central. It is a view of trade unions which we are eager to advance,' he declared.

The British Medical Association (BMA) has been moving in the opposite direction as it has grown into more of a trade union while upholding its professional purpose. As it explained in written evidence to the Commons Employment Committee: 'The BMA would exist as a professional association irrespective of its trade union status, but its recognition as a trade union has brought significant advantages both for the profession and the National Health Service,' it argued.

The value of the trade union function for doctors was spelt out by the BMA:

> The provision of clear negotiating arrangements; both sides are committed to using recognised channels for reaching clear agreements which, with the profession's democratic representative structure, means that negotiated outcomes are seen as fair by both sides. For the employer this means that the trade union can always 'deliver' its membership to accept negotiated changes in, for example, nationally agreed contracts of employment. The co-existence of professional and trade union functions within a professional organisation allows ethical and professional considerations to inform negotiations on employment matters; for example, negotiations are bound to take into account the profession's ethical position that industrial action which harms patients will not be countenanced – indeed, doctors would not accept negotiating machinery which did not do this.[24]

The BMA believes its trade union function has actually been enhanced and not weakened by the creation of the National Health Service Trusts. The ability of those bodies to 'introduce local terms and conditions of service makes the existence of a locally recognised trade union through which to conduct local negotiations even more important,' it told the MPs. The BMA fought hard but unsuccessfully to retain a national bargaining structure for doctors which was ended by the government in 1991. The association said it supported it because it had provided 'a reasonably uniform distribution of specialists throughout the country without noticeable problems of recruitment or retention.' The BMA admitted, however, that local bargaining had not made much of an initial impact. It had led, it said, to 'only minor changes in the peripheral aspects of a few doctors' terms of service.' The BMA went on to say: 'Individual doctors have neither the time, inclination, knowledge or bargaining power themselves to enter into detailed negotiations about terms of employment which may affect not just their income but their professional independence, which they guard jealously on behalf of their patients. The negotiating process requires the kind of expert professional and legal input which is best and most cost effectively provided by a national trade union.'

The BMA even suggested the growth of individual contracts of employment for doctors had not undermined trade unionism. 'Senior employees like doctors instinctively seek advice from their trade union/professional association on their contracts of employment and the complexity of the relationship between doctor, employer and patients has inevitably meant that in the few cases where individual contracts have been offered, the BMA's local negotiating machinery has become involved.'

A Union Federation Strategy

Another possible option for future trade union change lies through the development of federations. The most interesting example of this was established in 1990 by the Institute of Professionals, Managers and Specialists (IPMS) with the Communication Managers Association (CMA) and the Society of Telecom Executives (STE). The resulting joint body was established for a number of reasons which were explained by the IPMS in a policy document it presented to its 1994 conference.

> The first was the need to respond effectively to pressure from members to maintain and indeed extend the current level of services, particularly negotiating support, in the face of an increasingly hostile and complex bargaining environment. The second was to develop a form of organisation whereby each partner union could maintain its independent identity and bargaining autonomy before the threat of diminishing memberships and as a result diminishing resources. Thirdly, all three founder unions have been concerned to emphasise the potential for increasing union membership in other parts of the managerial, professional and specialist workforce. Traditionally such areas – largely in the private sector – have not been organised by unions, but this is one of the growth sectors in the United Kingdom and European labour market. The three

> founding unions of the federation want to eventually move to what they call its 'mature stage', which will involve the creation of a single union federation with members organised in autonomous, industrially based unions.

The IPMS strategy paper stressed that although constitutional change would be required to allow this to happen, union members' rights would 'remain unchanged'.[25]

Still All Kinds of Everything

The emergence of the super unions through mergers and amalgamations does not mean that the rest have only a limited future. In fact, the evidence suggests that many medium and smaller sized trade unions will flourish and not feel the need to seek absorption in a larger organisation. As the 130,000 strong CPSA civil service union has explained:

> It remains to be seen whether or not workers will want to join or remain members of unions which are so large and seek to represent so many different types of occupations. The enduring advantage of the smaller, specialised unions is that they are able to offer a distinctive sense of identity, mainly through industry or jobs which the union organises and with which the worker can associate and feel a genuine part of. We feel that this is still a very important factor when workers make decisions about joining or remaining a member of a trade union and one which may be lost if enough unions go down the road of large-scale mergers.[26]

The CPSA also pointed out that many workers might become suspicious 'of what they may perceive to be amalgamation for the sake of it.'

> Given the cynicism which still exists among the public about trade unions in general, particularly trade union leaders, workers will want to question closely the motives behind any mergers. Are they taking place because the leaders of the unions genuinely believe that the new union will be more modern, relevant and more able to provide an important service to them? Or are they just as concerned about the size of the organisations that they run and the political and industrial influence they will have? These are legitimate questions which are being asked and which will be increasingly asked in the future if the current trend continues.

Indeed, there are a number of impressive trade unions who did not give evidence to the Commons Employment Committee appealing to different segments of the labour market with some success. The FBU, the Fire Brigades union, fought a highly self-confident, measured and enthusiastic campaign in 1993 against any government threat to its special pay formula – provided after 1977 – that links firefighters' wages to the upper quartile of male manual earnings. The FBU may have ended up with a wage award less than the government's 1.5 per cent 'norm' for the public sector, but the union was able to ensure the sanctity of the precious pay formula by demonstrating to the government – with widespread public sympathy – that it was in earnest in its determination to take industrial action if necessary to uphold it.

The national leaders of the UCW (Union of Communication Workers) has cooperated over many years with the Post Office to modernise the service. They have been staunch allies in the fight to secure greater commercial freedom for the service although the union is opposed to privatisation. Early in 1994 the membership narrowly defeated an agreed productivity deal but the UCW has shown a positive willingness to agree to workplace reform in the name of efficiency. Recognising the threat of competition, the union has sought to convince its often sceptical members that they ought to embrace change and not dig in their heels in defence of antiquated rules and regulations. There has been a similar strategy followed by the NCU (the National Communications union) in its response to radical change in telecommunications after British Telecom's privatisation in 1986. Despite substantial cutbacks in the size of the labour force, the NCU has tried to establish negotiated deals that can link job security and pay increases to changes in working practices.

Conclusion

As always British trade unionism continues to have something of everything. The richness of its diverse traditions persists in more difficult times. But the trade unions have shown a readiness to adapt to imposed change in a variety of ways. They have begun to look at how to launch recruitment campaigns among women, blacks and deprived groups. Their finances are better than might be expected in the circumstances. They appear to be developing a more professional approach to problems of structure. The wave of mergers and amalgamations in recent years have perhaps too often been over-defensive, a response to falling memberships and squeezed finances. But some unions have modernised themselves in different ways. Those that seem most likely to prosper are those who share a clear identity of purpose. In focusing on a particular segment of the labour market or seeking to become more professional and discerning in their approach, they stand a better chance of growing in what looks like becoming an increasingly competitive market place for trade unions.

NOTES

1 GMB Journal January 1994, p 4.
2 TUC supplementary evidence, p 25.
3 USDAW written evidence, p 121.
4 TUC oral evidence.
5 Black Workers Report, TUC 1994.
6 Trade Union Involvement of Black Workers, CRE Report 1993.
7 TUC 1994 ibid
8 CRE ibid
9 Labour Research Department,
10 P Willman et al, Trade Union Finances, Cambridge University Press 1993, p183
11 ibid, p 207.
12 P Smith et al., Ballots and Union Government, BJIR Vol 3, Sept 1993, p 380.
13 TUC written evidence, p 23.
14 Labour Research, July 1993, p 3.
15 UNISON written evidence, p 128.
16 ibid, p 129.
17 J Edmonds, ibid, p 58.
18 GMB written evidence, p 45.
19 Towards The 21st Century, MSF 1994.
20 ibid.
21 RCN written evidence, p 202–203.
22 C Hancock oral evidence, p 224.
23 AUT written evidence.
24 BMA written evidence.
25 IPMS document to conference 1994.
26 CPSA written evidence, pp 52.

CHAPTER FOUR

Trade Unions and the Collective Bargaining Agenda

Trade unions remain very much collective bargainers. They continue to agree with the words of the 1968 Royal Commission on Trade Unions and Employer Associations that collective bargaining 'properly conducted is the most effective means of giving the workers the right to representation in decisions affecting their working lives, a right which is or should be the prerogative of every worker in a democratic society.'[1]

'The prime function of trade unions is collective bargaining,' the TUC argues. 'It is the distinctive activity of trade unions and employers. Collective agreements typically have the virtue of flexibility. With strong collective bargaining systems, employees are guaranteed the best deal on offer which may be tailored to their needs while employers are given flexibility to meet local needs and market conditions.'[2] The TUC argued that collective bargaining is a superior way of determining the wages and conditions of workers to one based on the individual determination of contracts by an employer.

As it explained to the MPs: 'Collective bargaining minimises resentment caused by distinguishing between individual workers. From the point of view of the workforce, collective bargaining takes the individual worker out of the difficult position of having to face the employer with demands and face the consequences. It is backed up by professional expertise from unions.' There is also evidence that collective bargaining provides a wage premium for unionised workers of between 8 and 10 per cent, although in the late 1980s an erosion of the average union/non-union wage differential appears to have taken place.

Collective bargaining arrangements do not only cover trade

union members. In some sectors general levels of terms and conditions of employment are effectively set by 'leading' collective agreements. Wage comparability and the 'rate for the job' remain powerful arguments in the determination of the terms and conditions of employment for many workers. Moreover, although in recent years a growing number of companies have introduced performance related pay in a controversial attempt to relate wages more closely to individual effort, suspicious trade unions have been reasonably successful in ensuring that many of those merit schemes are based on a negotiated framework and contain acceptable appeal mechanisms to ensure fairness. Performance related pay (PRP) has been used more as a complement than a substitute to bargained pay agreements with unions negotiating the general principles of a scheme and appeals machinery. Increasing difficulties in the implementation of such schemes has led to managerial reappraisals of their efficacy in determining pay. Now there is a new emphasis on wage deals that focuses on team work effort and a perceptible move away from the more individualistic approach.

The extent of collective bargaining in Britain has undoubtedly fallen sharply since it reached a high watermark at the end of the 1970s. Six years earlier in its previous study, 71 per cent of all establishments employing twenty-five employees or more had been covered by collective agreements; now the proportion was down to only 54 per cent. In the private manufacturing sector the drop was from 64 per cent to 51 per cent and in private services from 41 per cent to 33 per cent. A contraction had also taken place in the public sector – down from 95 per cent to 78 per cent, mainly due to the loss of collective bargaining rights for teachers and nurses although those two groups remain highly unionised.

In 1980, 55 per cent of manual workers had their wages negotiated by collective bargaining. The proportion rose to 62 per cent in 1984 but six years later it was down to only 48 per cent. The position was even worse for white-collar staff where 47 per cent had their pay collectively bargained in 1980. After a rise to 54 per cent in 1984 it dropped back to 43 per cent by 1990. The workplace survey calculated 47 per cent of establishments had no employees covered by collective bargaining (at all 72 per cent were covered in 1978) while 4 per cent had low coverage (1 to 19 per cent) and a further 7 per cent under half. Only 18 per cent of the establishments had 100 per cent collective bargaining coverage of their employees. The WIRS survey also revealed signs of growing partial trade union de-recognition. It found that around one in five industrial and commercial workplaces reporting they had recognised unions in 1984 had none by 1990. Those withdrawing recognition agreements made up 9 per cent of all workplaces. On the basis of these figures Dr Neil Millward and his colleagues suggested it was 'not unreasonable to conclude that the traditional, distinctive "system" of British industrial relations no longer characterised the economy as a whole.'[3]

Collective Bargaining Still Lives On

The relative decline of collective bargaining should not, however, be exaggerated. It is estimated that nearly half the country's workforce still have their pay and conditions determined by collective bargaining. Although collective bargaining is much less in evidence than it used to be in the years of trade union dominance during the 1960s and 1970s, recognised trade unions continue to cover a substantial part of the employed labour force. Britain still has a long way to go before it becomes a trade union free country. Moreover, many employees who are not members of trade unions or covered by collective agreements continue to have their wages and conditions determined by the indirect influences that stem from what happens among the organised workforce. Negotiating the terms and conditions of employment for their members with employers therefore remains a key trade union task.

It is also clear from the evidence of the 1990 WIRS survey that the contraction in collective bargaining which has taken place since the middle of the 1980s was not caused by any concerted employer offensive to drive the trade unions out of existing establishments. The main explanation for the change has come from the fact that the trade unions have been 'unable to replace the unionised workplaces that have closed down with similar numbers of newer workplaces where they have established full recognition.'[4] Only 29 per cent of workplaces established since 1984 had recognised unions, compared with 40 per cent for all workplaces in 1990. The lower level of trade union recognition among newer workplaces is restricted to those establishments which belong to large organisations. Newer independent establishments did not appear to be any less likely than older ones to have union recognition. But new site workplaces belonging to large companies were almost twice as likely not to recognise trade unions.

The smaller incidence of trade union recognition in new workplaces has been largely due to the fact that those created over the period tended to have characteristics associated with low levels of unionisation. They were generally smaller workplaces, more likely to be in the private service sector, employing fewer skilled workers and having much higher proportions of part-time and female employees. But Dr Millward has argued that these factors alone are not enough to explain the decline in collective bargaining. 'Prime candidates appear to be the removal of the statutory support for union recognition and decline in the presumption by management and the state in favour of collective bargaining between trade unions and employers,' he has argued.'[5]

A study published in 1993 by Dr Paul Marginson and colleagues at Warwick University's School of Industrial and Business Studies, which examined industrial relations in Britain's largest 1,000 companies, confirmed many of the 1990 WIRS survey findings but it also emphasised that the trade unions have maintained a strong presence in multinational enterprises. Trade unions were recognised for the largest group within the workforce in 69 per cent of the companies the Warwick study surveyed; in a quarter of companies recognition covered all establishments while in 17 per cent unions were recognised in most establishments and in 27 per cent in some establishments only. Trade union recognition was found to be more common in manufacturing companies than those in the services sector (occurring in 84 per cent of them compared with 54 per cent).

The Warwick University study discovered some large private companies had carried through partial trade union derecognition, at least for collective bargaining purposes: 19 per cent reported recognition for negotiating purposes had been partially or wholly withdrawn on existing sites. But the main explanation for the contraction of collective bargaining stemmed – as in the 1990 WIRS survey – from the decision by existing or newly created companies to open plants without recognising trade unions in them. As many as 80 per cent of enterprises in the Warwick survey reported opening at least one new site. But among them only 24 per cent had agreed to recognise trade unions at all the sites they had opened and 17 per cent at some or most of them. In 59 per cent, however, no trade union recognition had been granted to the largest group within the workforce. 'Comprehensive recognition of unions across all sites within a company now occurs only in a minority of large companies,' the report concluded.[6]

The Decline in Multi-Employer Bargaining

A more significant shift in the pattern of collective bargaining over recent years has been the rapid demise in multi-employer single industry agreements. The decentralisation of wage negotiations to company and increasingly to establishment level is a trend that goes back to the 1960s. But since the middle of the 1980s it has become much more widespread with the collapse of national sector-based wage determination, symbolised in particular by its demise in the engineering industry in 1990. The Warwick University survey found that pay is negotiated at establishment level in half of Britain's largest companies. 'Single employer bargaining has overwhelmed industry-wide arrangements,' it argued.[7]

An important consequence of the triumph of establishment based collective bargaining has been to strengthen the strategic position of employers in securing more uncontested control over what is covered in the negotiating process. The 1990 WIRS workplace survey indicated there had not been any noticeable decline over the previous six years in the workplace issues determined by joint regulation in unionised companies for either manual or non-manual workers. These covered physical working conditions, staffing levels and redeployment within plants. But there has been clear evidence of a marked decline in the willingness of companies to introduce joint consultation committees.

Another important change in the industrial relations system has been the increase, not in single union collective agreements which remain relatively rare in Britain, but in the growth of single table bargaining, especially where companies have sought to negotiate workplace structural change. A study carried out by Dr Gregor Gall at Manchester University's Institute of Science and Technology in 1993 discovered over sixty companies had moved to single table bargaining during the previous three years. These included British Steel, the Rover group and Vauxhall, most of the privatised water companies,

Power Gen and National Grid and forty-three National Health Service hospital and ambulance trusts. Dr Gall estimated as many as 300,000 workers had been covered by single table agreements in 1993. In his opinion the growth of such deals has stemmed from competitive pressures on employers facing the creation of single union or no strike deals in new green field site agreements. 'Employers want to reduce the amount of time and money spent on union negotiations by dealing with them all at the same time,' he wrote. 'They hope this streamlined bargaining will allow them to respond more quickly to changes in their markets with changes in production. They also want in their negotiations to achieve consistency with regard to pay and conditions in order to stop leap frogging and avoid any potential problems with the changes in equal pay law.'[8]

Single table bargaining is also seen as a necessary pre-condition by innovative companies who want to introduce new systems of workplace organisation. The introduction of single table bargaining has also been of real value to trade unions by helping them to eradicate the once traditional sectionalist rivalries and divisions between them and help to strengthen a sense of workplace solidarity. Many of the employers and trade unions who gave evidence to the Commons Employment Committee could point to the success of reaching unified and comprehensive collective agreements at the same time with both white-collar and blue-collar trade unions. The process of trade union mergers and amalgamations since the mid-1980s has also encouraged this development as general manual trade unions in particular have sought to widen their appeal across the traditional occupational divisions that used to protect a form of social apartheid in too many British workplaces.

Why Collective Bargaining?

The trade unions remain convinced that collective bargaining must continue to be at the core of their activities. They also insist that this approach is neither obsolete nor irrelevant in the new decentralised workplaces but, on the contrary, crucial in maintaining cohesion which is so necessary for companies who want to secure workplace cooperation in carrying through organisational change. Nonetheless, the trade unions have to justify the value of collective bargaining to employers and workers alike in ways they have not had to do in the past. The most important factor, stressed by the TUC, has been its achievement as a force for stability in enterprise wage-setting. 'Hand in hand with the demise of many national agreements and decentralisation of pay setting to the level of the firm has been the corresponding increase in the opportunity for confusion in pay determination arrangements and inflationary pay pressures, especially in non-union firms,' it explained. 'The presence of a union allows the problem to be internalised and solved in a stable way.'[9]

The TUC sought to demonstrate the validity of that approach by contrasting the difference between a) a unionised company and b) a non-unionised one. As it explained:

> In firm A the representative of management sits down and negotiates with the union representatives on the basis of a wage claim drawn up by the union and agreed to by all the workers. The wage claim takes account of past and expected profitability, productivity changes, the retail price index, the need to recruit and retain workers and wider economic pressures. The management submits an offer based on its own analysis of these core issues. Both sides have several short meetings and agree a settlement acceptable to all concerned.
>
> In firm B where there is no union, management representatives have to negotiate separately with many groups of workers or indeed with each individual worker. Negotiations would be protracted, occur in working time and disrupt the production process (far more than in firm A) and could lead to undesirable outcomes for the company. This would be especially so where small groups or indeed individual workers held 'insider power', eg scarce job specific skills. The threat to exit the company, especially in an economic upswing would increase their bargaining power. If this phenomenon was generalised across the company it would lead to fragmentation and leapfrogging.

The TUC maintained 'decollectivisation is more costly in terms of general transaction costs such as adminstration and economies of scale give way to fragmentation and leapfrogging.' It also means a loss of social solidarity in the firm, weakening worker identification with the company 'as selfishness becomes the norm.' 'Unions would take account of the need to retain profits for investment, whereas individual "insiders" would not. The costs associated with non-union bargaining are reduced by a union presence.'

A number of the trade unions reasserted the importance of collective bargaining in their written evidence to the Commons

Employment Committee. The TGWU argued it not only brought 'benefits to union members through improvements in terms and conditions' but that it had a 'broader benefit' for industry because it provided the means by which negotiations could be 'conducted in an orderly and efficient way.'[10] The union suggested attempts by companies to move away from collective bargaining would increase their costs because of the time and resources needed for local or individual bargaining.

Collective bargaining is also likely to produce more equitable pay systems, the trade unions argue. The 1990 WIRS survey found overall earnings dispersion was much narrower where trade unions negotiated with employers than elsewhere. 'Unions compress the wage structure between blacks and whites, women and men, the disabled and the able-bodied and the unskilled and skilled,' argued Professor David Metcalf of the London School of Economics.[11]

Goodbye to Collective Bargaining?

The general arguments deployed by the trade unions to support the value of collective bargaining as a system of wage determination however are no longer seen as self-evident by a growing number of employers. As the CBI has pointed out: 'collective bargaining is no longer seen as a universal desideratum.'[12] 'It is not universally the case in the unquestioning way it used to be that collective bargaining is the centrepiece of the employment relationship,' agreed Mr Geoffrey Armstrong, the Institute of Personnel Management's Director-General.[13]

New forms of work organisation – driven by a mixture of competitive pressures and technological innovation – have also helped to undermine collective bargaining, employers have argued. As the IPM explained to the Commons Employment Committee:

> Increasing competition, growing productivity and substantial job loss – in a sense the greater urgency of economic activity – in the primary industries, the utilities and manufacturing has led to new forms of work organisation aimed at increasing customer satisfaction. Pressures for improved performance have contributed to the erosion of cohesiveness of many bargaining groups as the emphasis at the workplace has shifted from the behaviour of occupational groups as a whole to the responsibility, performance and development of the individuals and teams within functional areas and between cross-functional groups.[14]

The IPM went on to argue that as a consequence of such developments an important shift has been taking place in the workplace in 'the objective of mutual reliance between members of teams' from 'the protection of occupational areas to the achievement of organisational aims through mutual support for organisational aims.' The IPM suggested this was part of a much wider phenomenon that went beyond the workplace to society in general. 'A growing emphasis on individual responsibility within the workplace has been reinforced by increasing home ownership which has limited the propensity of trade union members to make economic sacrifices in pursuit of collective aims,' it argued. 'These changes may indeed reflect a more profound move away from collective representation, security and action within society; a move which for good or ill throws more responsibility on individuals and their families for their own welfare.'

Such an observation may be exaggerated and it underestimates just how important such feelings have proved to be in the past. But the IPM went on to press home the uncomfortable logic of its view by pointing out that collective responses to managerial authority in the workplace were no longer so apparent. As it argued: 'From being a day to day check on management activity, conventional trade union activities have tended to become marginalised. Where in the past strong resistance would have normally been offered to change, sometimes in an almost ritualistic way, a more pragmatic approach is now taken.'

> There has always been a tension in the relationship between employers and employees, between their mutual wish for economic success and the concern of each not to give too much ground to the other. Recent years have seen a clear adjustment to this balance. Mutual interests in economic success now appear to be paramount. For some employers and employees this represents a cultural change and not just a temporary recognition of the dangers to both parties of the old approach. It appears to be quite consistent with this picture to find, on the one hand, the development of a more flexible workforce with more part-time working and shorter contracts and on the other hand, a greater sense of mutual reliance, need for the development of individuals and commitment to longer-term relationships. In this context, the more that employees appreciate that both the benefits and insecurities of employment relate in a tangible way to the results of mutual efforts to

improve performance and less to the adversarial relationships enshrined in the collective bargaining process, the less important trade union membership will appear to be. This will hold true until collective bargaining has something substantial to offer to the improvement of performance.

The Trade Union Role in Consultation

Employer organisations such as the CBI like to argue that a growing number of companies have introduced new systems of consultation with their employees outside recognised trade union channels of communication. 'Progress on employee involvement has been substantial and the evidence is of widespread success in achieving a good flow of information and consultation on the big issues,' the CBI has argued. 'As is to be expected from a successful, voluntary approach tailored to the needs of individual organisations and their workers, variety is the key characteristic.'[17] The CBI quoted from a survey it carried out with KPMG in 1991 that discovered no less than twelve methods of communication in general use in companies, from briefing groups to electronic mail. It found 47 per cent of company respondents said they operated some formal consultative machinery in their establishments and the employee representatives sitting on those committees were elected directly by the workforce. In 57 per cent of cases where formal committees were recognised by employers, the employee representation was 'chosen by trade unions'.

However, it would be quite wrong to deduce from this evidence that consultation is most effective and widespread in non-union settings. A survey carried out by ACAS in 1990 on consultation and communication found most progress had been made in improving employer-employee contact in those companies that practised collective bargaining with recognised trade unions. As it explained: 'Union establishments have been more likely to witness an increase in the range of consultation during the past three years and currently consult on a wider range of issues than their non-union counterparts. Where consultation has expanded we found no evidence to suggest that the increase has been at the expense of bargaining. Our evidence supports the view that in both British and foreign owned establishments, increases in consultation have supplemented and broadened the nature of discussions between management and unions rather than producing a decisive change in their character.'[18] The ACAS study found as many as 40 per cent of the establishments it covered used joint consultative committees that were created outside the management – union structures but these were in no way alternatives or threats to collective bargaining. On the contrary, the survey pointed out that 'in many instances recognised trade unions make a significant contribution to employee representation on these committees though they do not monopolise it.' Those observers who believe the introduction of new methods of consultation in the workplace can replace the collective bargaining system are mistaken.

Moreover, the ACAS survey also found that, contrary to popular belief, there had been a growth in the range of issues under consultation in the companies it covered in the late 1980s and not a decline. In 45 per cent the range had increased and 44 per cent stayed the same, with only 8 per cent of establishments reporting a decrease in the range of issues for consultation. It is true that consultation covers issues such as the introduction of new equipment, safety and welfare that are not subject to local collective bargaining. On staffing and working conditions there was a mix of consultation and bargaining. On pay, redundancy and welfare matters, however, the most common approach was consultation followed by collective bargaining.

The Changing Role of the Bargaining Shop Steward

It is unfortunate that hardly any of the trade unions who gave evidence to the Commons Employment Committee made use of any of their lay activist members, let alone ordinary rank and file in their representation. Nor, perhaps even more surprisingly, was there much evidence in their submissions on what has happened to workplace trade union organisation in recent years. This curious omission may be an oversight or it could suggest a significant shift is taking place inside modernised trade union structures towards a greater negotiating role for the full-time official and a corresponding decline in the position of workplace-based convenors and shop stewards. As we shall see in examining the transformation of the workplace, this may be only a partial explanation. After all, trade unions are not going to survive if they do not continue to motivate their lay members through the collective bargaining process. Indeed, if the more decentralised industrial relations system is going to work effectively it will require more and not less involvement by lay activists in the actual process of collective bargaining in the workplace even if local and national union officials appear to be taking a much more direct and active role in establishment-level bargaining than they used to do.

The 1990 government commissioned WIRS survey provides some insights into this missing dimension from the trade union evidence. It revealed there had been a noticeable contraction in the existence of lay trade union representation. 'The fall was widespread, affecting workplaces of all types, but particularly smaller workplaces and those with low levels of membership,' it argued. The survey found lay union representatives in only 38 per cent of workplaces, compared with 54 per cent in 1984. 'The most basic building blocks of local trade union organisation' are in retreat, it suggested. However, the survey also indicated that 'stability rather than change' characterised most workplaces with strong local unions although there was a clear trend to greater outside union servicing of lay representatives.[19] Moreover support for local unionism remained high among employers as measured by the facilities they provided for trade union work. There was no dramatic decline in statutory time off work and information gathering from management for lay representatives.

But the world of the shop stewards has changed since the 1970s. A fascinating insight into their activities was published in the September 1993 issue of the AEEU union's journal based on interviews with two of that union's 30,000 lay representatives who were both convenors – Keith Cardwell at GEC/Alsthom's plant in Preston, Lancashire and Mick Langley at Vauxhall in Luton.

Both agreed their jobs were much harder than they used to be. 'Members expect more of shop stewards today,' Langley explained. 'In past days when there was a dispute you'd just walk off the job. Today members don't want to do this. They can't afford to do it, in fact. So as shop stewards you have to talk your way to a solution. Once your heart ruled your head. Now you have to use your brains more. It's not only in a dispute situation that members expect more of stewards. They expect you to know everything about every subject under the sun. Members like to use the union's free legal services which is great but it all means more work for the stewards.'[20]

Mr Langley has sixty-one stewards reporting to him and Mr Cardwell as many as forty. Both hold other posts within their union and they feel over-worked. But as Mr Cardwell told the union journal:

> We must never forget that we are there to serve the members. I was elected works convenor in 1985. I can honestly say that ever since then I have been fighting a rear-guard action against job losses and the threat of closure. In the meantime we have to deal with the introduction of new technology – just-in-time principles, quality concepts and the various spin-offs – and these created many problems for us, including a certain amount of de-skilling. Only too often these days I'm seen to be – and I sometimes feel – that I am just a go-between the management and the shopfloor, perhaps even a management mouthpiece. I'm fighting every inch of the way.

However, Mr Cardwell also pointed to the problem of apathy among the rank and file of the union. 'Frankly people are demoralised. There's good machinery and good men lying idle. The government's all but killed off the manufacturing industry. They can't seem to understand that manufacturing is the only way we're going to turn the country round economically.' 'The biggest trouble lies with the younger workers,' he confessed. 'Frankly most of them don't want to know about union work, let alone taking office. So many are under many pressures outside the workplace.'

As Mr Cardwell further explained: 'Young married men want to spend evenings with their wives and families rather than working overtime for the union. You can understand it from the wives' point of view too – it's not easy for them to be supportive when they're being left on their own.'

Mr Langley admitted recruiting new members was difficult. 'Young people have been brought up without any appreciation of what a union is or why they need one,' he said. 'Mind you, recruitment was never easy. But today, whereas once you needed five minutes to get over the message, you now need half an hour.' Mr Cardwell added: 'We have to strive to get the message across to all youngsters who are lucky enough to find a job in industry. We've got to get them to join, to encourage them to participate, to take office. They are our future hope.' Despite their problems, both men like being convenors. As Mr Langley put it: 'There is still great satisfaction in getting problems resolved and assisting our members. If anyone is thinking of volunteering, I urge them to do so.

It's tough but it's tremendous.'

Progressive Bargaining in the Chemical Industry

Industry-wide national collective bargaining in Britain is not completely obsolete. It still persists in the chemical industry even though in recent years a growing number of companies have abandoned conformity to the national agreement so that less than half the members of the Chemical Industries Association (CIA) are now covered by them. 'Bargaining at national level is the area where the role of trade unions is most likely to change in the future,' the CIA told the Commons Employment Committee. 'Both sides have acknowledged that the system has its problems and the likelihood is that it will be greatly modified or stopped altogether in the next few years.'[21] But the association also suggested collective bargaining would continue in the chemical industry down at company level. As it explained to the MPs: 'The role of the trade unions in bargaining at company level seems unlikely to change in the vast majority of cases, even though there may be fewer unions involved. Cases where companies cease to recognise any trade unions for collective bargaining purposes are likely to remain confined to a very small number of companies. There will, however, be some instances in the white-collar area where declining membership renders the collective bargaining process obsolete.'

The CIA also suggested that trade union involvement at national level would continue no matter what happened to collective bargaining in the chemical industry. 'Both employers and unions have good reasons for cooperating in the area of health, safety and environment, training and economic development, which are independent of the national bargaining process,' it argued. 'In fact, additional reasons for maintaining national level activities in these areas might arise from developments in European Union social affairs.'

This favourable view towards trade unions by the industry employers is not surprising in the chemical industry, where traditionally industrial relations have been relatively consensual and trouble-free since national bargaining first started in 1917. It is estimated that as many as 85 per cent of blue-collar workers in the chemical industry belong to trade unions and about 25 per cent of white-collar staff.

The New Collective Deal in Printing and Publishing

The other important industry in Britain where national collective bargaining remains substantial is printing and publishing. Here opinions among the employers are more divided than in chemicals but there has been a lack of a consensus on bringing a permanent end to the industry-wide pay agreement. After a year's suspension a centralised deal was achieved in 1994 between the employers and the GPMU print union that has paved the way for full worker flexibility in the industry – to the delight of the British Printing Industries Federation. 'Returning to national negotiations has not been easy for the Federation following the breakdown of talks last year,' admitted Mr Andrew Brown, the Federation's Employee Relations Director. 'In agreeing to do so, our members made it clear that any settlement this year had to involve a low cash increase only and be recoverable at house level in 1994. Not only does this settlement meet these pre-conditions, but it also provides for full flexibility of working across all occupations. This is a significant advance which will allow companies to make substantial gains in productivity.'[22]

The new national agreement that came into force on 24 April 1994 spelt out the GPMU's explicit commitment to improve the industry's efficiency and competitiveness. It said very clearly that both sides had agreed 'the industry's workforce, plant and equipment' would be 'deployed fully and effectively in order to increase efficiency, provide a quick and flexible response to customers' requirements and improve profitability.' This also involved the need for 'a reduction of unit costs' through the introduction at individual company level of new technology and its use to its full potential. 'Management and chapel representatives will cooperate fully in identifying, discussing and implementing any changes necessary to achieve increased output and lower unit costs through the most effective use of people, materials and machines,' declared the agreement.[23]

The new deal spelt out in clear detail the end of demarcation lines in publishing and printing. 'Subject to suitable training and the necessary health and safety requirements, full flexibility of working between all occupations and the elimination of demarcation lines is accepted,' stated the agreement. 'To this end management and chapels will agree arrangements to achieve those objectives, including full flexibility and where appropriate establish arrangements for the necessary training and retraining of GPMU members.' This meant that in future GPMU members can be called upon by their employer to carry on duties within and between the craft classes laid down in the industry and transfer between machines, equipment and departments. 'The parties recognise it is the duty of GPMU members to cooperate with and, where required, assist in the training and retraining of other GPMU members,' said the agreement. 'It is accepted that changing production requirements of companies will require, from time to time, the redeployment of GPMU members to other departments on a short or long-term basis. Every cooperation shall be given by GPMU members where this is necessary and appropriate training shall be given as and when required.'

The agreement spelt out in detail how printing machine crews will cooperate as a team and share out the various tasks involved in the operation of their machines 'to reduce downtime and keep machines running in the most efficient manner.' 'Machine crews will take all practical steps to achieve optimum running speeds, minimal downtime and full utilisation of their machines,' it said. Manning levels in future are to be determined by the kind of machine being used, the product and the technological developments. But the agreement added that manning levels would also 'take account of the ability of an individual company to compete in domestic or international markets.' Both sides also accepted the introduction of integrated press rooms which would 'seek to maximise job opportunities' so that 'no existing employee will be made redundant as a direct result of the implementation' of such a move.

The New Deals in the Privatised Utilities

Collective bargaining has also survived virtually intact in the privatised utilities of gas, water and electricity. The old industrial relations culture of the nationalised industries may have gone in the more competitive environment in which they operate but, with a few exceptions, the new private companies have seen the value of cooperating with the trade unions and most of them have not sought to abandon collective bargaining. However, what they have done is negotiate wide-ranging agreements that have balanced improvements in pay and conditions of employment with a commitment to workplace innovation. As UNISON, the main trade union involved in the utilities sector, explained:

> The 1980s and 1990s were an era of unprecedented change in the public sector. It was dominated by the subjection of services to competition and the concept of moving public authorities from providing services to managing their provisions. There was continuous reorganisation. Rising demands and government determination to cash limits put enormous pressure on services and those who provided them. Although trade unions opposed privatisation of gas, electricity and water, believing their essential services should remain in public ownership, they have worked hard to assist in the peaceful creation of the new enterprises.

It claimed that the replacement of national negotiations could not have been achieved by the privatised companies without the 'positive approach' of the trade unions. 'UNISON has invested significant resources in training to familiarise workplace representatives with the private sector and company dynamics. Individual members have received advice from the union on personal contracts and other new working arrangements. UNISON sees itself as an indispensable part of the management of change at work and provides the machinery for consultation with staff where the law or good sense requires it.'[24]

The negotiated new settlements in the privatised utilities have a number of common elements that mark a clear break with past practice.

These include:

- The introduction of an integrated pay structure to cover all employees and a move from a weekly wage to a monthly salary.
- The removal of demarcations and increased flexibility.
- New job descriptions for manual and craft employees under new job evaluation schemes.
- The introduction of flexible hours of work with nine day fortnights, annualised hours, banked hours, shift work rotas and reduction in the working week for manual and craft employees.
- The introduction of single-table trade union bargaining.
- The harmonisation of terms and conditions of employment between all employees.

- The introduction of new pay systems with elements of individual performance and company performance remuneration.
- The provision of training and career development opportunities for all employees.

The New Collective Deals in the Public Services

In the face of often unwelcome change in the public services, the trade unions have sought to maintain momentum. Opposed to market testing, compulsory competitive tendering of work, performance related pay and other elements in the individualistic agenda, they have nonetheless not opposed blindly but embraced reform when necessary.

The most radical transformation is taking place in local government industrial relations with the emergence of a new employer strategy that has secured the full support of the trade unions. In response to competition from the private sector, devolution of management and the growth of a performance culture there has been a shake-up of trade union attitudes. As the employers explained in their January 1994 strategy document: 'Local government has had to become quicker to adapt, leaner and more effective. More from less is the familiar watchword. The focus has switched from administering stable, procedure-bound organisations to managing fluid outcome-oriented teams. The nature of local government is changing. There are fewer manual workers and more part-timers. Career paths are being opened up on a wider basis than the traditional professional routes. There is more emphasis on life-time training and development.'[25]

But the employers, like the trade unions, want to continue with nationally negotiated industrial relations with flexible changes in its existing collective bargaining machinery. The creation of UNISON in 1993 has opened the way to the possibility of workplace transformation through collective bargaining with the 'increasing perception that the artificial split between white collar and manual workers can hinder sensible management, particularly in situations vulnerable to competition and customerised delivery of quality services.'

The establishment of single status between white- and blue-collar workers is seen by the employers and the trade unions alike as an opportunity to increase job opportunities in local government, simplify staffing administration, enable the creation of a single training and development strategy for all employees, encourage recruitment and reduce managerial complexities. It is also going to enable local government to establish common core conditions with a single pay spine, common hours of work and the provision of common annual leave, sick and maternity pay, equal opportunities, treatment of part-timers and other conditions of employment. This is also seen as a way forward to the establishment of single-table bargaining in local government and the creation of a common pay review date.

The 1994 pay claim in local government was jointly submitted for the first time by UNISON alongside the TGWU and GMB. This revealed the new approach that looks likely to bring an end to the traditional trade union rivalries, leap-frogging and sectionalism that has bedeviled local authority industrial relations in the past. It also provided an insight into the importance of collective bargaining as an organisational response to the increasingly deregulated labour market in the public services. As the claim explained: 'In order to achieve our joint aims of a quality workforce providing a quality service, the employers must negotiate with a view to making substantial progress in ending low pay, discrimination and the different conditions for manual workers. The staff side claim is based on the three principles of fairness, equality and forward thinking.'[26]

The factors behind this new approach were partly the government's three year public sector pay bill freeze policy and the substantial cut in take-home pay suffered by many local authority workers due to the April 1994 tax and national insurance contribution increases. But the claim was also motivated by a 'growing realisation that the current outmoded differences in the conditions of service of manual, craft and white-collar workers are unsustainable' as well as recent High Court rulings on equal pay and part-time workers, coupled with an EOC report showing unfair treatment of women workers by local authority employers.

The public service trade unions have grown much more sensitive in their collective bargaining strategies to the needs of the customer. 'We have come to realise that local government services must aim for excellence and must win greater respect and affection,' TUC General Secretary Mr John Monks told a local government management board conference in January

1994. 'We cannot just assume that the public appreciate the services. We have to gain their active support and regard.'[27] The local government employers and the trade unions see the commitment to collective bargaining as necessary in the growth of a partnership approach. Trade union leaders like Mr Alan Jinkinson, UNISON's General Secretary and his colleague Mr Rodney Bickerstaffe are keen to make sure that the quality of public services are improved within a new culture of opportunity and achievement without diluting collectivism. They are well aware that many people remain unsympathetic to those working in the public sector outside the health service. The trade unions need to continue making the case for properly funded, high quality, cost effective public services through their deeds and not just in their rhetoric. In 1992 the TUC took the initiative in pressing the cause of public service trade unionism and collective bargaining by launching a campaign for high quality bargaining which placed a new emphasis on the needs of the public.

UNISON and other public service trade unions have also been able to negotiate a growing number of impressive agreements in the newly emerging National Health Trusts. The most important have been those that have ensured a framework for consultation and collective bargaining. Following a common pattern these deals have spelt out in detail the nature of the collective relationship between the employer and recognised trade unions. Both sides agree on general principles including an acceptance of 'a common objective to ensure the effective delivery of health services and the prosperity of the trust for the benefit of patients, the public and employees'; 'that management has a responsibility to plan, organise and manage the operations of the trust in order to achieve and maintain maximum efficiency in the organisation'; that while both sides recognise 'trade union membership is not a condition of employment, will recognise the right of staff to belong to an appropriate trade union/staff organisation and its benefits.' The agreements lay down that the trust will not just recognise trade unions for negotiations on pay, pensions and other terms and conditions of employment but also cover 'significant workplace reorganisation issues, broad job grading and design matters' along with equal opportunities issues, disciplinary procedures, time off and individual grievance and collective disputes procedure.

Conclusion

Collective bargaining may be on the defensive in many industries but it is unlikely to go away in the near future. On the contrary, there are enough examples in manufacturing and the services sector to suggest that collective agreements continue to have the flexibility and breadth needed for companies to innovate and workers to secure improvements in their living standards and relative security. The current interest in individualising pay schemes like those that are performance related can be expected to dwindle with a move to more group or team based wages systems. There is going to be further efforts by management who want to carry out internal workplace reform to bargain trade-offs between job restructuring and better pay and benefits. A return to national or industry-wide collective bargaining seems unlikely but greater corporate coordination might be expected in the larger companies. There is little reliable evidence to suggest that existing employers in practice want to replace collective bargaining with an alternative way of deciding the pay and conditions of workers, but it seems probable that wage systems will grow more complex and the range of benefits provided become more diverse to cater for different needs. This combination of the collective and the individual will not exclude the need for trade unions. On the contrary, they will be able to provide the necessary counter-weight to ensure the emergence of any wider agenda for bargaining has the consent of the workplace. As in the past, collective bargaining is seen rightly by many employers as a useful and effective mechanism to propitiate change with the least danger of conflict.

NOTES

1 Royal Commission on Trade Unions and Employers' Associations report, Cmnd 3623 HMSO 1968
2 TUC written evidence p 2.
3 N Millward et al, Workplace Industrial Relations In Transition, Dartmouth 1992, p 350.
4 ibid
5 ibid
6 P Marginson, Management of Large Enterprises, Warwick University Business School 1993
7 ibid
8 G Gall, Labour Research March 1993
9 TUC written evidence, p 31.
10 TGWU written evidence, p 195.
11 D Metcalf, Industrial Relations and Economic Performance, British Journal of Industrial Relations, Vol 31 No 2, June 1993 p. 262.

12 CBI evidence, p 319.
13 G Armstrong verbal evidence, p 402.
14 IPM written evidence, pp 389–391.
15 G Armstrong verbal evidence, p 400.
16 IPM written evidence, p 391.
17 CBI written evidence, p 10–11.
18 Consultation and Communication, ACAS 1991, p 21.
19 N Millward
20 AEEU journal, September 1993, pp 9–11.
21 CIA written evidence
22 British Printing Industries Federation press release, April 1994.
23 GPMU – BPIF National Agreement 1994.
24 UNISON written evidence, p 131.
25 Harmonising Employment in Local Government, January 1994.
26 Joint UNISON, TGWU and GMB claim 1994.

CHAPTER FIVE

Trade Unions in a Changing Workplace

The future of trade unions in Britain's private sector depend in the immediate future on whether or not they can develop strategies to win representation and recognition from employers inside new workplaces and uphold existing collective agreements. In short, they must establish a broad market appeal not just to workers as potential members but perhaps more importantly to employers as well. As long as Britain lacks any legal right of employee representation or of trade union recognition, trade unions must try to persuade companies that they ought to have an organised workplace because it will actually provide them with a strategic advantage in their efforts to achieve greater competitiveness on both domestic and global markets.

The Department of Employment explained this in its written evidence to the Commons Employment Committee:

> If trade unions wish to stem the tide of decreasing recognition by employers, they will need to demonstrate their worth to them. Most employers in the UK have no recognised union. In our voluntarist system, employers are not obliged by law to recognise trade unions. Unions therefore need to persuade employers why they should establish or retain recognition and that there can be benefits to them in discussing and negotiating employment issues with trade unions. Unions must demonstrate that just as they can assist individual members in dealing with complex employment issues, so employers can benefit from an informed dialogue with union representatives on such topics. In developing their case for recognition, unions need to understand the competitive context within which companies operate. It is by demonstrating that they can assist companies in coping with these competitive demands that unions will be most successful in winning recognition. In particular unions should adopt approaches which show unequivocally that they

share management's desire to raise competitiveness and adapt to change.

The Department of Employment acknowledged that 'unions, of course, need to preserve their independence from management to safeguard their protective role. On occasion, unions may find it necessary to criticise or oppose management initiatives. Too frequently in the past, however, unions have resisted change as a matter of course and sought to preserve outdated working practices.' It suggested the trade unions should show they wanted a 'partnership' with employers by 'sharing a commitment to business goals and by adopting forward-looking strategies towards change which assume that most proposals for change have the potential to be beneficial rather than the reverse.'[1]

The commercial success of any enterprise is of obvious mutual benefit to employer, shareholder and employees alike. If working together produces increased levels of improved productivity, higher wages, lower unit labour costs and healthy profits there is no sensible reason why anybody should question the idea of an industrial partnership. This is not just pious talk. Indeed, if the Department of Employment read the accumulated evidence from the many private sector companies presented to the Commons Employment Committee on the future of the trade unions they would realise the government's own exhortation is already far behind the times. There are a growing number of companies, under the stimulus of the need for global competitiveness, who have improved their productivity and overall business performance by working closely in alliance with trade unions and not trying to destroy or limit their influence in the workplace. A transformation is taking place in British industrial relations over large areas of industry as a result of a renewal in management-trade union cooperation. This represents a dramatic shift away from the traditions of the past, from the essentially adversarial system where trust between employers and employees was so often lacking and conflict resolution lay at the heart of so much joint consultation and collective bargaining. Defence of hallowed customs and practices through the policing of demarcation lines, the maintenance of both pre- and post-entry closed shops and restricted entry for young workers into skilled trades were once widespread, but not any longer. The country's changing workplace reveals a revolution has been taking place across many large unionised companies. By force of enlightened example, many of Britain's trade unions have begun to demonstrate to employers that they can be a vital and positive force in increasing workplace competitiveness.

'There has indeed been a very substantial "wind of change" blowing through our offices and across our shop floors in recent years,' said ACAS Chairman John Hougham. He believes the productivity improvements made in much of British industry during the late 1980s stemmed from 'an acceptance of the need for organisations to take tough decisions and a growing acknowledgement of the need to become competitive to survive.'[2]

The Commons Trade and Industry Committee, in its April 1994 report on competitiveness, emphasised the vital importance of the change that has been taking place in British industrial relations. 'A report such as this written a decade ago would have devoted considerable attention to the United Kingdom's adversarial industrial relations and the effects in terms of stoppages, the obstruction of change and the absorption of management time. No other area has changed so much. The United Kingdom's industrial relations are now widely regarded as a competitive strength.' The study suggested that the dramatic decline in the number of strikes and days lost because of industrial disruption was due in part to the growth of 'good' industrial relations in manufacturing with the greater commitment by companies to the 'empowerment' of their own employees in the production process. This word was used to describe the devolution of decision-making and responsibility to the lowest possible level in the workplace, often to self-managing teams: 'effective employee consultation'; 'the promotion of 'a spirit of continuous improvement'; 'commitment to long-term employment though not a guarantee and not necessarily in the same job' and the introduction of 'extensive training programmes and continuing professional development.' The Committee acknowledged that 'empowerment' had taken root in only a minority of British manufacturing firms and that it was 'far from being the norm', but its report suggested the most successful companies were those that were establishing trust in their employee relations through negotiation with trade unions. The Committee unanimously endorsed the view that 'successful manufacturing companies are likely to be those which have constructive relationships both with their workforces and with the trade unions representing them and that trade unions can contribute to the successful implementation of change within companies.'[3]

Trade Unions as Innovators

'Modern trade unions recognise that companies must be competitive in global markets if they are to be successful and provide secure employment for their employees,' the TUC declared in its March 1994 renewal document. 'That is why unions in Britain, as much as in Germany and Japan, are committed to high quality employment as an essential ingredient of economic success. Unions play a positive role in the investment decisions of companies. A union presence makes it more difficult for employers to adopt a "hire and fire" mentality and to treat their employees as disposable assets.'[2]

As the TUC suggested in its written evidence to the Commons Employment Committee: 'Trade unions have a strategy for the management of change to meet the competitive conditions of the 1990s. The focus must be on the production of competitive, high quality products and services. Employers need the commitment of their workforce to meet the challenges ahead. Commitment is best obtained through the involvement, participation and agreement of the workforce, not by management edict or through the courts. Winning the support of the workforce requires commitment from employers to provide good quality jobs and to consult with the workforce.'[3]

Many of Britain's trade unions have become workplace innovators and not obstacles to corporate change. 'Unions are willing to bargain in good faith to introduce changes in working practices and production methods,' the TUC has argued. 'Unions are interested in enhancing the skills of their members and have a commitment to the development of higher value added products leading to improve company performance. Trade unions also play a positive role in the investment decision of companies,' claimed the TUC and quoted the findings of Professor David Metcalf at the London School of Economics who revealed in his analysis of the 1990 WIRS survey that 'if anything unionised workplaces use more and invest more in advanced capital equipment and human capital than do their non-union equivalents.'[4] There is some evidence, however, to suggest that foreign multinational companies are attracted into Britain not just by the country's relatively low labour costs as well as the lack of statutory rights for workers in pay, benefits and length of working time compared with the other advanced European Union economies but because they have more opportunity in a less regulated labour market to introduce innovatory labour practices that have become 'an essential part of their production and management systems'.[5]

In their joint manifesto – A New Agenda: Bargaining for Prosperity in the 1990s – John Edmonds of the GMB and Alan Tuffin of the UCW communication workers emphasised that trade unions want to create partnerships with employers in a joint response to the competitive challenge. As they explained: 'Price cutting is fast becoming a relatively ineffective means of winning back lost markets. Recent experience and forecasts for the future suggest non-price considerations like innovation, design, reliability, prompt delivery and after sales service are now overtaking price as the key determinants of success. Quality performance will matter most in the 1990s.'[6]

Their document stressed this meant giving 'even greater weight to team work, motivation and commitment. Success and security, profitability and prosperity require that management and labour work together to make the best use of the talent available in each enterprise.' 'We envisage Britain's trade unions developing a joint approach with the employers to create the conditions for economic success and social cohesion,' they explained. 'It would mean talking to Britain's employers about how to achieve quality performance, cost and price competitiveness and a fairer society.'

The two union leaders emphasised this would mean widening the collective bargaining agenda from its traditional concern with pay and conditions. Employers and union negotiators would have to deal with vital questions such as company investment strategy, its research and development spending programmes and plans for new product development, as well as embrace the restructuring of work organisation for maximum mutual flexibility, equal opportunities for women, measures to prevent racial discrimination in the labour market and the strengthening of health and safety policies in the wider work environment.

> The New Agenda would make the quality of output rather than the price of inputs the centrepiece of talks between trade unions and employers. Inevitably pay would be one item on the agenda. But work organisation, training and quality should form

> the focus. Discussions should concentrate upon productivity and ways of bringing the ingenuity of employees to bear on questions of quality. Unions should press management to discuss how they intend to discover and develop the talents of their workforce, what investment they propose to put into innovation and product design and how they hope to encourage the commitment of employees to ever higher standards of service to the customer.

This meant, they agreed, the abandonment of outdated methods of work and defensive shop floor traditions of labour practice. 'Unions must escape from a self-defeating fixation with tightly specified job descriptions and embrace the adaptability that comes from broader job definitions.'

The GMB itself has been particularly innovative in its response to the changing workplace of Human Resource Management and Total Quality Management. In 1993 its productivity services centre published a fascinating account of how trade unions should respond to these developments. The document acknowledged that trade unions, especially their shop stewards and staff representatives 'may be marginalised deliberately by management' through the introduction of HRM strategies such as team working, multi-skilling, direct management communication to the workforce, performance related pay and suggestions that workers' interests were the same as those of the company. The GMB pointed to a 1992 study by Dr John Storey of Loughborough University that examined HRM techniques in fifteen large companies and laid out as many as eleven key elements of the new corporate strategies. 'All of these initiatives pose serious questions for unions as they result in significant change in the working lives of members. Developing a trade union agenda to deal with these challenges is critical in ensuring that we remain relevant to members and are able to secure improvements for them from these changes,' argued the GMB.[7] The union acknowledged companies who introduced the new methods of management 'may not be out to weaken union organisation specifically within the workplace' but warned 'that may well be the consequence unless unions can show they still have a vital role to play in promoting the interests of workers.'

The GMB has acknowledged that 'many of the new management techniques have proved popular with employees.' But it added they could undermine trade unions by changing the workplace culture through direct communication with employees, individualising the workforce through the use of appraisal and performance related pay and marginalising the shop stewards by changing the role of supervisors and bypassing traditional consultation procedures via teamworking and briefing. However, the GMB also suggested these problems could be avoided if trade union activists 'kept on top of developments' and trade unions improved their own communications with their members.

As the union concluded:

> HRM techniques pose fundamental challenges both to the organisation and very relevance of trade unions. In the 1970s unions had to learn how to cope with work study and job evaluation. In the 1990s we have to do the same with HRM. HRM potentially has plenty to offer workers – job security, more interesting work, better training, more involvement in the decisions that affect them. But HRM also has its negative side – increased work rates, more stress, discriminatory recruitment systems, fewer jobs in the long term and, if we are not careful, a weaker role for unions. In any given situation where HRM techniques are proposed, it is our job to maximise the opportunities for our members and minimise the threats.

The GMB quoted a recent US study on the activities of employee involvement committees across twenty-one industries which concluded: 'Without a strong union such committees tend to offer solutions that enhance the power of managers at the expense of workers. The resulting deterioration of trust and demoralisation of the workforce may be what saps productivity. Most unions, on the other hand, constitute an independent voice for workers.'

'This study emphasises the key point – that the role of trade unions is not irrelevant or out of date but can continue to be a positive one for both working people and the organisation employing them,' said the GMB.

The TUC suggested in its evidence to the Commons Employment Committee that there were three good reasons why unionised enterprises were more likely than non-union companies to be innovators with impressive investment records. Firstly, it pointed out the very presence of trade unions in the workplace made it harder for employers to pursue a 'hire and fire' mentality and treat their employees as disposable assets. 'This tends to encourage them to take a longer term view of employees as a resource to be invested in rather than a cost of production,' the TUC said. 'It acts as an incentive for employers to raise the productivity of their workforces by, amongst other things, investing in technology and new capacity.'[8] Secondly, the TUC asserted that trade unions 'encourage companies to invest in skills and higher skill levels in turn make it more worthwhile for them to invest in capital; in economic terms they increase the marginal productivity of capital.'

Thirdly, the TUC claimed trade unions 'act as a positive force for change, particularly in the introduction of new technologies.' The role of trade unions was to provide a sense of security to workers who faced the fears and uncertainties of workplace reorganisation. 'By helping to solve problems before they become confrontations and by giving employees confidence that changes will benefit them as well as the company, unions smooth the way to change.' In essence, the TUC suggested the trade union presence in the workplace establishes 'the climate of trust and cooperation in which new working practices can be introduced most effectively. Contrary to popular myths, trade unions are a force for change.'

The future of the trade unions in the private sector will depend on their ability to get that message across to new employers; that having an organised workforce is good for their business performance. Assisting companies in coping with the competitive challenge is clearly a successful strategy for many trade unions who can demonstrate negotiated workplace change is of mutual advantage to both the company and their employees. This is not a new perception. Contrary to popular assertion, trade unions (with some atypical exceptions) as institutions have not, in the recent past, resisted technological change. It is no coincidence that the British private companies which have been the most successful on global markets in recent years have been those whose workers have been organised in recognised trade unions.

As the AEEU engineering union explained in its evidence to the Commons Employment Committee: 'It is significant that the world class inward investors into Britain like Sony, Bosch and Toyota have all decided to recognise trade unions in their British operations. They were not required to do so; on the contrary, our government has boasted that inward investors into Britain are not bound by a minimum wage, the 'social chapter' of the Maastricht treaty or the requirement to recognise trade unions. Yet, unlike the British government, world-class companies clearly see good wages and conditions, together with a constructive dialogue with employee representatives, as integral to, rather than contrary to, corporate success.'[9]

Most trade unions have warmly welcomed the flow of inward investment into Britain and they have sought to cooperate with foreign owned companies who have established plants in the country. The positive trade union attitude can be seen in the growing range of impressive collective agreements reached with multinationals.

Bill Jordan, the AEEU's president, is a particularly effective champion of the new workplace trade unionism where employees establish a relationship with the companies they work for aimed at improving their business performance. 'Unions act as a positive force for change, particularly when this involves new ways of working,' he has argued. 'In larger organisations in particular, change is bound to bring with it fears and uncertainties amongst the workforce. By helping to solve problems before they become confrontations and by giving employees confidence that changes will benefit them as well as the company, unions smooth the way to change. Any list of Britain's largest industrial world class companies would reveal that the overwhelming majority are unionised.'[10]

In its written evidence, the AEEU laid emphasis on its view that trade unions must become involved in helping to turn the companies their members work in into world-class performers.

> World-class manufacturing centres on the concepts of teamwork and flexibility. The skills and knowledge of the workforce must be recognised and put to maximum use; this means implementing quality circles where workplace representatives come together to discuss ways of improving the product. It also means putting a great emphasis on the importance of communication and consultation between management and workforce. World-class producers compete by raising the standards of all aspects of manufacturing while second-rate companies seek to compete through lower costs on wages, training, research and development etc. World-class companies know that in order to attract and retain a high quality workforce, excellent pay and conditions are required.[11]

Mr Jordan admitted that the kind of 'new' industrial relations approach he advocated would not have been possible in the

1970s. 'At that time I think we were too happy kicking the stuffing out of each other and gladly doing that, and that was to be regretted,' he said. 'If anything has encouraged the acceptance of the new approach by unions and for it to be copied by other management it is the despair that came out of the early 1980s when so many jobs were lost, so many companies were closed and we started to look for better ways of doing business. That has been reinforced in the last three years. Again, more trade unions and more managers are saying we need to look at best practice. What has pleased us is that at the core of this best practice is the recognition that without a good partnership arrangement between the management and the workers through representation you are seriously undermining your competitive edge.'[12]

The AEEU's outlook on workplace innovation draws heavily on the industrial relations experience to be found in three of the United Kingdom's main competitors – Germany, Sweden and Japan. As the union pointed out 'those countries in the world that currently have the best long-term trading records in manufactured goods have well developed employee representation systems, predominantly through trade unions and/or works councils.' It emphasised that in the three countries highlighted for their good work practices, had all enjoyed greater economic success and stronger manufacturing industries than Britain in the past thirty years. The AEEU believes that the common denominator that accounts for the contrast lies in the partnership-based approach to industrial relations to be found in Germany, Sweden and Japan.

In the past the complex structure of multi-unionism in the British workplace has proved to be an obstacle to innovation, but in the past few years a substantial increase has taken place in both the existence of single union collective agreements with companies and the use of single table bargaining where trade unions combine together to negotiate directly with an employer.

The AEEU, as a supporter of industrial unionism, is a strong believer in single union deals in companies. 'It is no coincidence that Germany and Japan, whose differing industrial relations structures nevertheless both encourage just one union in any one company, are two of the most successful industrial nations in the world,' it has argued. The AEEU maintains that the introduction of single unionism in the enterprise ensures flexibility. 'Multi-unionism, where various unions represent workers whose tasks increasingly overlap, is industrially illogical in the flexible firm,' it pointed out. The AEEU believes if Britain is to emulate that success, we must match the flexibility of Germany and Japan. Single union agreements greatly assist this process. If a single union agreement is not possible, single table bargaining is the next best thing. Inward investor companies frequently insist on single union agreements and given Britain's current employment laws, can refuse recognition altogether if such an agreement is not forthcoming. In this negative sense, it might be argued that the future of unions depends upon our signing single union agreements and establishing single table bargaining. From the AEEU's point of view, however, this would misinterpret our reasons for reaching such agreements.'[13]

'We have signed a number of single union agreements with inward investors such as Nissan, Toyota and Sony and we find their approach to HRM gives us no reason for complaint,' said Mr Jordan. 'Team-working, flexibility and multi-skilling have been central to the competitive edge that these companies have established but they have never sought to exploit their workforces by using these techniques.' He added:

> Whether we like it or not, these practices amount to a modern industrial development that is here to stay. It must be our job to ensure that they are introduced in a way that is of maximum benefit to our membership. A refusal to acknowledge HRM would give the opponents of social partnership an opportunity to cast the trade union movement as negative and as being stuck in the past. Frankly, in my view, there would be some justification to this charge. Our adoption of an oppositionalist line would also deny us the opportunity to differentiate between good and bad management. At present AEEU support for HRM in its form at Toyota, Nissan and Sony allows us to be critical of those companies that try to use these techniques as a cloak for attacks on their workforces. In reality, companies will introduce these techniques regardless of our opposition. Let us not leave our shop stewards with the unenviable task of trying to respond to change with no guidance or practical support from their union or from the wider trade union movement.[14]

Other trade unions with many members in the private manufacturing sector have also displayed a strong enthusiasm in embracing the cause of change in the workplace. Mr Bill

Morris, the TGWU's General Secretary, asserts his union has been at the forefront of the important workplace reforms that have been introduced in recent years at the main car companies – Ford, Vauxhall and, above all, Rover. 'Partnership for us is about cooperation,' said Mr Morris. 'What we will resist is the imposition of a one way model which does not in any way make provision for any other view except the company's view. We would argue that the successful companies in Britain are those companies, in terms of long-term success, which work with the trade unions, which develop a partnership.'[15]

The TGWU has accepted the need for change while recognising the challenges this has imposed on older forms of work organisation. As it explained in its 1993 strategy document, Focus for The Future: 'TGWU members are having to deal with human resource management every working day. A recent survey by Warwick University of the union's officials and shop stewards revealed this, with 44 per cent of stewards reporting the use of team-briefings and multi-skilling over the past three years.' The union is now adopting a 'positive agenda' to face workplace change and pre-empt any moves to de-recognition by employers. 'The crucial point for us is to maintain independent union representation and to engage in jointly determining change at work,' it argued in 1993.[16] The TGWU has pressed the cause of single status in the workplace with the harmonisation of sick pay and holidays between manual and non-manual employees, keeping national negotiating rights as part of the package. The union has also been developing its own concept of quality in the workplace.

Trade unions are translating their good intentions into practical action. It is no exaggeration to talk of a new cooperative spirit between management, trade unions and workers in many areas of British manufacturing industry which were once a byword for industrial conflict.

The TGWU published a study in the spring of 1994 that pointed to the key role cooperative industrial relations played in the building of the Channel Tunnel. It concluded that 'from the management side TML has achieved its goal of completing the tunnel more or less to schedule, if at a higher cost than initially envisaged. There have been no major disputes and productivity has been consistently high. The price that has been paid for this has been high wages, an abandonment of an ideological right to manage and an acceptance of joint determination of rules and procedures increasingly as the project has developed.'[17] The company gave 'direct encouragement to trade union organisation'. It even commended the TGWU's professionalism. TML gave the unions 'privileged access' and the stewards and their unions 'responded with a level of hard work and dedication' which amply repaid membership commitment. 'Management preferred to rely on joint regulation and the acceptance of strong trade union organisation as the realistic way to achieve their goals,' the report indicated.

The New Deal at Rover

One of the best examples of the positive workplace approach can be found at the Rover group, now a subsidiary of the German conglomerate BMW. Ten years ago many of its plants were riven with bitter unofficial disruption. Now many of them are showplaces for enterprise unionism.

It was in April 1992 that the company signed an important agreement with five recognised trade unions known as the New Deal. It has quickly become an oft-quoted example of the new consensual approach to industrial relations apparent across British manufacturing industry. Shop floor support for what was being proposed was not easy to achieve. When the deal was put to the workforce in a ballot vote it was accepted by the narrowest of margins: 11,961 votes for, 11,793 against. 'The agreement is a positive example of the way in which unions can contribute to the process of introducing changes in working practices while retaining employee protection to the advantage of employers and employees alike.'[18] As the union explained in its 1993 biennial conference report, the Rover agreement maintained the company's 'main requirement of being able to compete with the Japanese transplants, all of whom practise lean production methods,' but still left 'the old trade union structure for recognition, representation and negotiating rights in place.'[19] 'Rover is perhaps one of the most significant agreements in Britain,' Mr Jordan told the MPs. 'It is a giant step forward for British industry. Here we were taking a company with perhaps one of the worst industrial relations histories of any in the country and through a partnership of the management and the trade unions brought in the most radical change that has ever beset that company. Rover is not the Japanese doing what they are good at; it is the British showing that they too can be as good as the best in the world.'[20]

In his evidence to the Commons Employment Committee, the then Rover Group Chairman Mr George Simpson confirmed the positive view of the trade unions for the deal. 'The fact we have been able to enrol the trade union people at Rover in the company's mission and objectives has allowed us to move at a pace which would have been impossible without trade union collaboration, so we see the relationship we have with trade unions at Rover as a very positive thing for the company,' he told the MPs.[21] 'Having the trade unions understand what the company's mission is in life and working with us in partnership, we have been able to make tremendous strides in terms of productivity and costs.'

Rover pointed out that the 1992 agreement 'works on the basis that the company, the recognised trade unions and employees are all stakeholders in the business and all have a direct interest in Rover becoming and remaining a successful world class company.'

In the view of the company the agreement's 'key thrust' lies in the fact that 'the job security and prosperity of employees can only be achieved by everyone being committed to radical changes to the traditional ways we have designed, manufactured and sold our products.' As it explained: 'The agreement focuses on individual contribution and self-development, the essential need for flexibility to accommodate rapidly changing business needs, the constant challenge of eliminating waste by concentrating our efforts solely on added value work and the fact that we are now a single status company.'[22]

In separate evidence, the Rover Group sought to place the company's new approach into a wider context. It argued:

> The pursuit of greater productivity and efficiency have caused the majority of managers in the European car industry to believe that attainment of these objectives will not be possible, without a dramatic shift in company cultures away from the bureaucratic, authoritarian and hierarchical patterns that have characterised mass production industries throughout most of the twentieth century.
>
> The change from the old 'managers manage; employees do what management tells them to do' style stems from recognising that the real experts on many activities within a company are not its managers but employees throughout the firm. Successful businesses are increasingly those that can attract, retain and

> motivate all employees to develop and use their full talents in the interest of the firm.[23]

The Rover New Deal is worth examining in some detail. Its first part is concerned with the creation of 'single status' in the company between manual and non-manual employees. 'We are all employees and the only distinction is the contribution we make,' declares the document.[24] This has meant introducing a number of important changes that have eliminated the old invidious status distinctions that used to separate the shop floor from the office.

These involve:

- The phasing out of clocking-on for work attendance by all employees.
- The introduction of a single status sick pay scheme.
- Allowing all employees to have a regular health check-up provided by the company.
- Everybody working within Rover except those employed on outside plant activities to wear the same company workwear.
- The arrival of single status catering facilities, ending the different level canteens.
- Allowing production workers to progressively have the opportunity to take part of their annual holiday entitlement outside shutdown periods.
- All workers to be paid by credit transfer.
- A guarantee of no lay-offs by the company. (The agreement states: 'In the event of a problem which disrupts production all employees will be engaged in worthwhile activities and be required to cooperate with efforts to maintain productive output.')
- The introduction of minimum notice period for all workers to be one month.

In return for these reforms Rover workers are expected to cooperate with management in workplace change. Clause two of the New Deal emphasises that 'continuous improvement' is to be 'a requirement for everyone'. 'The company must continually improve its performance and competitive position through the elimination of waste, increased levels of efficiency and reduced levels of manpower – working smarter rather than harder.' The agreement makes it clear that work planning and changes in production schedules will be carried out in consultation with the work teams who 'will consider all alternative ways of satisfying customer demand' and accept overtime working is 'allocated fairly' based on skills and the number of employees required 'with no restrictive practices applied or sought'.

The New Deal also brings an end to the existence of job demarcation lines on the shop floor that used to segment the British car industry with disruptive consequences. Paragraph three of the document states that Rover workers 'will be expected to be flexible subject to their ability to do the jobs after training if necessary and subject to safe working practices being observed.' 'Every employee will have unrestricted access to the use of company tools and equipment necessary for them to make their contribution.' A strong emphasis is placed on empowering the individual worker who enjoys 'the maximum devolution of authority and accountability'. The New Deal makes it clear that the work teams are responsible for a wide range of issues including ensuring work quality, routine maintenance and housekeeping, process improvements, cost reductions, work allocation, job rotation, training of each other and material control.

The document also promised the introduction in November 1992 of a single grade structure for the workforce to replace a five grade hourly paid and six grade staff structure. By integrating everybody on the same grade structure, Rover ensured advancement up the salary range would 'be achievable by everyone through skill acquisition.' In addition, productivity bonus schemes were to be phased out and everybody would instead participate in a bonus system related directly to company performance based on attendance.

Paragraph seven of the New Deal lists expectations of future improvement in creating a 'good working environment'. This involves ensuring plant and office layout is 'safe and easy to work in', 'continuous improvement of medical and catering facilities', 'the minimisation of activities causing unnecessary stress or discomfort' and 'production of the highest quality products'.

One of the most important parts of the agreement lies in a company commitment to avoid compulsory redundancies. 'Employees who want to work for Rover will be able to stay with Rover,' argues the New Deal. 'Necessary reductions in manpower will be achieved in future, with the cooperation of all employees through retraining and redeployment, natural wastage, voluntary severance and early retirement programmes,' it insists.

There is a strong emphasis on the need to keep employees fully informed on company policy. 'Constant open and honest two-way communications with employees throughout the company will be the norm,' states paragraph nine. 'The process of daily, weekly, monthly and annual employee briefings will be strengthened.'

The commitment to company training is absolute. 'All of us will participate in identifying training needs and giving and receiving training to improve skills/knowledge and to continuously improve the processes on which we work,' declares the New Deal. Rover says it wants to make training opportunities open to all its employees who will be encouraged to 'develop themselves to their full potential'. Everybody is expected to take part in discussion groups, quality action teams, suggestion schemes and the like to improve company performance.

The New Deal also spells out the function for recognised trade unions in the company. It emphasises the need to enhance consultation with union representatives 'to ensure maximum understanding of company performance, competitive practices and standards, product and company plans and all areas of activity affecting the company and its employees.' Bi-annual reviews take place between the company, union national officials and joint negotiating committee employee representatives.

In the area of conflict resolution, the agreement virtually rules out the use of the strike weapon. As paragraph fifteen makes clear: 'In the event of any grievance or dispute which any employee or group of employees may have, the full company/trade union procedure will be used to resolve the problem. In the unlikely event of any grievance or dispute not being resolved in this manner, if both parties agree, it will be referred to arbitration, the outcome of which will be binding on both parties. There will be no disputes outside this procedure.'

The Spread of Progressive Deals

It would be wrong to suggest the Rover deal is an exception. Across much of British industry, forward-looking, legally non-binding collective agreements have been reached between companies and their recognised trade unions.

A report by ACAS on industrial relations in Wales instanced the achievement of the Ford Motor Company at its Bridgend engine plant. In 1986 local management and plant trade union officials from the TGWU, AEEU and MSF reached agreement on a new approach to save the plant from closure. 'The Japanese manufacturing model of lean production techniques leading to the generation of profits, ongoing investment and the protection of jobs became uppermost in the minds of management and trade unions alike,' said ACAS. 'The plant viewed quality as the major initiative to build its reputation. This along with changes in management style, employee attitudes and overall relationships was seen as the key to the future.'[25]

This involved a complete change in the plant's industrial culture. A continuous improvement programme was introduced with the creation of integrated manufacturing teams of skilled and production workers, area foremen who were made responsible for production and maintenance and total process improvement groups to underpin the team arrangements. All the old traditional demarcation lines have been swept away with spectacular results, according to Ford, so that Bridgend is now in Europe 'top of the league for productivity, quality and unit cost.'

As ACAS explained: 'Naturally, not all things have gone smoothly for all of the time and there have been moments when achieving full agreement has been difficult. However, the results of the strategy of jointly involving trade union representatives and their members together with all levels of management has kept the plant profitable. Strong personal inputs from the convenor and his stewards and the plant manager and his team, particularly in the area of employee relations, have been major factors in this success.'

John Edmonds of the GMB, instanced the example of the Norwegian company, Kvaerner, when it acquired the troubled Govan shipyard on the Clyde in Scotland in 1989. 'They brought a participative management style that was not particularly common in parts of the shipbuilding industry,' he explained.[26] The company agreed with him. 'Since setting in place a new, more accountable local industrial relations framework in 1990, we at Kvaerner Govan have found that the role of our trade unions has been an integral ingredient of transforming what was a loss-making and uncompetitive shipyard into a viable and competitive shipbuilding operation,' it wrote to MPs.[27]

As the company explained:

> In their new role, the trade unions act in a responsible manner, particularly constructively in collective bargaining, problem solving, productivity improvement, health and safety, and training initiatives etc. They also have a significant role in the administration of disciplinary procedures, company restructuring, manpower balancing, redundancy and communication.
>
> We view industrial relationship as an important aspect of managing our business given that, to compete effectively, we require a motivated and committed workforce to ensure that their energies are channelled effectively in the overall interests of achieving the twin aims of shipyard profitability and competitiveness.
>
> The local trade unions have a key role to play in creating the culture, environment and workplace attitudes which enable us to achieve these twin aims. This, of course, requires a management style that recognises the value of organised labour and the benefits that the trade unions' role and 'voice' can bring to a company.

Early in 1994 Kvaerner Govan introduced Britain's first adult apprenticeship scheme with the cooperation of the trade unions. The agreement enabled semi-skilled workers whose jobs were redundant to gain a second chance by being able to learn a range of skills with better job security prospects as welders, fabricators and pipefitters. 'Traditionally in British industry, if you are not apprenticed to a skilled trade by the age of seventeen or so you are marked for life as unskilled or semi-skilled,' said Mr Bobby Gordon, Kvaerner's Personnel and Employee Relations Director. 'Our adult apprenticeship programme is a landmark in industrial relations because it breaks some eighty years of custom and practice in the shipbuilding and engineering industry. It is another example of how our approach to manpower utilisation is changing in response to the challenges of a highly competitive market-place in which we have to beat worldwide opposition to win orders.

It clearly made no sense to let men with years of knowledge and experience of shipbuilding walk out of the gate, probably never to return, just because they were not apprenticed in their youth.'[28]

HP Foods Ltd., which since 1988 has been a subsidiary of the French multinational food and drink group BSN, has a robust and positive view of trade unions, particularly the TGWU, who have 100 per cent membership at the company's Birmingham and Worcester plants for process and engineering workers, with similar representation and recognition rights at the company's Norfolk plant where the AEEU also have 100 per cent membership for engineering staff. The company has a 'strong personnel policy embedded in its core values and operating style'. This 'in essence sees the company's economic and social missions as interlinked, with economic success flowing from a strong involvement and personnel development philosophy in which employees are viewed as equal stakeholders with shareholders.'[29] As HP told the Commons Employment Committee: 'BSN believes that collectivism is an inevitable wish of the workforce, therefore trade unions are not only legitimate but they are needed as a counterbalance to the economic pressure on management and as a constructive partner in the management of change. This belief reflected the views of the management team in HP at the time of its acquisition in 1988 – unfortunately under its previous parent (Hanson Plc 1986 – 88) there was no real room for the expression or funding of such progressive involvement policies.'

Now the company says it regards the recognised British unions as 'social partners' and it has widened the traditional agenda of collective bargaining and grievance handling.

It now covers:

- Profit-sharing which has been introduced and makes up around 5 per cent of a workers' basic pay. As a result there is a 'meaningful economic dialogue' every month with shop stewards at plant level that leads to 'greater economic understanding'. Company results are published each month to all employees.
- Two pension fund employee trustees (including one from the unions) have been introduced and have played a major role in the development of improved pension benefits for the lower paid.

- Trade union safety representatives at all the company's sites make an important contribution to its safety record with British Safety Council awards at all sites.
- A meeting every six months between HP's Managing Director with senior stewards and full-time officers for a business review.
- One British steward attends BSN's annual European level union meeting with group board directors at which 'major economic developments and social policies are discussed'.
- Major investment projects are progressed in detailed dialogue with employees and their representatives.
- Joint management, union training and upskilling programmes. 'Major changes to working practices, including voluntary job reductions have been successfully negotiated with the TGWU, coupled with outplacement support, revised pay structures and job training.'

HP emphasised that the 'joint involvement philosophy' ensured 'direct face-to-face communication between managers and employees is no longer seen as "trying to subvert the right of the union to talk to its members", the individual and collective approaches exist in harmony.' The 'relationship of trust' developed between the company and the unions has allowed 'the introduction of progressive social policies for all individuals (suggestion scheme, employee assistance programme of information and counselling and an occupational health initiative) to proceed without suspicion that they are substitional for pay and without automatic insistence on union negotiation in their design/management.'

HP stressed that the key to its successful partnership with its workers developed at local level. It admitted that 'paradoxically at national level the TGWU has been slower than, for example, the GMB or the AEEU in embracing the "new agenda", yet our involvement initiatives have outstripped the pace of progress in sister companies where the GMB and the AEEU are the dominant unions.'

Innovation in Older Companies

A number of enlightened companies who have long-standing collective agreements with recognised unions intend to change their approach to industrial relations in the future. Nestlé, the food manufacturer, has pointed out that the trade union's traditional role in the company that covered pay bargaining, resolution of grievances and job security arrangements has grown less in recent years. As it explained to MPs:

> In recent years the power and influence of trade unions has diminished partly as a result of the legislation enacted by the government but also as a result of changes in our management style and the focus on initiatives aimed at making employees feel involved, informed and valued. Briefing groups, quality circles etc. and a whole range of various communications to employees on company performance and objectives have reduced the influence of the trade unions at shop steward level as well as nationally. The unions have reacted to these influences by seeking to justify their existence by offering their members new, improved services such as financial advice, discount arrangements and particularly in the legal field with support for claims in respect of industrial accidents, deafness, RSI etc.[30]

Nestlé also told the MPs: 'Our view of the future role of trade unions is significantly influenced by our long tradition of working with recognised trade unions and history of good industrial relations. We see a continuing role on traditional lines but with a further diminution of their influence at both local and national level. Although we see negotiations continuing with trade unions these are likely to become increasingly plant-based in the future. Union mergers are expected to continue and single table-plant bargaining is likely to replace the current separate negotiating groups. The company foresees a "continuing consultative role" for trade unions at plant level in areas like health and safety. But it also said it could, "over time", see the union role becoming "superfluous".'

The Boots Company told the Commons Employment Committee it had worked with trade unions for over thirty years. The most significant deal was with USDAW but the company also has agreements with five other unions. However, it estimates today only around 6,000 out of its 80,000 staff are covered by trade union recognition. The company explained it had worked towards de-recognition in some areas, very recently replacing a full negotiation agreement with a consultative agreement for its semi-skilled and skilled engineering staff.

> We believe this trend will continue and such transactions are possible in companies where an effective infrastructure of consultation and cooperation exists. We have for many years had a fully comprehensive structure of staff councils, reflecting the company's management structure in which all staff are represented and in which our trade unions have seats as of right. Such environments are probably more likely to exist in medium to large companies (say, with more than 1,000 staff). We suspect that in smaller companies, for various reasons, the environment is not as conducive to a less formal relationship between employer, trade unions and employee. It is likely that in these companies there will continue to be either formal trade union agreements or no unions at all, with the latter more likely.[31]

The Japanese Experience

The Sony corporation, in its written evidence to the Commons Employment Committee, summarised twenty years of experience of manufacturing operations in Britain: 'We believe the historically adversarial relationship of unions and employers is an outdated concept and in our rapidly changing environment, industrial growth and prosperity can only be achieved through consensus and partnership. The employer and the employee share the same objectives: the creation and growth of prosperity and wealth.'[32]

It is true the company suggested 'only a limited number of trade unions (such as the AEEU) embrace this concept' and 'only such unions have a useful future in British manufacturing' but Sony emphasised the value of having an outside force involved in the company's affairs. As it explained: 'Within the manufacturing sector, progressive labour relations require an independent window into the workforce for manufacturing management and the best window is that provided by an independent union espousing the values of consensus and partnership. A representative system helps to ensure that employees' interests are taken into account and this could be a major factor in the satisfactory achievement of change. In disciplinary issues, for example, a representative system is the best way of ensuring that justice is done and is seen to be done.'

Toyota began production in Britain in December 1992 with a single union agreement with the AEEU. It explained to the Commons Employment Committee why it decided to recognise a trade union for collective bargaining purposes.

The company argued that its 'philosophy' contained 'two fundamental principles' that were of 'central importance' for employee relations – 'respect for the value of people' and 'mutual trust and respect'. 'Toyota respects the existing British trade unions, their long history, and their valuable contribution to the development of society,' it argued.[33]

The company approached five trade unions in the car industry to 'find a partner who was willing to work together with both Toyota members and the company to put these philosophies into practice.' In October 1991 it decided to conclude an agreement with the AEEU. Toyota said the deal provided the company with 'the platform of understanding and practical arrangements on which we are building (with hard work) the daily practice of respect for all members, mutual trust and a stable, prosperous company which can provide long term employment and good working conditions.' The company argues that its agreement with the AEEU has enabled it to establish 'specific structures' which are 'designed to maximise fairness and balance in representation, involvement, information sharing and the discussion of issues of common interest.

> The situation is that the company should be able to take full account of members' views in arriving at business decisions. The partnership between the company and the union created these structures and now together provide the strength which underwrite and support them. It is still early days but we are building the basis for durable, positive relationships, based on partnership and constructive, non-adversarial practices. We find the common interests of the people employed at Toyota are far greater than their differences (whether they are shop floor or office) and a single union best represents this common interest, as we had thought it would, in our situation.

One of the most interesting examples of the new enterprise unionism in Britain can be found at the Nissan company where the management took the initiative in seeking a working alliance with the AEEU. In his thoughtful evidence to the Commons Employment Committee, the company's Personnel Director Mr Peter Wickens spelt out what the partnership approach meant to Nissan. 'Successful trade unions in the future must be committed to the success of the enterprise and the people who work in it,' he explained. 'Change is now the only constant. Trade unions must encourage and support change. We are past the time when every change of technology, working practice or staffing level can be the subject of negotiation. Indeed when decisions affecting these issues are being pushed way down into the organisation the unions have a real opportunity not to resist such changes but to facilitate them in a manner beneficial to both employees and the company.'[34] Mr Ian Gibson, Nissan's Managing Director and Chief Executive told the committee the company found that 'trade unions are cooperative and eager to make sure we are a successful company because they believe that this is for the benefit of their members.'[35]

Toshiba's television and air conditioner production plant at Plymouth provides further evidence of the success of trade union-management relations. It explained its achievement in a paper presented by its headquarters in Japan to Professor John Dunlop's management-union commission in the United States in March 1994. As the company argued:

> When it was established in 1981, Toshiba Consumer Products had a management team of six, of whom only one was Japanese, the engineering director. This team was charged with developing a corporate plan for the new company that had to win approval from Toshiba corporation. Its role was positive, in that the members were to define TCP's management structure and practices and therefore the company's culture, rather than to put in place practices imported from Japan. A primary element in this was the approach taken to human resources management.
>
> The team's key phrase was 'Automatically assuming the traditional approach is necessary is abdication of responsibility.' In other words, TCP was looking for a new approach to human resources management. In practice this mean 'attitude first, skill second', the idea that people with the right attitude could be trained in appropriate skills. Reflecting the same philosophy, line workers and office employees all receive monthly salaries and the same benefits. The joint venture's six cafeterias for different grades of employees were replaced by a single cafeteria for everybody. This undoubtedly helped to reinforce a sense of equal status and fosters part of being part of a team.[36]

But from the start the company was keen to blend a trade union into the structure of its organisation. It recognised the AEEU and gave it sole representation rights. Around 60 per cent of the 1,000 workers are members of the union. Toshiba explained however that within the company's framework 'the trade union has a different role from that of the union in most British companies.' The 'traditional role of collective representation of employees' was 'mainly accomplished' through the seventeen strong elected Company Advisory Board chaired by the Managing Director and made up of two directors and the rest elected shop floor representatives. The senior shop steward is automatically a member of that board, which is 'free to discuss anything and given the information it needs to do so.' Toshiba said the board was given information on industry wage rates, the economic situation and the company's performance to help in pay negotiations. 'Decisions are passed on to management by the board as non-binding recommendations,' explained the company. 'If a management policy does not find support, the system provides for further discussion at the board. If that fails to produce agreement, the union has a right to negotiation. After this there is a final arbitration phase by an independent third party through pendulum arbitration.'

Apparently 'the board system and pendulum arbitration appears to have won the confidence of everybody in the company, not least the union,' explained the company. 'All the evidence shows that the overall system works well. Not a single day of work has been lost in disputes and there has yet to be a disagreement that reaches the arbitration phase.' In both 1992 and 1993 the company's Plymouth plant won high awards for performance. Productivity has climbed by 17.5 per cent annually over the last ten years.

Inward Investors and the New Unionism

Trade union involvement in industrial change is not just confined to the establishment of new greenfield plants. Many companies have carried out fundamental reforms in their existing British plants with strong trade union cooperation.

Iveco Ford is a recent good example. Formed in 1986 as a joint venture between Ford Motor Company and Iveco, the commercial vehicle division of the Italian conglomerate Fiat, its plant at Langley in Buckinghamshire switched from the production of a unique model range to the standard European Iveco product. Nearly all the hourly-paid workers are unionised and three quarters of the staff. In recent years the Langley plant has endured hard times. In 1989 it withstood a six week strike and it took seven months of intensive negotiations to achieve a new agreement. Two years later the unions were compelled to accept a six month deferment in pay and last year a six month pay freeze was followed by a 3 per cent basic wage rise with no further negotiations until 1 January 1995.

As Iveco Ford told the Commons Employment Committee: 'Clearly the unions' position has altered significantly. They have come from a confrontational "fight for everything we can get" approach to one of having to fully appreciate the adverse market conditions facing the company and the influence of Iveco's European situation. They have had to understand that if industrial relations are seen to be unstable in the United Kingdom this could negatively influence Iveco's decision regarding sourcing the British market.'[37]

The range of collective agreements linked to workplace change suggests trade unions in the 1990s can often be successful and vital partners with management in achieving global competitiveness. Certainly recent performance indicates companies that have recognised trade unions can secure sweeping change in their plants without disruption. The view of foreign owned multinational companies operating in Britain is extremely positive about the industrial relations scene. In March 1994 KPMG Peat Marwick, the consultants, published a wide-ranging survey of 800 international firms operating in the United Kingdom. It found that the British workforce 'consistently exceeded the expectations of the companies' expectations in the areas of labour relations, productivity, adaptability, quality, skill and training.'[38] 'With over two million people employed by foreign owned companies in the United Kingdom it is encouraging that our labour relations are specifically highlighted for praise, something that would have been unheard of twenty years ago,' said Mr Colin Sharman, United Kingdom senior partner of KPMG. 'The survey clearly demonstrates that the quality of our workforce plays a significant role in attracting overseas companies to this country. Productivity is also highly rated.'

The Limits of Workplace Innovation

Unfortunately much of the country's manufacturing sector does not provide a similar picture of positive change in alliance with trade unions. As the AEEU's President Mr Bill Jordan has argued, 'Britain has a two-tier industry, a layer of excellent to moderately good companies on a substantial underclass of low performance companies.' In his view, the Japanese industrial relations model can be and has been adopted in Britain as a 'partnership of management, unions and employees' when it is viewed as 'an integral part of the whole new manufacturing and management technique package.' There is no inherent resistance from workers to the concept but it needs 'a cultural conversion' starting at senior management level and working down through the enterprise.[39] As Mr Jordan argued: 'In relatively few cases where companies have gone for the full world-class package, it took strong and farsighted management and trade unions to agree to end the age-old war game over the power to determine the level and quality of production and give that power to those who could do most with it: the workforce.'

The AEEU President pointed out that there are still not enough managers and trade unions who are willing to pursue the Japanese best practice model. Indeed, he admits there is 'no simple model that can be adopted and it would certainly be a mistake to attempt to transplant an approach developed in the circumstances of another country.' But while admitting developments in Japan and continental Europe, especially Germany, must be seen in the context of different cultural backgrounds to that of Britain, the concept of 'partnership' in manufacturing had been put into practice with tremendous advantage. Mr Jordan argues:

> Our challenge in Britain is to develop a partnership that meets our own needs. It will not be an easy task. Industrial development in Britain has seen both sides of industry cultivate and refine conflict for their own advantage. This conflict has shaped Britain's political landscape. It has written itself into our laws and it has corrosively affected our competitiveness. It has also given rise to a paradox at the heart of our industry that our competitors find both puzzling and gratifying. Virtually every successful company in Britain will say that people are their most important asset, that they need to involve and communicate with their employees and that it is only by building a spirit of partnership at work that they can hope to compete.
>
> And yet the standard response from British employers is to resist any legal or industrial relations system designed to encourage such partnership. How many companies will recognise that the worthy talk of valuing their employees does not sit easily with a hire and fire mentality among

> company managers or with a legal framework to encourage it. Clearly, the firms that espouse a partnership with their employees do not see the existence of fair labour standards as an obstacle to the success of their own competitiveness. So why should they be worried about them being required of other firms in the same position. I find it hard to believe this is an act of generosity towards their competitors. So I am forced to the conclusion that it is really no more than an ideological conviction that any imposition on employers must be resisted, especially if it impinges on the right to take instant, arbitrary and unchallenged decisions.

He believes it needs 'the German model of the institutional stick of imposing higher standards to get the rest of British industry moving.'

Trade Unions are Good for Business

Mr John Hougham, the ACAS Chairman, has observed from the service's own experience that 'where unions are recognised they generally make a positive contribution to working relationships especially in the current economic and industrial climate, where the management of change is a major preoccupation.'[40]

The Involvement and Participation Association, in their written evidence to the Commons Employment Committee laid particular emphasis on the key role it believed trade unions could play in the management of workplace change through the provision of a collective voice.

> Change is only possible today with employee support and it is essential for survival. Unions have a particularly important role to play in creating a better balance between job security and job inflexibility. The IPA would like to see trade unions playing a much more proactive role in developing real involvement within companies. This could, for example, be through ensuring that training budgets and employee involvement activities are not trimmed back when times become difficult. Trade unions could also achieve much by encouraging members to develop mobile skills, thereby giving them both greater flexibility and variety. Just In Time management gives added power to the workforce because the margins of time are so narrow – it is essential that this power is used to good and not to harmful effect.[41]

Conclusion

The wide range of evidence presented to the Commons Employment Committee indicates that trade union participation in workplace innovation has gone far beyond the level of rhetoric. Surprisingly the decentralised and uncoordinated industrial relations system that has emerged in much of the private sector has provided a flexibility and willingness to change on the shop floor that makes the battle zone mentality of the 1960s and 1970s an unpleasant and distant memory. A genuine new partnership is developing in the workplace and it is producing tangible and impressive results. The trade union presence has become – in the view of many companies – a vital ingredient in the achievement of shop floor stability and cooperation through a period of extraordinarily swift technological change. This is not enterprise unionism. On the contrary, sensible employers and trade union officials recognise that the value of having trade unions in the workplace is to provide employees with an autonomous, collective voice. This is not seen as a threat to the well-being of the company; through mutual consent trade unions and employers can work together in improving corporate performance. But the existence of an external institution in the workplace does provide a necessary safeguard for employees against any potential dangers of autocratic management. The majority of the best employers value trade unions as allies in the workplace and they are still prepared to give them structural support as they have done so in the past. After all, it is thanks to trade unions that companies have always been able to carry through change with stability.

NOTES

1 Department of Employment written evidence, pp 5–6.
2 John Hougham speech, 21 April 1994.
3 House of Commons Trade and Industry Committee Report, Competitiveness of British Industry, Vol 1, pp 88–89.
4 TUC Campaigning for Change, 1994 p 6.
5 TUC written evidence, p 13.
6 J Edmonds and A Tuffin, The New Agenda: Bargaining for Prosperity in the 1990s, GMB/ UCW, 1991.
7 GMB, HRM/TQM, 1993, p 6.
8 TUC supplementary evidence, p 31.
9 AEEU written evidence, p 43.
10 Bill Jordan AEEU oral evidence, p 59.
11 AEEU supplementary written evidence, p 69.
12 Bill Jordan, ibid, p 61.
13 AEEU evidence, ibid, p 69–70.
14 Bill Jordan, AEEU presidential speech, April 1994.
15 Bill Morris, TGWU oral evidence, p 180.
16 Focus for The Future, TGWU

1994, p 22.
17 The Channel Tunnel Project, TGWU 1994, p 22.
18 TGWU written evidence, p 166.
19 TGWU 1993 biennial conference report, p 134.
20 B Jordan, AEEU oral evidence, p 62.
21 G Simpson, Rover Group Chairman, oral evidence, p 247.
22 Rover Group written evidence, p 231.
23 Competitiveness of UK Industry, Commons Trade and Industry Committee May 1994, p 130.
24 Rover Tomorrow: The New Deal, pp 232–246.
25 Best Practice In Industrial Relations, ACAS March 1994
26 J Edmonds oral evidence, p 58.
27 Kvaerner-Govan written evidence
28 Kvaerner-Govan press release, February 1994.
29 HP Foods Ltd written evidence.
30 Nestlé written evidence.
31 Boots written evidence.
32 Sony written evidence.
33 Toyota written evidence.
34 Nissan written evidence.
35 Nissan oral evidence
36 Toshiba written evidence to US Dunlop Commission, March 1994.
37 Iveco Ford written evidence.
38 KPMG Peat Marwick Report.
39 B Jordan, speech, February 1994.
40 J Hougham, April 1994 speech.
41 Involvement and Participation Association, written evidence, p 5.

CHAPTER SIX

Trade Unions as Service Providers

Trade unions have always been servicing organisations for their members. Before the creation of the welfare state they used to perform the invaluable role of friendly societies that provided a wide range of benefits for their members in need. As Sidney and Beatrice Webb explained in their classic work, *Industrial Democracy* published in 1897, 'all activities of trade unionism' are forms of mutual insurance. Whether the purpose be the fixing of a list of piecework prices, the promotion of a new factory bill or the defence of a member against a prosecution for picketing, we see the contributions subscribed equally in the past by all the members applied in ways which benefit unequally particular individuals or particular sections among them, independently of the amount which these individuals or sections may themselves have contributed.'[1] Indeed, the Webbs pointed out 'friendly mutual insurance' was 'in many industries the oldest form of trade union activity'. This was one of the crucial reasons why the trade unions were anxious to secure legal immunities as a protection for their funds from attack through the courts that might endanger their financial viability and their capacity to offer benefits.

A great deal of evidence, especially from employer organisations, to the Commons Employment Committee in 1994 stressed the urgent need for the trade unions to refocus their activities away from collective bargaining and onto the needs of individual union members. The Department of Employment suggested the trade unions would 'need to work with the grain' of the changes taking place in the labour market and 'modernise if they are to prosper'. It argued that the trade unions had to make themselves more adaptable to the demands of individual employees. As it explained:

> Individuals are free to become members of a union but of

course there is no obligation for them to do so. With the ending of closed shops, joining a union has become a matter of choice and personal preference. In exercising this choice, individuals do not start out from the assumption that by definition unions are beneficial for them. People are taking an increasingly individualistic attitude and are less inclined to belong to traditional mass organisations like trade unions. It seems likely that individuals are taking a much more pragmatic attitude when deciding on union membership and are less influenced by traditional allegiances. They are now influenced by value for money considerations, just as they are when they buy any other service. If they are to attract and retain members, unions will need to demonstrate those areas where their services are beneficial and cannot be supplied more cheaply or effectively by other organisations. In other words, unions will have to sell themselves to individuals more effectively. They will have to focus more on the individual and the individual's requirements at the workplace and, to a lesser extent, elsewhere. This mirrors the increasing emphasis by companies on the individual and the move away from collective bargaining towards more decentralised systems of management.

Value for money will always be a consideration for union members. This means that members or potential members will need to be satisfied that their unions are efficiently run as businesses. Some of the services – legal and pensions advice – can be provided from other sources. Individuals will turn to these sources, if they feel that unions are poor providers of services. It has been rare for senior union figures to rise to the top because of their managerial abilities. The impression is given that unions have often been weakly managed and financed on a shoe-string. The modernisation of unions would require the modernisation of their management, as well as the redefinition of their role.[2]

Many trade unions in recent years have streamlined their organisational structures, become more professional and established a much closer rapport with their members. But this does not mean that they are about to become or should become purely business organisations in the way the Department of Employment has suggested for hardly altruistic motives.

The CPSA agree the trade unions have to be much more concerned with servicing their members as individuals if they are to survive and in doing this they should seek inspiration from the formative years of the trade unions during the last century. As it explained: 'The founding fathers built up the trade union movement largely on the back of undertaking friendly society functions and in doing so they established a very strong and direct relationship with their members. Wage negotiations were very important but there were a whole host of other roles in which the union played a part in, such as organising sick and burial clubs, collecting information on job vacancies, right through to providing access to libraries.'[3]

The CPSA said it believed the trade unions have lost touch with their members:

> From being the centre of the workers world, unions have in recent years perhaps wrongly been perceived by both members and non-members to be essentially concerned with wage negotiations and the provision of services that they may not regard as essential to them. This, together with the rise of the number of employees on individual contracts – a trend we are told that is set to intensify in the future – and the increase in the use of performance related pay is said to represent a major threat to the unions. 'The most credible option' certainly in the current circumstances of endemic decline is for them to attempt to restore a more direct relationship with their members, perhaps by reasserting their friendly society functions in a way that is valid for the 1990s and beyond. The key point that the trade unions must address is how can they become again organisations which provide enough of the types of services which are directly concerned with the interests and daily working lives of employees.[3]

The TGWU takes a more cautious position. 'Representation of individual members over disciplinary matters and grievances has always been and will remain a major part of trade union work,' argued the TGWU. 'Individual benefits such as accident and sickness payments are also a standard trade union benefit though not a major function of trade unions.' But it went on to suggest that individual negotiation over pay and conditions was not a primary role for the TGWU, nor did it see it 'developing into a primary role'. 'We are responsive to the needs of our members and the need to offer a range of attractive services to current and potential members. Evidence shows that those employees who have to negotiate individual contracts prefer to do so within a tangible framework and that they believe trade unions can provide a valuable service in this context. Therefore, we do provide individual services to members as appropriate. In our view, this is an additional role and not a substitute for collective representation.'

The TGWU concluded:

> There is no doubt that individual benefits and services can be used to encourage membership retention. However, survey evidence shows that the primary reason for joining a union is to improve terms and conditions and to offer protection at work. Furthermore, the main reason why people leave the union is that they retire, become unemployed or take another job where another union is recognised or where there is no union recognition. The TGWU is always alert to the need to develop new services in order to provide an appropriate service to all of our members, whatever their individual circumstances. However, we do not believe that concentrating on individual benefits at the expense of collective representation will enhance our success in retaining members. Indeed, it is more likely to have the opposite effect.[4]

This does not mean the trade unions do not make a direct appeal in their campaigning literature to attract potential recruits by an appeal to them as individuals. The TGWU itself has issued a leaflet, for example, entitled 'Check into the best deals around. T and G too good to lose. Whatever your job, wherever you live – the T and G offers a great deal. You can be sure of it'. The union drew attention in the leaflet to its legal services, professional advice, cash benefits covering accident insurance and convalescence, representation at work or in industrial tribunals, good deals on mortgages and loans, life assurance, credit card, home and motor insurance. UNISON has published two attractively designed leaflets setting out membership benefits and services that emphasise the individual advantages of joining the union. 'Fast, efficient, friendly and the best value around', asserted one of them. 'You can save the cost of your UNISON subscription many times over.' This drew the worker's attention to free legal assistance with protection for the family; 'big discounts on holidays and travel'; special mortgage deals and savings schemes; 'huge savings on your household insurance premiums'; car breakdown and recovery services; personal loans, life and financial planning; a low fee for house conveyancing and making out a will. In other more focused recruitment material UNISON has emphasised three attributes for potential members – that it delivers protection for the individual, democracy and 'value for money'.

In the more competitive labour market trade unions cannot

afford to ignore or reject the need to widen their consumer appeals to potential members.

Fringe Benefits for Individual Members

The trade unions continue to provide a wide range of financial benefits to their members. In 1992 the total amount devoted to that expenditure amounted to £72 million out of a total gross spending of £601 million. This amounted to an average annual expenditure in benefits of £8.06 per member, compared with £59.25 per member devoted to administrative costs. More than half the benefit expenditure was accounted for by only seven trade unions. NALGO, now part of UNISON, was the most generous with its benefits provision (£9.7 million) followed by the TGWU (£8.5 million); GPMU print union (£7.5 million); the GMB (£4.5 million); MSF (£3.28 million); NUPE, now also part of UNISON, (£3.26 million) and the AEEU (£3.1 million). These aggregate figures provide only a rough indication of the financial resources devoted by trade unions to benefits. As the Certification Office explains, the distinction between benefits to members and administration and other expenditure is not always clear cut. Certain types of expenditure – for example the provision of legal and other advisory services – can fall under other parts of a trade union's accounts.

Unity Trust Bank and its ancillary companies are playing an increasing role in providing a range of services to the trade unions. Established in 1984, its aim is to become a significant financial power in the voluntary sector by the end of the century. More than 5.5 million trade unionists in thirty-two TUC affiliated unions have access to its services. As 87 per cent of trade unionists now have bank accounts, 26 per cent own shares and 56 per cent have a credit card, there is clearly a growing membership interest in the kinds of servicing Unity Trust can provide. Its member-benefit packages include motor and home insurance, personal loans and mortgages, discounted travel and the use of a Unity First Master Card. The bank also provides pension services to trade union members who do not have access to adequate occupational schemes. Through Jacques Martin Unity Ltd. – a joint venture with the Australian Colonial Mutual Group – it administers industry-wide pension schemes. It has also developed a life assurance policy for trade union members through Hambro Guardian Consultancy. Unity Trust is also keen to promote wider trade union interest in the concept of collective ownership through the development of employee share ownership and profit sharing schemes.

There is clearly considerable scope for expansion in the kind of sophisticated financial services and benefits trade unions can provide their members. This is a growth area and as trade unions compete with one another for members they can be expected to fine-tune what they can offer. But this is only a small part of a much wider new trade union agenda for servicing the members. Increasingly trade unions are seeking to develop functions related to the workplace which are of direct relevance for the members outside the traditional area of collective bargaining.

Trade Union Expansion in Legal Services

The trade unions are spending far more of their financial resources on the provision of a wide range of legal services to their members in what has become a more regulated industrial relations system. 'Winning compensation for industrial illness and injuries is a massively increased area of work for trade unions,' says the Labour Research Department.[5] In 1992 the TUC estimated that its affiliate unions dealt with as many as 125,000 personal injury cases and recovered over £300 million in settlements for their members. In April 1994 the LRD carried out a survey of eighteen of the twenty largest TUC affiliated unions, representing 6.6 million workers. It found nearly £175 million was recovered in compensation for work-related injuries and illness in 1993 by fifteen unions alone. Between them they dealt with over 51,000 personal injury claims.

The TGWU represents, on average, over 1,200 cases a year before industrial tribunals. 'One of the most important parts of the service is to ensure that members who have the misfortune to suffer an accident at work receive proper and full compensation for their injuries,' the union explains.[6] In 1993 alone its hired lawyers won over £81 million in compensation for members injured at work – far more than the total revenue raised in membership contributions. A total of 26,136 cases involving TGWU members were settled in 1992, the vast majority out of court and in the union's favour. The union estimates it wins as much as £2 million a week in compensation payments for its members. TGWU also provides members with half an hour's free legal advice with its solicitors on any subject in over a hundred different locations.

Other trade unions have equally impressive records of success in legal representation for their members. In 1993 the GMB's legal advisers helped to win £44 million in compensation for its members in occupational accident and disease cases. BIFU explained that the legal services offered to trade union members often involves 'professional advice and representation which individuals could not possibly afford but unions can provide through their collective resources.' The union pointed out that it was pursuing the case of a number of East African Asian members against Barclays Bank over alleged discriminatory treatment on their pensions. 'Without BIFU providing such a service it would be all too easy for employers to avoid the consequences of their actions by appealing to higher courts or tribunals, in every case exploiting the individual's ability to afford further proceedings,' it argued.[7]

Equal Opportunities: A Growing Service

Trade unions are taking an increasingly important part in developing and pressing for equal opportunity policies in the workplace. The TUC has argued that 'in many cases the promotion of equal opportunities is a joint employer/union initiative and the union plays an important role in ensuring that new equal opportunity policies and procedures being introduced by the employer are understood and accepted by the workforce.'[8] Indeed, trade union activities in this crucial area may well determine how well they survive as women are likely to make up perhaps half the membership of the trade unions by the end of the decade. As the Equal Opportunities Commission has explained: 'The ability of trade unions to organise workers, predominantly female in the service sector and to maintain or increase trade union density in the fragmenting public sector is the key to their influence in future years. With the projected increases in jobs being in the service sector, mainly part-time and occupied predominantly by women, there is a strong incentive, already recognised by many trade unions, to give due regard in recruitment initiatives and negotiating priorities, to the issues that most concern vulnerable groups of women, including many workers from black and ethnic minority groups.'[9]

In the EOC's opinion the growth of low paid jobs and lack

of statutory protections to prevent unfair dismissal as well as the abolition of the Wages Councils in 1993 has increased the need for effective trade union organisation. But their own research suggested that there remain 'low levels of awareness of equality issues' among many trade union negotiators, narrow bargaining agendas and a lack of priority being given to issues like childcare facilities which are of special concern for women workers. The EOC found, on the other hand, that there has been a growth in 'many trade union-led initiatives' on the review and reform of wage and salary structures, negotiated agreements to introduce pro-rata treatment of part-time workers and agreements on screening for cervical cancer. 'There remains a role for trade unions to monitor employment practices for sex discrimination and to challenge potential unlawful discrimination,' the EOC has argued. 'This need is stronger in the absence of a clear statutory framework of equality legislation and user-friendly procedures.'

Trade unions have shown in recent years that they are keen to represent women in equal pay and sex discrimination cases, acknowledging that the rights provided by law are difficult to pursue without the expert advice and support they can provide. 'In the absence of trade union support, many more women and men would be denied effective access to judicial processes,' the EOC admitted. 'Trade union assisted cases have also established important precedents that have had an impact wider than the individual case.' However the EOC added that the activities of the trade unions in the equal opportunities area has been 'uneven both between trade unions and within them.' 'There remains great potential for the legislation to be used on behalf of members, particularly where de-recognition has removed or diminished the prospects for negotiated settlements,' it said. Moreover, the EOC revealed just how crucial the trade unions have now become in helping to transfer knowledge on sex discrimination to other organisations and individuals. The EOC has run briefing sessions for trade unions on job evaluation and many other gender related topics and union legal officers are among the target audience for the EOC's guidance documents on legislation and developments in case law. The representational role of trade unions has also allowed the EOC to target scarce resources on complainants who are not trade union members or whose union is unable to assist them.

With around one million women in its ranks, UNISON is adopting 'structures and bargaining agendas' to reflect its female membership, many of whom are part-time and low paid. As it argued: 'Confronting low pay and unequal pay should be a priority for itself and for every citizen who is concerned about social justice. The United Kingdom remains in the top ten of the world's richest countries, yet the gap between wealthy and poor is greater now than at any time this century. Between 1979 and 1990 pay at the highest point grew at least 25 per cent more than at the lowest. Earnings across occupations increased by 190 per cent but only 140 per cent for low paid public sector employees.'[10] The union added that it was committed to 'building on success already achieved in equal pay for work of equal value cases. A nationally co-ordinated strategy has been pursued with the electricity companies in order to change wage structures which traditionally discriminate against women.' UNISON is giving a high priority to dealing with cases of sexual harassment in the workplace and negotiating policies with employers to ensure there is adequate counselling, training and procedures to deal with the problem.

Since 1988 the GMB has taken a number of initiatives aimed at changing its image and character. John Edmonds, the General Secretary, said he intended to make the 'feminisation' of the union one of his main objectives. The GMB has launched a 'winning a fair deal' initiative designed to confront the problem of discrimination against women in areas covered by the union's collective agreements. As it explained:

> Equal rights have moved closer to the top of the GMB bargaining agenda nationwide. The national agreement covering local government workers is currently subjected to an equal opportunities audit in cooperation with the employers. The new British Gas career support scheme contains a range of provisions designed to assist employees with family or domestic responsibilities to continue to develop their skills and further their careers and covers maternity, paternity, career breaks and childcare support. Maternity leave and maternity pay have been improved with several major employers covered by the GMB Food and Leisure section, cancer screening arrangements have been improved.[11]

Health and Safety at Work

Health and safety at work has become, after pay and conditions of employment, the largest single cause for concern among workers. It is not hard to understand why. Every year there are around 1.6 million workplace injuries in Britain and 2.0 million cases of ill health either caused or made worse by working conditions, of which 750,000 result in time off work. Between 400 to 500 workers die every year from work-related injuries or illness. Early death as a result of work related ill health totals 10,000 cases annually. The economic cost of accidents and ill-health is estimated to amount to 30 million lost days of production a year which cost employers between £4 – 9 billion and the economy as a whole from £10 to £15 billion, amounting to as much as 1.75 to 2.75 per cent of gross domestic product.

The trade unions continue to exercise a positive influence over health and safety at work issues. Representatives nominated by the TUC sit with others from the CBI on the governing council of the strongly independent tripartite Health and Safety Commission. Nor is the trade union presence on that body a token one. No safety or health regulations are accepted by the Health and Safety Executive unless they have secured the approval of both trade union representatives as well as employers. It is estimated more than a hundred TUC representatives work on the HSC's industry and advisory committees as well as ad hoc groups dealing with specific health at work questions. In its restructuring programme the TUC has made health and safety one of its five priority areas. At present an estimated 7,000 trade unionists participate every year on health and safety at work courses, mainly organised through the TUC on ten day, one-day-a-week work releases. Since 1978 an estimated 100,000 safety representatives have been trained for work on the shop floor.

Under the 1974 Health and Safety at Work Act, health and safety committees are a statutory requirement where trade unions are recognised by employers but they are not in non-union companies. The 1990 workplace survey found a growing number of establishments especially in the private and public services sector, where workers have no collective voice at all on health and safety questions. It has been estimated only 9 per cent of workplaces in Britain have health and safety committees. Moreover, the TUC found in a recent inquiry that 'despite considerable guidance and publicity, there was still a wide ignorance among safety representatives of the extent of their rights and functions.'[12] Instead, employers enjoy unquestioned authority. The unilateral assertion of management over health and safety rose dramatically from the late 1980s. In 1984, 22 per cent of establishments were in that position but six years later that figure had risen to 37 per cent.

There are some signs that this reassertion of managerial power has weakened health and safety provisions in the workplace. In the TUC's opinion 'the single most common underlying cause of work related accidents and ill health' stemmed from management failure. Trade unionists could point to the inadequacy of management systems for disasters such as the capsizing of the Herald of Free Enterprise outside Zeebrugge harbour, the fire at Kings Cross tube station in London, the train crash at Clapham Junction and the explosion on the Piper Alpha oil rig in the North sea. But it was not just the incidence of headline-catching disasters that concerned trade unions. The TUC has said it believes 'there are worrying signs that health and safety performance is deteriorating due to government cuts, competitive pressures, privatisation, the spread of self employment and subcontracting – as well as in the growth of small firms. In many traditional industry sectors major injury rates remain alarmingly high and little or no effort is being made to address health risks.'[13]

However, Britain continues to have much stronger health and safety regulations in force than most of the other European Union countries. In 1993 the Trade Union Reform and Employment Rights Act even strengthened the position of workers on health and safety questions with a provision that not only protected safety representatives from unfair treatment by their employer but safeguarded workers from employer attack 'in circumstances of danger which the employee believes to be serious and imminent and which he or she could not reasonably be expected to avert', and led them to leave the job or refuse to return to it while they believed the danger persisted.

Here is one area where trade unions continue to enjoy a substantial influence if they are prepared to use it. Safety representatives appointed by recognised trade unions retain considerable legal powers. They have the right to represent their members in industrial injury and sickness cases, to investigate potential health hazards in the workplace, deal with members' health and safety complaints. They have the right to make formal workplace inspections at least once every three months, liaise with the factory inspectorate or other enforcement officers and require the formation of joint management-union health and safety committees. For their part employers also have legal obligations towards safety representatives. They must allow them time off work with pay to fulfil their jobs and for trade union approved training as well as provide workplace facilities and assistance such as access to a telephone, photocopying and filing. The most important right enjoyed by safety representatives is their access to company information as specified in the regulations. This enables them to establish clear procedures with management on the reporting of health hazards, accident investigation, grievance and disputes and inspection rights. The legal regulations enable safety representatives to communicate directly with workers through informal discussion, the circulation of surveys and questionnaires, production of newsletters and formal meetings in work-breaks or during working time when and where possible. Under the 1977 regulations that are still in force an employer is required by law to establish a joint safety committee where two or more representatives request there should be one. He must then consult them about the composition of the committee and form it within three months.

The TUC is opposed – as is the CBI – to the government's decision to withdraw public funding from trade union health and safety training. 'The Safety Representative and Safety Committees system has proved very effective, although little publicity has been given to the positive effects which this approach to workplace involvement has had on British industrial relations,' argued the TUC.[14] What worries the trade unions is the lack of statutory rights for consultation on health and safety matters for workers who are not trade union members. 'The main route to overcoming this must be a removal of existing barriers (both legal and industrial) to trade union membership and recognition to allow employees to make use of the law on health and safety representation,' added the TUC.

A survey of safety representatives carried out by the Labour Research Department in 1993 gave a mixed view of their activities. Only 55 per cent of the sample were exercising their right to carry out workplace inspections every three months or more while 37 per cent said they did not have adequate health and safety information from their employer due to lack of access or because the information was inadequate. On the other hand, 73 per cent of the safety representatives had negotiated paid-time off for meeting with their colleagues in other plants. The vast majority had an office, access to a telephone, typing, photocopying and other administrative facilities. The LRD survey found widespread lack of interest and apathy among workers on health and safety issues and the trade unions have difficulty in recruiting members to take on the task of safety representative. But the unions are taking an increasing interest in the environmental audits that companies are now beginning to carry out.

The TUC is giving a high priority to the problem of Work-related Upper Limb Disorders (RSI) which affects an estimated 200,000 people a year and is believed to cost the economy over £1 billion a year. A campaign was launched in March 1994 'to raise the profile' on RSI among workers, employers, opinion formers and policy makers. 'We want to prove the relevance of trade union membership and strengthen union health and safety organisation,' said the TUC.[15] The campaign reflected the new TUC concern to build alliances with other bodies, such as the Chartered Society of Physiotherapists, the Association of Personal Injury Lawyers and the RSI Association. The TUC held a joint conference with them in May 1994 on the RSI issue. Lobbying of Members of Parliament has also taken place and a national media campaign organised.

Trade Unions and Worker Training

The training of workers has a high priority on the bargaining agenda of most trade unions. One of the most impressive approaches came in 1993 from the trade unions in the Confederation of Shipbuilding and Engineering Unions (CSEU), spearheaded by Mr Bill Jordan, the AEEU's President. He has described its plan – Engineering The Future – as 'the most far reaching training initiative ever to emerge from the trade union movement'. 'A thorough shake-up of engineering training is vital if British manufacturing is to compete in world markets,' he argued. 'The new manufacturing techniques that are sweeping world production, including just in time, quality circles and team-working, demand continuous improvements in the skills of every employee.'[17] The CSEU proposed a new series of National Vocational Qualifications from levels one to five should be set as essential targets for the engineering industry. 'We believe no one should be allowed to set foot in a workplace to perform even the simplest task unless they have a level one NVQ in basic safety and awareness skills,' argued Mr Jordan. 'This would be a minimum qualification but would offer a foot on the ladder to employees who were not expecting an opportunity to undertake workplace training.' He proposed the development of a National Manufacturing/Engineering Foundation Qualification available to every worker including all sixteen- and seventeen-year-olds not specifically contracted to an apprenticeship. The trade union approach is far away from the old defence of craft sectionalism. 'Broad based rather than task specific skills are required if engineers perform to their maximum potential,' said Mr Jordan. 'The content of our foundation qualification should be as broad as possible. The backbone of world class companies will be the range of skills offered by the craft-technician employee.'[16] He also called for more highly qualified managers at NVQ level five.

The AEEU President spelt out his vision of the future for training:

> We need company training schools, training officers and college places, similar to those that existed during the best years of the apprenticeship system. Any new structure must be clear and easy to understand. This is particularly important for small firms that usually have neither the staff time nor the level of technical knowledge to produce an adequate training system for themselves . . . All employers must be made to contribute in a constructive way. We think an updated levy system must play a part. There have to be proper rates for trainees. There must be training opportunities for the whole of the engineering workforce. We must prioritise training for women, for all employees irrespective of age and grade. Gearing a strategy to the needs of new recruits is short-sighted. Eighty per cent of the workforce of the year 2000 is already in work and these people must obviously be targeted for training.

The CSEU proposed the creation of joint management/trade union workplace committees in all large and medium-sized companies which would liaise with their local TEC's who would offer advice and assistance to maximise their effectiveness. 'In a world of escalating competition and rapidly changing industry, only the companies and countries that have the highest and most flexible skills will survive,' said Mr Jordan and Mr Alex Ferry, the CSEU General Secretary.[17] The trade unions in the engineering industry have demonstrated that they are in the forefront of the effort to carry out a radical transformation of the training system.

The TGWU and the GMB have produced a joint statement of intent on training signed by their General Secretaries Bill Morris and John Edmonds that underlines their commitment to the issue. As they explained: 'Training is increasingly important to Britain's industrial and economic success. As capital becomes more mobile, technology improves, international competition intensifies and quality becomes more important to customers, it is the skill invested in human beings that makes the difference between success and failure. Developing the talent of our people is the key to future prosperity.'[18]

The two unions argued that Britain needs 'a training culture where lifetime training is provided and accepted as the normal requirement of a modern industrial economy.' 'Our members understand that job security will depend more and more on meeting rising expectations of product quality and customer service,' they explained. 'This demands the development and regular improvement of skills through training.'

The TGWU and GMB argued forcefully that individual worker training is 'a way of achieving ambitions, of equalising opportunity and a route to a more interesting job.'

The old notion of trade unions as jobs-for-life protection agencies is no longer relevant. As Morris and Edmonds proclaimed:

> Britain's workers want jobs that are interesting and worth doing well, that offer both a challenge and an opportunity for promotion. Too many workers feel trapped in poorly paid, humdrum, dead end jobs, performing routine and repetitive tasks. Many face little choice but to save their energy and their enthusiasm for after work when their real talents can be deployed in helping to run social clubs, voluntary groups, sports clubs, local councils and the like. Training is not just the key to economic success. It is the means by which our members can achieve a happier and more satisfying life. Training should be regarded as an individual right as well as an industrial necessity.

The two unions called for a right for workers to have a minimum five days a year paid education or training, which they described as a 'only a small step towards a new training culture.' They emphasised that protection of income and job security is not enough to ensure opportunities for all. It was also necessary, they argued, that there was sufficient provision of education and training available in subjects and at a time and place suitable for potential students; equal access with improved facilities for people caring for children or other dependents; training open to part time workers and the unemployed; fair rules and arrangements to monitor performance and combat discrimination.

The TUC has set aside an additional £25,000 to help support existing programmes with the objective of doubling the number of unionised workplaces in which unions and management work together on training from 20 to 40 per cent. It has also thrown its backing behind the national education and training targets, the national vocational qualifications and the Investors In People scheme. As the TUC explained in evidence to the Commons Employment Committee:

> Training and development is an issue of mutual importance to government, employers, unions and individuals. However, trade unions have a number of specific roles to play. They encourage employers to offer broad based training which leads to recognised qualifications, they make sure all groups of workers have access to training opportunities and they monitor the training that is offered. They also have a role in encouraging and supporting individual employees. Many of the workers most in need of training are those who are most reluctant to make use of the opportunities, fearing it will reveal their weaknesses or threaten their jobs. Unions can protect and support such workers. Equally massive reorganisation, restructuring and redundancies within industry have left many workers deeply suspicious of initiatives from managements. Unions can help to allay their fears.[19]

Trade unions would like to play a more active role in the Training and Enterprise Councils (TEC), established by the government in 1988 at local level to provide opportunities for workers to train. At the time of their foundation the TUC took a critical view of the TECs. It disliked the dominance of employers on the new bodies, the lack of both a national and sectoral framework within which they could work and what it saw as their inadequate powers to ensure the delivery of appropriate training for workers and disadvantaged groups.

But the TUC has welcomed the devolution of executive power to local level and the right of TECs to assess local skill needs and their right to devise local training programmes. It now believes there would be considerable advantages in the creation of partnerships between trade unions and TECs. 'Through unions TECs can gain access to groups of employers and employees they cannot reach through their normal channels,' argues the TUC. 'They can use union expertise on equal opportunities to help deliver their own equal opportunity strategies and they can work together to make sure that local training opportunities are of high quality and broad based. Unions gain access to local expertise and knowledge on training and in particular NVQs which is in great demand among workplace representatives.'

The best example of a partnership for quality training can be found in the south Thames TEC's relations with the TUC. Since its creation, the South Thames TEC has taken a positive view of trade unionism. It explicitly committed itself to work with trade unions in its corporate plan, supporting trade union rights and training needs of its own staff. An initial attempt to mobilise local union interest in TEC activities failed but the TEC then approached the TUC for help. Congress House responded positively. It seconded one of its own full-time education and training officials for six months to work with the TEC. The aim was to 'encourage unions to put training and employee development near the top of the negotiating agenda in all unionised workplaces in the area.'[20] Five other TECs have made similar partnerships with local trade unions on the South Thames pattern and many more are working with trade unions on NVQs, Investors in People, equal opportunities and special needs strategies. As the TUC has explained: 'The benefits for members and local people are the increased number and quality of local training opportunities, improved performance in relation to access to training for those with special needs and the advantage that the TEC becomes more clearly a local body operating in the interests of the whole community and not just private sector employers.'

With active trade union encouragement, a growing number of companies are encouraging the personal development of workers through the provision of a range of learning opportunities for them. These are especially found in larger companies with a strong trade union shop floor presence such as Peugeot Talbot, Rover and Vauxhall. One of the most effective is at Ford Motor Company. It was introduced there in 1987 as part of the national pay settlement through negotiations with the trade unions. Known as EDAP (Employee Development Assistance Programme), it offers all its 31,000 workers sponsorship for voluntary work or study undertaken after working hours for personal and career development. This is not a substitute for on-the-job training. The scheme at Ford is run jointly by management and the trade unions and it is funded by the company. Over its first five years Ford ploughed £10 million into EDAP. Local joint programme committees administered the scheme in each of the company's twenty-one plants. By 1991 – 92 a third of the 21,399 applicants received EDAP assistance. The largest proportion went on aerobics courses followed by learning a foreign language. The scheme has also enabled shift-workers to attend further education courses. Other notable management-union schemes have also prospered at Jaguar Cars, Leyland Trucks, Sainsbury's and Unipart.

Conclusion

The trade unions do not need to be told by employers or the government that they have to position themselves more effectively in the market-place to attract and hold onto members. In fact, as this chapter has shown most of them are seeking to refine and develop a wide range of services inside and outside the workplace that might provide them with the edge in recruitment over their rivals. Many are utilising modern techniques of communication to spread their message more effectively among employees whether they are in a trade union or not. Their journals and magazines have grown more glossy and they appeal more than they used to do to the members as consumers. The GMB, MSF and AEEU have been particularly effective in doing this. The use of video film, display advertising and mail shots of trade union leaflets and offers is growing apace. Of course, none of this may be particularly new. Trade unions have never enjoyed a captive market. They have always had to actively seek members all the time in order to stay alive. But the mere provision of attractive packages of financial and other services targeted at the individual member or potential member is not going to be enough to reverse the trend of trade union decline. That 'mutual insurance' described so well by the Webbs covers much more than that. Nor does it seem likely that the trade unions can revert to the friendly society role they played in the last century unless Britain is going to see an end to its welfare state. It is true that in the Nordic countries trade unions play an active and vital role in administering the social welfare system and this gives them an added value to workers which is why trade union density is so much higher there than in other parts of the western industrialised world, but the British unions do not want and nor can they expect to shoulder a similar responsibility. Making trade unions more attractive to workers makes sense and their servicing function may well grow more important in our deregulated labour market although it seems unlikely to eclipse the other purposes of trade unions.

NOTES

1 B and S Webb, Industrial Democracy, Longmans 1897, p 152.
2 Department of Employment written evidence, pp 4–5.
3 CPSA written evidence, p 54.
4 TGWU written evidence, p 195.
5 Labour Research, April 1994
6 TGWU written evidence, p 8.
7 BIFU written evidence, p 82.
8 TUC written evidence, p 8.
9 EOC written evidence
10 UNISON written evidence
11 GMB written evidence, p 49.
12 Health and Safety At Work, 1993 TUC
13 ibid
14 ibid
15 RSI Campaign, 1994 TUC
16 B Jordan, February 1994 speech.
17 Engineering The Future, CSEU 1993, p 1.
18 J Edmonds and B Morris, Training For Needs, 1993, pp 4–5.
19 TUC written evidence, p 21.
20 Working in Partnership For Quality Training, TUC 1994, p5.

CHAPTER SEVEN

The Changing Public Face of the Trade Unions

Britain's more active trade unionists have always sought to play an important role in the making of public policy beyond the workplace. They regard themselves as representatives who should provide a collective voice for workers on public questions. 'Trade union representatives, often unpaid volunteers, perform a wide range of functions in the wider society, nationally and internationally,' the TUC explained in its evidence to the Commons Employment Committee. 'Trade unions believe that there is such a thing as society and believe they should put something in for the common benefit. Formally or informally hundreds of thousands of active trade unionists bring their experience of workplace issues to bear on involvement in their local communities as school governors, justices of the peace, members of church and voluntary bodies and of course in local politics.'[1]

In local areas trade union activists are often among the pillars of the community who bring to policy-making a badly needed expertise and a practical understanding of a wide range of issues. Over recent years many of them have been excluded from a growing number of voluntary bodies as a result of government policy. It is local employers and not local trade unionists who have taken up most of the appointed posts on a wide range of organisations which have been established by the Conservatives, such as the National Health Trusts and the Training and Enterprise Councils. The deliberate exclusion of many trade unionists from participation in a number of public institutions has reflected a strong view in government that trade unionists should limit their activities purely to the needs of the workplace and then only to help companies grow more competitive. This ostracism is a disturbing development. For most of this century trade unionists were encouraged by the state to take part in public life as valued members of the community. There was a bipartisan attitude to the role of the trade unions. Now ministers and their senior civil servants seem hardly able to contain their indifference, and on some occasions contempt, for trade unionism.

Marginalising Trade Union Influences

The change in official attitudes has become a cause for genuine concern and regret inside the Trades Union Congress whose very existence was based on the premise that trade unions are important and should be influential, at least through a process of consultation, in the making of public policy. Indeed, the TUC has provided Britain's trade unions with a national focus for the expression of their collective opinions for over 150 years. It remains one of the largest free trade union centres in the world and Britain's biggest independent voluntary organisation. In 1994 it represented sixty-nine affiliated trade unions with a combined membership of 7.2 million workers. The growth of the 'super' unions in recent years through the wave of trade union mergers and amalgamations has not undermined the need for the TUC. As it explained in supplementary evidence presented to the Commons Employment Committee:

> Although this means that large unions have more substantial resources than in previous years it does not mean that there is no role for a national trade union centre. No individual union acting alone can exercise the same influence as all unions acting together through the TUC. It is through our lobbying and campaigning activities at national level that the TUC adds value to the work of individual unions. There is still a clear imperative demanding a single trade union voice on a wide range of economic and social policy issues. Equally there is a need for one organisation at national level advocating the benefits of trade unionism and campaigning for proper protections for people at work. Our public affairs role will therefore survive the advent of the so-called 'super unions'.[2]

The TGWU endorsed that view in its own submission to the Commons Employment Committee. It did not believe, it said, that the current trend towards the creation of fewer but larger trade unions undermined the TUC's role. 'The TUC provides a forum where the trade unions can develop common policies and strategies. This brings a strength and coherence to trade union industrial policy and by giving a common voice to the trade union movement makes for more coherent and predictable industrial relations.' The TGWU added that it was of 'great benefit to unions and employers that, unlike most European countries, Britain has a single and united trade union centre.'[3]

Since its birth in the Mechanics Institution in Manchester on 2 June 1868 as the world's first national trade union organisation, the TUC has become an influential and respected pressure group, lobbying governments of all political parties to further the interests of working people over the whole spectrum of public policy. The TUC explained its public consultative role with governments in evidence presented to the 1968 Royal Commission on Trade Unions and Employers' Associations: 'Governments treat the TUC as a sort of industrial Parliament; in the first place to obtain the benefit of the views and experience of the trade union movement in framing legislation or developing policies in general, and second, to secure the approval or endorsement of the TUC for the broad terms of legislation which will have a day to day influence on the work of trade unions.'[4]

As a result, the trade unions, through the TUC's representative function, have exercised a considerable impact on government domestic policy-making, particularly since the 1930s. The TUC's constructive influence was often vital during the Second World War and it continued to be in the immediate post-war period when its positive lobbying tactics across Whitehall departments were highly successful. The achievement of 'full' employment after 1945 and the creation of the welfare state both owed much to the TUC's pressure on successive Labour and Conservative governments. The TUC also played an important role in the development of Britain's public education and social welfare services. It took a keen direct interest in the nationalisation of the country's key industries such as coal, the railways and the utilities. It was a strong advocate of national social insurance and the use of redistributive taxation as a means of creating more equity. It also helped to secure legal rights for workers to receive redundancy payments, maternity pay and compensation for unfair dismissal, the right to equal pay for men and women, the outlawing of workplace discrimination on grounds of gender or race and the development of comprehensive health and safety laws.

Before May 1979 TUC delegations were regular visitors to government departments. The annual reports of the TUC over the years provide convincing, detailed evidence of the organisation's close involvement in public policy-making which used to go far beyond the demands of the workplace and the needs of collective bargaining. Congress House became an important part of an intricate network of power and influence at national level. No public inquiry or royal commission was complete without a TUC nominee sitting on it. From football hooliganism to Christmas bonuses for pensioners, the TUC had a view and it was one that was usually heard with respect by ministers and more often than not acted upon in Whitehall. Some critics, on both the right and the left, began to feel that the TUC had grown in the 1960s and 1970s into an over-mighty subject that could make or break democratically-elected governments and that it was shouldering too many burdens imposed upon it by a corporatist state. Over successive incomes policies from 1948 to 1978 the TUC was persuaded to help rescue Labour governments in economic trouble by agreeing to accept wage restraint or even a wage freeze on behalf of its affiliate members. This often led in turn to widespread discontent among trade union activists and workplace disillusionment which brought about the eventual rejection of incomes policies by many rank and file trade unionists.

But the TUC was never – nor did it claim to be – a highly centralised institution that could issue directives from on high that were accepted without question by obedient, submissive trade unionists. It has been for most of its history a loose confederation of disparate affiliate trade unions who have sought to protect their own autonomy over the years with often self-destructive consequences. Inevitably the TUC's pace has tended to be slow and circumspect. But its internal unity has often been impressive, showing that on occasion it can act with decisiveness as a representative body and not a collection of divided sectional interests. In a crisis the TUC has often responded with a much-needed sense of urgency although often in the past this proved to be much more effective at resisting external pressures than in creating its own unified position in an innovative way.

Since the Conservatives were elected to office in May 1979 the TUC's influence on government policy has waned drastically. 'Unions individually and collectively through the TUC have not had a scintilla of influence over government policies,' the CPSA civil service union complained in its written evidence to the Commons Employment Committee. 'Trade unions in Britain have been forced onto the defensive for so long because we have had to operate in an environment in which it has proved difficult to develop new ideas.' In no other country in Europe have unions had to face such hostility from their government. Uniquely Britain also remains the one country where the role of trade unions in national life is still questioned.'[5] In recent years the trade union's collective voice has either been silenced or gone unheeded over a wide area of government policy-making. 'Government departments no longer consider it automatic to consult the TUC on all matters of importance to the economy and employment,' admitted the TUC in March 1994.[6]

Prime Minister John Major's sudden decision at the end of 1992 to abolish the tripartite National Economic Development Council along with its secretariat deprived the trade unions, through the TUC, of access to what had often been an invaluable, consultative forum, which at many levels made a positive contribution to the analysis of macro economic policy and vital questions such as the future of manufacturing industry and the role of finance capital. The NEDC – created in 1962 by that patrician One Nation Conservative Prime Minister Harold Macmillan – was much more than just a forum for monthly meetings of trade union leaders and employer representatives with government ministers and others. Its real value lay in its unsung but important detailed work which was carried out through a network of committees and working parties covering a wide range of industrial sectors. For most of its life, the NEDC may not have played the central role in the management of the economy many first conceived for it in the early 1960s but its demise was yet another example of the government's short-sighted capacity to abandon institutions for no obvious reason.

Britain's trade unions also used to play an important part in the development of Britain's training and employment policies at least until as recently as 1987. Through the TUC, at national and local level, they helped to administer the government's labour market programmes with an often enthusiastic participation in the operation of the tripartite Manpower Services Commission (MSC), later the Training Commission. Lord David Young may have been an ardent Thatcherite, but as MSC Chairman in the early 1980s and later on as Employment Secretary, he demonstrated how much he valued the trade union contribution in that policy area as he worked amicably alongside the then TUC General Secretary, Mr Len Murray and his deputy Mr Ken Graham in the evolution of policies designed to reduce the high level of unemployment and equip young people and the long-term jobless with skills for the new world of work.

However, the government's abolition of the Training Commission in 1988 and its replacement by the local employer-dominated Training and Enterprise Councils brought a sharp decline in direct trade union involvement in labour market policy. The eighty-two existing TECs which now cover England and Wales are two thirds dominated by local employers and very few trade union officials or representatives sit on any of them. A recent study of TECs by Professor Robert Bennett at the London School of Economics underlined the limited involvement of trade unionists in their local activities.

Another smaller but no less significant example of the diminishing of the trade union presence in British public life was the Prime Minister's personal decision in March 1994 not to appoint a trade union leader to sit on the governing body of the Bank of England. Ever since its nationalisation in 1946, it had been the tradition to have a representative from organised labour at the bank. The governor of the bank Eddie George urged Mr Major to reappoint AEEU General Secretary Gavin Laird for a third four-year term. The bank had been impressed by the way Mr Laird had carried out his duties and did not want to lose him. But Mr George was overruled by 10 Downing Street and no trade union leader was appointed to replace Mr Laird.

Where Trade Union Public Influence Survives

However, the government's marginalising of the TUC and trade unions in public life has followed an often uneven and erratic pattern in recent years. A number of national tripartite institutions still survive from the 1970s where trade union representatives – recommended to the government by the

TUC – continue to play an important role. The most notable of them are the Advisory Conciliation and Arbitration Service (ACAS), the Health and Safety Commission (HSC), the Equal Opportunities Commission (EOC) and the Commission for Racial Equality (CRE).

All four tripartite bodies have TUC nominees as of right sitting on them and they continue to meet with apparent government approval, at least for the time being. Unexpectedly strong support for the TUC's role in these institutions has come from the CBI. 'Employers generally see merit in the involvement of trade unions in bodies which bear on their members direct interests and concerns in the workplace,' it told the Commons Employment Committee. 'Whilst they effectively articulate and offer responsible leadership on these concerns, TUC nominees can make a useful contribution in them.'[7]

Three TUC nominated trade union members are still members of the ACAS governing council. The contribution they make 'to the service's operations has been and will continue to be essential both to its effective governance and to ensuring its acceptability to a wide range of opinion,' its Chairman, Mr John Hougham told the Commons Employment Committee. 'The changes which have been occurring in industrial relations institutions in recent years have not altered this situation and nor, in my judgement, are they likely to do so in the future.'[8]

TUC nominees also continue to play an important part in the national work of the Health and Safety Commission. There are still three TUC nominees on the governing body while other trade union officials serve on its various advisory committees, covering subject areas such as toxic and dangerous substances, nuclear installations, and occupational health.

Three TUC nominees remain on the governing body of the EOC where they exercise considerable influence over the evolution of equal opportunities policy. 'Trade unions make a valuable contribution to public debate on social and economic policy and it is difficult to identify alternative sources of equivalent input in the event of a decline in this role,' the EOC told the Commons Employment Committee.[9] Until May 1993 the TUC used to nominate two commissioners to the Department of Employment for membership of the Commission on Racial Equality's board, but now it is down to one. The CRE, which has a non-voting member on the TUC race relations advisory committee, regards the TUC connection as a 'useful point of contact, allowing a regular exchange of information.' 'It also enables us to influence policy,' the CRE added.[10]

TUC nominees also still have places on the Monopolies and Mergers Commission, the National Council for Vocational Qualifications and the British Overseas Trade Board. A small number of public advisory bodies survive: like those covering broadcasting complaints; the collection of distribution statistics; the retail price index and the seas fish industry authority. In 1989 – when the last exact count was taken – TUC nominees and trade union officials continued to provide representation on as many as forty-eight different government committees and outside public bodies. This may have been far fewer than in the 1970s but it suggested that there were still limited but important areas of public life where the trade union presence continues to exist.

The TUC: A New Campaigning Role

The TUC accepts that it has lost much of the direct influence it used to enjoy with governments – both Conservative as well as Labour – in the post-war period. For its part, the Conservative government appears to envisage that the trade unions have only a limited public role left to play. Mr David Hunt, the Employment Secretary told the TUC in March 1994 that his door was 'always open for dialogue' with the trade unions. 'But they must recognise their own limitations,' he added. 'The corporate state is a wholly discredited concept. It will not be restored. There will be no preferential status for unions on the inside of government and no direct role in the determination of policy.'[11] Although he spoke of his wish to see the development of what he called a 'partnership' between government and the trade unions, it remained very unclear whether this might amount to much of substance.

Many trade unions are sceptical whether any constructive engagement is possible with a Conservative government. The CPSA was not alone in questioning the validity of occasional ministerial assurances that they wanted better relations with the trade unions. The Civil Service unions suggested that John Major's failure to lift the government ban imposed in January 1984 by Margaret Thatcher when she was Prime Minister on trade unionism at the government's Communications Headquarters in Cheltenham was indicative of his refusal to consider any new relationship with organised labour. Although he said he was willing to try and find a way out of the impasse over GCHQ, Mr Major used the same central argument as his predecessor to justify continuation of the ban on trade unionism there, namely that membership of a trade union and employment at GCHQ would place workers under an impossible conflict of loyalties.

Nonetheless the TUC still remains keen to re-establish a dialogue with whoever is the government of the day, however limited this might turn out to be in practice. In refocusing its public policy strategy, the TUC has returned to an old and respected trade union tradition that predates the TUC's informal and special relationship with the Labour Party. During the 1970s the TUC appeared to many outsiders to grow much too close to the Labour Party through the development of the ambitious Social Contract, although it was Edward Heath's Conservative government that went the furthest in offering the TUC a direct role in the management of the economy in the autumn of 1972.

Mr John Monks is following very much in the footsteps of his distinguished predecessors as General Secretary – Sir (later Lord) Walter Citrine and George Woodcock. Indeed, he appears to be taking the TUC back to the aspirations of its founding fathers. 'The creation of the TUC was one way of facilitating a role as a pressure group within the existing political system. It was the expression of the belief that gains could be made by the rational representation of grievances backed up by an indication of the scale of support that the unions enjoyed,' Professor Chris Wrigley has written.[12] Mr Monks believes the TUC should expect to act in its own right unbeholden to any political party. It is in the business of establishing an important and respected role in public life but what particular forms this should take will depend always on the circumstances of the time and vary from issue to issue.

Congress House is keen to establish broader alliances and coalitions of concern in society with members of all the political parties, as well as voluntary organisations, pressure groups and other independent bodies. The TUC is building up its own lobbying activities in Parliament to try and influence MPs on specific legislation of concern to working people. 'We need to build an understanding of trade union work and objectives right across the political spectrum,' declared the TUC relaunch document.[13] In the recent past Congress House made very little effort to search out support for its point of view among Conservative backbenchers but this is no longer so. Even if many Conservative MPs may not sympathise with the TUC on broad policy issues, some are more willing to listen to the TUC's point of view and perhaps, on occasion, be influenced by it.

Direct overtures have been reciprocated by the TUC to the Liberal Democrats, who for their part, have displayed a much more sympathetic attitude to the future of the trade unions. Discussions have taken place between the party's leadership and the TUC on matters of common interest. Mr Paddy Ashdown, the Liberal Democrat leader, told a meeting of the Involvement and Participation Association (IPA) in March 1994 that he found a 'refreshing willingness' inside the TUC to adopt a 'positive and creative way' in creating 'a consensus in social policy', based on a new relationship at the workplace that balanced the needs of employers with the individual rights of workers.[14]

It is true that close historical links remain between many trade unions and the Labour Party and the broader Labour Movement. But the TUC has never been affiliated to the Labour Party and the majority of its affiliates are not either. The fact that most large trade unions are affiliated to the Labour Party as well as to the TUC does not mean the TUC is in any sense the industrial arm of a political party. Liberal and Conservative as well as Labour governments in the past have treated the trade unions through the TUC as a large and very important interest group whose views deserved a hearing. Mr Monks hopes that over the coming years the TUC can return to that position. He is keen to abandon the tendency of the trade unions since May 1979 who have wanted to keep on playing a waiting game for the eventual return of a Labour government to save them. Mr Monks wants the TUC to break free from those self-imposed constraints and regain its room for political manoeuvre.

This does not mean that many trade unions will not continue to have close organisational and financial ties to the Labour Party, based as much on personal influence as any remaining formal linkage through the size of their block votes at the party conference or election of some members of Labour's National Executive. But the Liaison Committee – the body that formulated and monitored the Social Contract – has gone and the TUC and the Labour Party are unlikely to hammer out such detailed joint programmes in the future. The careful words used to describe the relationship in the TUC's 1966 evidence to the Royal Commission on Trade Unions and Employers' Associations seem relevant once again. 'The existence of common roots yet distinct functions is the most important feature of the relationship,' it explained. 'That relationship becomes strained if either attempts to capitalise on the loyalties which exist, and the strength of the relationship lies paradoxically in the looseness of the ties.'[15]

The TUC's determination to refocus itself in order to maximise its influence over public policy was evident at its relaunch on 1 March 1994. 'By shaking off the practices which impede achievement and setting ourselves clearly defined objectives focused on the world of work, I believe we can move forward effectively and decisively,' John Monks said. 'The challenge for the TUC over the foreseeable future is to make itself more relevant and make itself count – with working people, with unions, with government and with the wider community.'[16] 'We want the TUC to be widely respected, widely representative of working people, and playing a major part in the nation's affairs – certainly as they affect the world of work, economic development and social justice,' he declared. 'We want the TUC to be interesting and attractive – the kind of organisation people are proud to be part of, activists strive to work for and government and other important interest groups seek to meet and do business with.'

This new, more open strategy has brought an important change of direction for the TUC. It is moving away from being a Fifth Estate concerned with shadowing government departments through a large number of committees that used to eat up too much of the TUC's limited income as well as the time of its secretariat. 'Too much resource is consumed in preparing for meetings and not enough on following through on decisions,' said the TUC in its report on structural reform.[17] The TUC has asserted in its new mission statement that it wants to become 'a high profile organisation which campaigns successfully for trade union aims and values, assists trade unions to increase membership and effectiveness, cuts out wasteful rivalry and promotes trade union solidarity.[18]

A fresh emphasis has been placed on the TUC's transformation into a campaigning body whose voice can 'count in the public affairs world'. Three campaign task groups have been formed in key areas. One is designed to promote 'a renewal of confidence in the concept of full employment'; the second is to develop 'trade union responses to the human resource management agenda'; the third is campaigning 'for the right of representation for workers in relation to their employers and rights for trade unions in relation to trade union organisation and recognition'.

Sweeping administrative reforms were carried out in the spring of 1994 to reflect that shift in TUC strategy. The TUC general council meets only four times a year now instead of every month. All the TUC's departmental committees have been suspended and replaced by an executive committee. Joint committees have been formed to cover women's issues, race relations, regional councils and trade councils and young people. The industry committees have been scrapped and replaced by a series of forums covering energy, public services, manufacturing, transport, construction, entertainment, private services and education. TUC task groups have been formed to deal with issues like trade union education and public sector pay. The traditional departments have been broken up. The staff at TUC headquarters have been retrained in the use of new technologies and the organisation has sought to achieve Investors in People status. A fresh emphasis has been placed on making the TUC's communications and policy presentation more professional and appealing to the general public. The TUC wants to shake off that lovable old carthorse image depicted by David Low in his famous cartoons. It is determined to drop its defensive attitude, born out of the recent period of setbacks and decline by carrying through its biggest internal shake-up in over seventy years.

One of the most significant changes in the TUC's public face has been the much greater willingness it has started to display in reaching out to voluntary organisations and associations on specific public policy issues in a more systematic and coherent way than it has done in the past. The TUC is in the business of establishing networks with like-minded and sympathetic interest groups on a wide range of questions of relevance to working people. The days have gone when the TUC would look down complacently and at times arrogantly on the world beyond Congress House and spurn the construction of such networks of influence. 'Trade unionism should be recognised as a more important force throughout British politics and the TUC needs to be knocking on as many doors as possible on behalf of working people,' it pronounced in its March 1994 relaunch document.[19]

The TUC Public Policy Agenda

The TUC is keen to establish its own distinctive policy agenda independent of any political party. Congress House may no longer feel the need to provide an instant view on every topic in the daily news but the TUC retains a strong and committed position on the broad issues of the moment that is based on a strong core of shared ethical values. It articulates the pain and anxiety of much of contemporary Britain. Church leaders have been impressed by the TUC's new role: 'A vigorous and outward looking trade union movement is of great importance to the health of our nation,' declared the Rt Rev David Sheppard, Bishop of Liverpool. 'The future of work is one of the most fundamental issues of our time, encompassing both the dignity of labour and the blight of unemployment. I respect and value the contribution to justice and integrity in our economic life which has been made by trade union members locally and nationally for many decades.'[20] 'Millions of working people continue to need effective organisations to articulate their interests and give them a voice,' said George Carey, the Archbishop of Canterbury. The Rev Brian Beck, President of the Methodist Conference welcomed the TUC's 'renewed contribution to the development of civil society' and added that he believed there was 'scope for cooperation' between the Methodists and the TUC.

The TUC's ethical values are well expressed through its main public policy priorities. The return to full employment lies at the heart of the TUC's economic strategy just as it did in 1942 – 44 when both John Maynard Keynes and Sir William Beveridge exercised an undoubted influence over TUC economic and social thought. 'This should be the central objective for government policies,' the TUC told the Commons Employment Committee in October 1993. It believes 'full employment is both possible and can be achieved in the

1990s.'[21] It is the social destructiveness as much as the economic and industrial waste of having more than 2.5 million people out of work that concerns the TUC. As it explained to MPs: 'The pressures on social stability from continued high levels of unemployment are growing. As particular groups in the labour market (and increasingly ethnic communities) are excluded from any chance of a job, or have access to only the most insecure and worst paid jobs, so the sense of social alienation will become deep-rooted, especially amongst the young. The social problems associated with the growth of poverty, unemployment and under-employment (including crime and the threat of social disorder) will worsen.'

The TUC acknowledged that 'it would be wrong to say that unemployment is the only cause of social tensions or that this can somehow excuse lawlessness', but it warned: 'The erosion of a sense of social solidarity and the traditional checks and balances which a strong sense of local community produces help create the conditions in which social disorder and breakdown proliferate.'

The TUC remains very much an organisation that believes in the concepts of social justice and solidarity. It wants to see Britain become a much fairer society where the widening gap between the rich and the rest of the population can be narrowed. The TUC favours a revival of social citizenship with its assumption that people have obligations to one another as well as individual rights. It believes that the trade unions still have a positive role to play, 'not least in representing the interests of those who have lost out from economic and industrial change and the impact of government social policies.' In this it remains unashamedly committed to collectivist answers to contemporary economic and social problems. As the TUC asserted in its March 1993 submission to the Commission on Social Justice: 'Social justice is about what the community can do to meet the legitimate aspirations of all of its citizens to opportunity, choice and security. There are limits to what the community can do, and providing for individual initiative and achievement will always be a crucial element of social justice. But the trade union movement is founded on and committed to the belief that collective provision offers the only way to ensure that individuals can realise their aspirations.'[22]

In the TUC's opinion this must involve a recognition that the foundation of social justice lies through redeveloping the concept of community. The commitment of trade unions to the principle of solidarity derives not only from feelings of compassion but because they also believe it is 'crucial to the efficient functioning of society'. The TUC continues to support universal benefit provision in welfare policy. 'The only way to ensure that the people most in need of childcare, education and training, housing, employment and so on actually get what they need is to offer the same opportunity to all,' it told the Commission on Social Justice. 'Universality not only increases take-up rates (whether in the case of free libraries or child benefit), it ensures that everyone, however different their need for provision, has a stake in protecting that provision.'

The TUC also remains a strong believer in using the social welfare system as an instrument for the redistribution of income and wealth. 'It is an effective way of redistributing income across the life cycle, particularly to those who are at times of their lives when they are least likely to benefit from paid employment (such as childhood and old age),' it argued in evidence to the Commons Social Security Committee in 1993 on the government's social security expenditure review.[23] The TUC also supports social insurance as 'the most equitable way of insuring against loss of income.' As it told the Commission on Social Justice:

> If social insurance were abolished, insurance against loss of earnings would not disappear – workers' desire for social security is such that it would be replaced by occupational or private insurance. Occupational insurance tends to be confined to relatively privileged groups of workers, who are able successfully to negotiate substantial employer contributions. Private insurance is only open to those who can afford it, and those with greater risks (such as disabled people) face higher premiums. Social insurance by spreading risk across the whole working population and by its nature as a compulsory scheme, is capable of reducing these inequalities as well as the costs.[24]

Full employment and the restoration of a practical sense of social justice are not the only TUC public policy objectives. It has also been at the forefront of campaigns to support a revival in manufacturing industry and the creation of world-class companies. The future of the public services is also a question that the TUC wants to focus on more vigorously, not through a short-sighted defence of the producer self-interest of public service unions but by securing the wider support of consumers in the achievement of high quality public provision for everybody. 'We reject any attempt to divide workers in the public from those in the private sector,' Mr Monks told a TUC public service conference in March 1994. 'We reject any attempt to divide users from providers. We all have an interest in seeing quality public services delivered by quality workers.'[25] The TUC's identification with the cause of good public services has been important in developing a positive alternative to the government's privatisation and market testing approach. It has helped to shift the emphasis in debate among public service unions from the interests of the producer to those of the citizen. The introduction in 1992 by the TUC of union-led Quality Work Assured Servicemark schemes is a pointer in the new direction.

On many other public policy questions the TUC's collective voice has also been growing louder and clearer. It is taking, for example, a highly principled position against racism in our society. In March 1994 the TUC organised a well-attended demonstration and march in the East End of London to protest against that evil. Its commitment to the cause of ethnic equality was also seen in the decision to provide three seats on the TUC general council for black representation from September 1994.

The TUC has joined hands with a number of women's pressure groups including the EOC in campaigning for equality of retirement age at sixty and not at sixty-five as the government has proposed. In March 1994 the TUC backed bodies such as Opportunity 2000, the IPM, Midland Bank and the Industrial Society in the launch of a 'family friendly employment agenda' that called on employers to introduce working practices more compatible with family life. The TUC has also thrown its still considerable weight behind a campaign to provide more opportunities for the disabled to participate on public bodies like industrial tribunals.

No coalition or alliance dealing with issues of moral or social concern should underestimate the importance of the TUC's position. It may no longer wield the kind of power and influence over governments it used to do when it grew into an Estate of the Realm. Its political objectives are also more modest now. But under the sensible and calming leadership of John Monks the TUC remains an important force that needs to be reckoned with. As a social institution representing the interests of 7.3 million working people, it cannot easily be ignored. Since May 1979 the TUC has often been driven onto the sidelines of public life as a result of deliberate government policy, but there are some belated signs that the national mood is changing. With an honourable involvement in public policy that goes back to the middle of the last century, Congress House looks set for an overdue revival of its involvement in the public policy area. In the current debate over the future of democratic rights, the reform of the welfare state, the reassessment of the meaning of fraternity and equality in practice, the TUC promises to re-establish a radical voice in the national debate that nobody intent on change can afford to ignore. During the 1980s it became fashionable in some quarters – on the left as well as on the right – to deride or ignore trade unions and by implication the workplace in any political discussion. There was a widespread belief that the way forward lay through adapting to 'the new individualism', to 'alternative lifestyles', to the demands of the affluent consumer. Trade unions were seen as part of an old, discredited agenda of failed corporatism. The new public face of the TUC in the 1990's suggests such dismissive and patronising attitudes are without foundation. By shifting its focus to a more open, campaigning style and displaying genuine enthusiasm in allying with other voluntary associations on social and moral issues, the TUC is placing itself once more in the mainstream of public policy-making.

The affiliated trade unions too are also widening their interests and campaigning on public policy questions. The clear approval from the majority of their members for the maintenance of political funds – shown by ballot votes in favour of their retention – suggests they believe the trade unions should continue to take an active interest in the world outside the workplace. The 1984 – 85 political fund ballots turned into a surprisingly triumphant affirmation of the trade union role in public affairs. As many as 51 per cent of their members voted on those ballots with 83 per cent backing the continuance of political funds. Eight trade unions even won ballot votes from their members to establish political funds for the first time. This was not a firm endorsement of the link between the trade unions and the Labour Party which remains more controversial, but a clear signal that members believed it was quite legitimate of their trade unions to campaign and press Parliament on political questions as lobbyists, a role that the law appeared to threaten. The political fund ballot results of 1994–95 also suggest that the trade unions continue to have the support of their members for the existence of such funds.

The Conservatives argue that the trade unions in Britain should break whatever formal ties they have to the Labour Party. They claim the deadening weight of trade union power has made Labour fundamentally hostile to the existence of the social market economy. But no trade union movement in the world can be described as non-party political. Ever since the New Deal of the 1930s the American labour movement has moved very close to the Democratic Party and no Democrat aspirant to the White House could afford to alienate the trade unions. In mainland Europe trade union national organisations as in Germany, Sweden, France and Italy pursue political objectives and insist they should continue to pursue a dual strategy – to protect and improve the material interests of workers they represent and also campaign for change in the wider society.

However, the best relationship trade unions should have with any of the political parties is one where both sides can pursue their different agendas in a spirit of mutual tolerance and understanding. Too close an identity of interest is likely to weaken them. The Swedish and German Social Democrats have shown it is possible to maintain a fruitful association with their country's trade union movements without undermining the freedom of either. The TUC, under John Monks, has its own policy agenda. It wants to establish much more room for manoeuvre. No party political connection is going to be allowed to stand in the way of what is needed in the transformation of the public face of British trade unionism and that is as it should be.

Conclusion

Britain's trade unions have not been very effective in recent years in presenting a public face to the world. Too many of them for too long were careless of what people thought about them. They were concerned for their members as producers but not consumers. Their political outlook was not very representative of their divided memberships. Trade unions may have been involved in the activities of the wider community at local as well as national level but they did not give it enough close attention. Now the TUC has begun to adopt a more focused and concerned public policy agenda which should appeal to the intelligence and imagination of many people beyond the ranks of the trade unions. Under John Monks the TUC will attempt to develop a cohesive and clear-cut identity of public interest independent of any political party. This may not produce any immediate results with the current Conservative government that seems to question whether trade unions should have any public role to play at all. But that is not its purpose. Far more important for the TUC is to become the main lobbying group in our society for the interests of working people and their families. Through coalitions and alliances, the TUC should shape the public policy debate. On a wide range of social and economic issues, Congress House has a practical but also idealistic voice. Too often in the recent past that voice has been muted or confused. Now there is an opportunity for the TUC to seize the initiative. With more self-confidence and a greater readiness to take calculated risks, the TUC should then be able to return to its historic purpose.

NOTES

1 TUC written evidence, p 4–5.
2 TUC supplementary evidence, p 25.
3 TGWU written evidence, p 194.
4 Trade Unionism, TUC 1966, p 66.
5 CPSA written evidence, p 53.
6 Renewal for Change, TUC 1994, p 3.
7 CBI written evidence, p 323.
8 J Hougham letter to Commons Employment Committee, 1994.
9 Equal Opportunities Commission written evidence
10 Commission for Racial Equality written evidence, p 4.
11 D Hunt, Industrial Society speech, 17 March 1994.
12 Working for the Future, TUC 1993, p 10–11.

13 TUC Relaunch ibid, p 3.
14 P Ashdown, April 1994 speech to Industrial Participation Association.
15 J Monks, TUC 1966, p 57
16 TUC Relaunch, March 1994
17 Future of the TUC, TUC 1993
18 Campaign for Change, TUC March 1994, p 9.
19 ibid p 57
20 Messages of Support, March 1994, TUC.
21 Full Employment, TUC evidence to Commons Employment Committee, p 1.
22 TUC Submission to Commission on Social Justice, March 1993
23 TUC Submission to Commons Social Security Committee, 1993
24 ibid, Note 22
25 J Monks speech to TUC public service conference, March 1994.

CHAPTER EIGHT

Trade Unions and the Outside World

Britain's trade unions – once among its most vociferous critics – are now enthusiasts of the European Union. 'In the trade union field, the European dimension has opened up exciting and daunting challenges,' argued TUC General Secretary John Monks.[1] 'The TUC must not miss the opportunity to play a pivotal role in the shaping of the new agenda in Europe,' declared TGWU General Secretary Bill Morris at the 1992 Congress.[2] 'The GMB understands full well that its members' livelihoods depend increasingly upon developments in the European Community,' said Mr John Edmonds.[3] 'There are more doors open in Brussels to the trade unions than there are in the United Kingdom,' said Mr Tony Dubbins, the GPMU's General Secretary at the 1993 Congress. Although he suggested the EU 'put financial and commercial priorities well ahead of social issues', he agreed the EU provided the only opportunity for trade unions to influence legislation which, in turn, will affect working conditions and the social wages of working people and their families throughout the whole of Europe.'[4] Hardly any trade union leader in Britain nowadays would like to see the country leave the EU.

The reason for such widespread enthusiasm among most trade unions is not hard to understand. Confronted at home by an unsympathetic government eager to marginalise them, they have found inspiration can be drawn from the EU and other trade union movements on mainland Europe. The EU has provided not just a lifeline for the trade unions but the means for a potentially effective counter-offensive by organised labour for the rest of the 1990s. The emergence of 'social' Europe onto the British trade union agenda has brought renewed hope and a sense of direction to at least partially mitigate the despair of recent years. For many of the trade unions, involvement with the EC has come as a sudden and unexpectedly pleasant surprise and gone a long way to eradicate much of the insularity and chauvinism that used to characterise their attitudes to mainland Europe. As the AEEU has explained: 'Since 1979 trade unions in Britain have faced unprecedented government hostility. This attitude has not been shared by the governments of other EC member states; even right of centre parties such as the German Christian Democrats have sought to work in partnership with both employers and unions. The European Commission has also taken a positive attitude towards social partnership and this is the reason for much British government hostility to initiatives from Brussels.'[5]

The wider implications of the new development for the British trade unions are only just beginning to be understood. TUC General Secretary, John Monks explained:

> In the past, labour looked almost exclusively to the national government – in terms of either winning political power or securing corporatist influence – as the best means to obtain some or all of its desired ends. International federations were established to match international organisations but the action centre was at national level. Now, governmental sovereignty is under pressure – affected by political power going up to Brussels and, in some cases, down to the regions. At the same time economic power is more, not less concentrated, mainly in multinational companies. The only countervailing power available to this concentration of economic sovereignty is organised labour or the collective workforce and through groups of sections larger than the nation state.[6]

Trade Union Conversion to Mainland Europe

The strong and vigorous relationship between the British trade unions and the EU is a relatively recent phenomenon. Between 1961, when Harold Macmillan's government first applied to join the then European Economic Community, until the mid-1980s, the trade unions were at best ambivalent about their attitudes to mainland Europe. The TUC changed its collective mind about the merits of British EC membership no less than six times during that period. Many British trade unions were suspicious of the political character of other western European trade union bodies and maintained a false sense of their superiority as collective bargainers compared with their mainland counterparts.

It was really only in 1988 at the Trades Union Congress in Bournemouth that such deep-rooted trade union doubts about the European Community were finally laid to rest. Thanks to the initiative of TUC Assistant General Secretary David Lea, the EC's President Mr Jacques Delors accepted an invitation to address the delegates. This marked the crucial turning point in British trade union attitudes to mainland Europe. Mr Delors made an electrifying speech that won a standing ovation. 'Your movement has a major role to play. Europe needs you,' he declared. Describing himself as an 'architect' in the building of the new Europe, Mr Delors highlighted the need for a 'social dimension' to complement the creation of the integrated single market by January 1993 based on the free movement of capital, labour, goods and services. 'While we are trying to pool our efforts, it would be unacceptable for unfair practices to distort the interplay of economic forces. It would be unacceptable for Europe to become a source of social regression, while we are trying to rediscover together the road to prosperity and employment,' he told the delegates.[7] Mr Delors emphasised the proposed single market 'should not diminish the level of social protection already achieved in the member states.' On the contrary it was 'necessary to improve workers' living and working conditions and provide better protection for their health and safety at work.'

Mr Delors added that he wanted 'the establishment of a platform of guaranteed social rights, containing general principles, such as every worker's right to be covered by a collective agreement and more specific measures concerning, for example, the status of temporary work, to struggle against the dismantling of the labour market.' It was also necessary that the EU should have 'a statute for European companies which would include the participation of workers or their representatives,' he added. Finally, Mr Delors suggested workers in the EU should enjoy 'the right to life-long education in a changing society'. 'Social dialogue and collective bargaining are essential pillars of our democratic society and social progress,' he declared. It was not so much the detail as the spirit of his speech which captivated the TUC delegates. At last, after years of decline, the British trade unions had been shown there might well be a constructive way forward out of some of their domestic troubles.

Mr Delors' speech brought an immediate, positive response from the trade union leaders. 'The only card game in town at the moment is in a town called Brussels and it is a game of poker where we have got to learn the rules and learn them fast,' said Mr Ron Todd, General Secretary of the TGWU.[8] 'We have to put Europe much higher on our agenda,' declared Mr Todd. 'We must widen western European trade union cooperation so that every representative organisation that wants to play a part can do so. I do not just mean in words. I mean in deeds and effective action.' The then TUC General Secretary Norman Willis suggested that Mr Delors had offered an attractive deal to European labour. 'If we accept the dynamic of the single market the European Commission and businesses would accept the need to look after the rights of working people. In place of the free for all he was offering a vision of a society which was a fair for all.'[9]

Equally important as Mr Delors' address was the speech made immediately afterwards to the same Congress by Mr Ernst Breit, President of the European Trade Union Confederation (ETUC) and head of the German DGB trade union organisation. As he told delegates: 'The process of the completion of the internal market will decide what path Europe will follow in the coming decades. We have a responsibility to our members throughout the Community to find a common trade union challenge. We will only succeed in doing this if we develop mutual solidarity and unity in our countries and in Europe to make the voice of the workers heard.'[10]

The enthusiastic delegates at the 1988 Congress passed without dissent a wide-ranging resolution that laid out a detailed European strategy for the trade unions. This was also a turning-point in the TUC's policy towards the EC. The motion called for the creation of 'common European-wide bargaining', the establishment of a charter of European workers' rights including protection for workers's interests in mergers, industrial and economic democracy, right to health and safety, right to training, social protection and occupational equality.

But the 1988 Congress was more than just a rhetorical triumph for Mr Delors. It also demonstrated the TUC's interest in the EC was the start of a permanent shift in its strategy. Congress House itself produced a detailed agenda – Maximising The Benefits, Minimising The Costs – which revealed its European trade union strategy in response to the 1992 single market challenge. As the document explained: 'It is certain the creation of a single integrated market of 320 million people in the Community will lead to an acceleration of industrial and economic change which will have far-reaching effects on employment and living conditions. This is expected to bring benefits in terms of a faster rate of economic growth in the Community and new jobs; it will also bring disruptive change and create needs and social problems. The task of the TUC and the European trade movement as a whole is to make the most of the advantages of the change and reduce to a minimum the disadvantages to working people.'[11]

The TUC argued the European trade unions could and should establish a direct influence on the unification process. The 1988 document made it clear that the EU's developing social dimension could help to counteract Mrs Thatcher's deregulatory labour market programme and provide a new role for the trade unions. For Congress House itself it meant the refocusing of priorities. As the corridors of Whitehall were closed to TUC influence, the European Commission headquarters in the Berlaymont building in Brussels would provide a positive alternative. Already in 1988 the TUC foresaw what was likely to happen in the years ahead as the British government's position over social affairs came into conflict with that held by the rest of the EU.

As the TUC's strategy document explained:

> Views are divided within the Commission and between EC governments as to the place which market mechanisms should play in achieving economic unity together with social cohesion. But it is only a small minority among governments who would like to see the internal market programme develop with the philosophy of 'neo-liberalism run amok' to quote a senior commissioner recently. The British government, in particular, would prefer to see a completely open market of Europe to which competition would be unrestricted. It argues that labour market inflexibility is responsible for high levels of unemployment; employment protection inhibits job creation; and social security protection is a disincentive to work. That approach is not that predominating among other governments in the Council of Ministers.[12]

The conversion of the British trade unions to the EU now looks complete and irrevocable. As Mr John Edmonds, the GMB's General Secretary told the 1992 Congress: 'Trade unions are power-seeking organisations. Nowadays just about every road to power and influence leads through Brussels. The centre of decision-making has shifted, and it has shifted for good. Nowadays we get much more influence for our money if we lobby in Brussels than if we bang on the doors of the Tory ministers in Whitehall.'[13] 'Like all organisations, British trade unions must calculate where their influence is greatest,' the AEEU explained. 'In recent years the answer has been in Europe.'[14]

European Labour's Network of Influence

To an increasing extent, the TUC is developing an important role for itself inside the EU as a highly effective pressure group in the shaping of future European social legislation. In December 1993 it established its own office in Brussels to coordinate its efforts and make closer contact with the rest of the European trade unions in a more systematic way. The TUC has played a key role in the European Trade Union Confederation (ETUC) since its formation in 1973. That body has become an integral part of the EU's decision-making process, encouraged by the European Commission which has recognised the ETUC should be the representative 'social partner' for workers inside the EU. With its Network Europe programme the British TUC has established a highly effective lobbying operation through its contacts with the large British Labour Party contingent in the European Parliament and on the EU's Economic and Social Committee. It also provides a growing service on a wide range of European issues – through publications, seminars and conferences. A number of British trade unions have also established their own networks of influence on mainland Europe. MSF, for example, is affiliated to seven European-wide trade union industry committees. The union is playing an active role in the development of works councils in a growing number of European companies including Thomson Consumer Electronics, Bull, Siemens, GEC-Alsthom and Allianz. The TGWU has also established a wide range of contacts with mainland European unions through the trade union industry committees. The GMB opened its own office in Brussels in January 1993 with a full-time official to help expand links with labour organisations across the EU and keep GMB members abreast with the latest EU developments that might affect them. The AEEU plays a key role in the work of the European Metalworkers Federation. Other trade unions are following suit. In a remarkably short space of time the British trade unions have started to exercise power and influence in mainland Europe.

It may still be premature to suggest that all of these exciting developments signal the beginning of an irresistible convergence towards the creation of European-wide trade unionism. But the trade unions have established a permanent and increasingly influential presence in the EU to counter the strength of European multinationals and combat the British government's flexible labour market agenda.

Ideally the TUC and its partners from the other EU states, would like to see the growth of a voluntary system of cooperation at EU level between themselves and the employers who are organised in their own organisation – UNICE. Since 1985 – at President Delors' initiative – 'the social partners' represented by the ETUC and UNICE, have been encouraged to establish a 'social dialogue'. The so-called Val Duchesse process is an option based on consensus and voluntary cooperation through the establishment of European framework agreements on social questions instead of using the formal regulatory route of legally enforceable directives agreed by the Council of Ministers and the European Parliament in Strasbourg. This process for negotiated deals was eventually formalised after long discussions and became included in the Social Protocol to the 1991 Maastricht treaty. Under its terms the European Commission is obliged to consult the social partners before submitting any proposals on the possible direction of EU action and it can do so again when it decides on the content of its proposals. The social partners under this procedure initiate consultations that can last up to nine months to try and reach agreement between themselves without the need for recourse to legal regulation. At the end of that period the social partners will be able to decide that the most effective way forward is not through EU legislation but a framework agreement. The so-called 'social dialogue' procedures were finally ratified in July 1992.

As the TUC explained: 'At the European Community level, by contrast with current UK experience, the institutions of social partnership (joint union-employer work with the EC institutions) and social dialogue (discussions between unions and employers on specific themes) are valued across the political spectrum and supported by trade union and employers' organisations alike. The process of consultation of the social partners is now firmly in place in Community practice and enshrined in the Maastricht treaty.' The TUC added that the 1991 Maastricht treaty had introduced the new procedure to establish, if possible, European-wide standards by agreement. 'This is part of the Social Chapter from which Britain in theory has opted out,' it explained. 'However in practice such agreements will be concluded between bodies in which British unions and employers are represented. Indeed, the text of this provision was drawn up by a union-employer group which included the TUC and the CBI.'[15]

Britain's trade unions have become active members of a growing number of European industry committees at sector level, the first of which were established more than thirty years ago. There are sixteen of them now in operation which cover a wide range of industrial sectors including engineering, post and telecommunications, textiles, construction, transport, printing, the media and public services. Their progress in establishing so-called 'sectoral dialogues' has so far proved to be rather uneven, determined partly by the pace of integration in different industries but also by the reluctance or downright opposition of some employer organisations to participate in their activities. Few of them have yet developed into substantial forums with the potential for the effective creation of transnational industrial relations, but at least it is a start.

EU Influences on the British Labour Market

It is becoming increasingly apparent that the United Kingdom cannot be insulated from the consequences of the EU's evolving social affairs policy. 'Although the UK government has opted-out of the social chapter of the Maastricht treaty that does not mean that Britain can escape the influence of social legislation at European level,' the TUC has argued.[16] Legislation through the implementation of directives is 'only one of a number of tools at the disposal of the Community social policy,' explained the European Commission's Green Paper published in December 1993. 'Often it has complemented other instruments. Only rarely has it been used to prescribe certain specific actions in the social policy sphere.'[17] But nonetheless the Green Paper suggested legal provisions had 'furnished a sound basis for the guarantee of fundamental social rights for workers, rights which have been further consolidated in the case law of the European Court of Justice.'

The emergence in recent years of EU legally-binding directives on labour market issues has alarmed the British government, particularly since the passing of the 1986 Single European Act which effectively ended the veto power that could be used by a single member state to prevent the passage of particular legislation it disliked. A new article 118a was introduced as an amendment into the Treaty of Rome that introduced the concept of qualified majority voting into the Council of Ministers for the acceptance of directives that encouraged 'improvements, especially in the working environment, as regards health and safety of workers.'

The TUC has suggested there must be a 'measure of doubt about the legal status of the UK's Maastricht opt-out from the treaty's social chapter. A legal challenge on the grounds that the opt-out is itself anti-competitive cannot be ruled out. In sum, many observers believe the UK's position is legally, politically and economically untenable. The social legislation of the European Union will continue to shape British industrial relations.'[18]

The new importance of the role of the 'social partners' in EU policy-making was apparent in EU President Jacques Delors' White Paper on Growth, Competitiveness and Employment published in December 1993. The British trade unions favoured what they saw as the clear commitment by the European Commission in that document to a strong social dimension. The report recommended the creation of a European 'social pact', which would 'be adapted to the specific circumstances of each country and each business'. It also meant solidarity 'between generations' and 'between regions' as well as 'the fight against social exclusion'.

The Conservative government in Britain can be expected to fight all the way against much of the EU's emerging social agenda which it believes will undermine British competitiveness by adding to the burdens on business. But as EU commissioner Leon Brittan, the former British Cabinet Minister explained: 'Social protection alone does not make a country uncompetitive. A worker who receives high wages, long holidays, generous maternity leave and a good pension may still be comparatively productive if he or she is highly skilled, well educated and works in a country with high capital investment, good infrastructure and a strong emphasis on industrial research.'[20]

The Importance of Trade Union Rights

British involvement with mainland western Europe has brought a growing awareness among the country's trade unions that their threatened and insecure legal position is unparalleled anywhere else inside the EU and that workers on the continent enjoy greater social protections from the consequences of adversity in the labour market than in Britain. In their demands for the introduction of legal rights for worker representation and union recognition our trade unions are reflecting the lessons they have started to learn from their recent European experiences. 'Britain is the only European Community country – and probably the only country in the developed world – without a positive legal framework for employee representation,' explained the TUC.[21]

Interestingly, through their growing personal contacts and networks, Britain's trade union officials and shop stewards have recognised the advantages of the so-called continental industrial relations model compared to the Anglo-American neo-liberal system championed by the Conservative government. As Mr Monks wrote in 1993: 'In all other EU countries apart from Britain, the government of the day regards, however dubiously in some cases, employers and unions as social partners; they believe that, without partnership at work, the conditions for growth will be impossible to achieve or to sustain. Thus, instead of arguing, as the British government has done, that you must become competitive to provide job and income security, the other EU governments believe that measures to give workers security are a necessary precondition of change.'[22]

Mr Monks went on to explain that worker and trade union influence might be expressed in different ways in different EU member states but that all of them except for Britain had established a common approach based on 'a wish to impose checks on employer power and to give rights to workers and their union.' 'The European model is one which we believe has much to offer British industry. That is based on a fair framework of law, a role for positive and constructive trade unionism and a social partnership between employers and trade unions,' USDAW said.[23]

Increasingly the EU is not just seen by the British trade unions as a way of confronting John Major's government on social issues. It is also regarded by them as providing the practical example of a much more successful and enviable industrial and labour market model that ensures workers have the opportunity to participate more fully in its development. Mr Monks has pointed to the cultural chasm that separates the approach of the English speaking world to corporate business to that of mainland Europe.

Britain's employer organisations – at least in public – appear to be taking a sanguine view of the consequences of the European 'social dimension' for the country's industrial relations scene. The Confederation of British Industry may be a 'social partner' in the Brussels decision-making process but it does not seem to believe the EU will make any drastic inroads into the way the British labour market operates in the future. As it explained: 'The United Kingdom is not bound by the social protocol which makes the potential development (of European level agreements between employer bodies and trade unions) of less direct relevance to British trade unions. Nor does it sit easily with the UK's industrial relations tradition of voluntarism, non-binding agreements and devolved authority.'[24] It added there were 'two other trends across Europe' which reduced the likelihood of European-style agreements. These were 'the general management tendency towards settling more matters at local level' which was 'eroding industry-wide arrangements in a number of countries' and the growth of 'subsidiarity – the acceptance that most matters are better settled at local level' which the CBI claimed was 'gaining more sway in the European public policy debate.'

However, Britain's employer bodies appeared to be taking a rather short-sighted view of the multi-faceted and cumulative influences of the EU's social affairs agenda that are going to modify and quite possibly transform industrial relations practice in this country into the next century. Slowly but surely Britain is becoming involved in the emergence of a complex multi-layered legal system of social regulations that directly conflicts with much of the government's 'flexible' labour market strategy and the country's voluntarist tradition of industrial relations practice.

EU Influence: The First Results of the Social Agenda

The external pressures stemming mainly from Brussels have in fact already begun to make a profound impact on the British industrial relations scene. In 1993 the British government was compelled to legislate no less than seven EU directives into its Trade Union Reform and Employment Rights Act as a result of its need to meet requirements laid down by the EU.

These have enabled British women for the first time to enjoy legal protection from being dismissed by their employer on grounds of pregnancy. Statutory maternity entitlement was introduced for fourteen weeks regardless of a woman's length of service with the company on a rate no lower than that of statutory sick pay provision which came into force in October 1994. The legal entitlement for employees working more than eight hours a week after two months in the job to have written terms and conditions of employment were strengthened, though this will add to the costs of employers who will no longer be able to refer employees to a collective agreement or other document where the information they needed was available.

An important protection has been introduced for workers to encourage tougher workplace health and safety policies. The 1993 Act has provided workers with the right for the first time to refuse to work if they believe their working conditions to be unsafe. An employee will be able to secure unfair dismissal compensation from an employer before an industrial tribunal for taking action at work where he or she reasonably believes they are in 'serious and imminent' danger.

Provisions in the measure have also strengthened, at least in the short term, the contractual rights of employees in cases of a transfer of undertakings with an extension to cover those which were not commercial ventures. Again, under EU pressure the 1993 Act also strengthened the consultation procedures in cases of redundancy with a view to reaching agreement with trade union representatives.

As Professor Keith Ewing has observed, these changes 'offer some small consolation by adding not insignificantly to the employment protection of individual workers in a manner which may provide additional means to resist employer-imposed changes in working conditions. They will also be an irritant to employers in the hands of alert lay officials.'[25]

A growing number of British trade unions have also been able to use EU law effectively in securing victories for their members in the courts. One of the most significant was achieved by the TGWU over the highly complex and technical question of business transfers of ownership. The union represented Eastbourne refuse collectors whose terms and conditions had worsened when the council they worked for contracted out their services to a private company. Both the British and European courts found in favour of the Eastbourne workers, arguing that the EC's 1977 acquired rights directive applied where public services were privatised through the use of compulsory competitive tendering, market testing and other forms of deregulation. This meant the rights and interests of workers were safeguarded by the law when their employment was transferred from one employer to another. But the 1981 Transfer of Undertakings (Protection of Employment) regulations that gave effect in British law to the directive had excluded from its coverage the regulation of undertakings that were 'not in the nature of a commercial venture'. The European Commission used infringement proceedings against the British government over its interpretation of the directive in the European Court of Justice, which proved successful. The judgement has come as an unexpected blow to the British government's privatisation programme. As the TUC explained in a background paper on the highly technical issue in September 1993: 'The rationale behind programmes of deregulation is the ability for private contractors to offer a cheaper service. That usually means cuts in wages and other labour costs. If the directive and regulations apply to this type of transfer, it makes it more difficult for the new employer to undermine existing conditions. Therefore tendering becomes a less attractive option for private contractors.'[26] The UK Attorney General was compelled to introduce amendments in the 1993 Trade Union Reform and Employment Rights Act to bring non-profit making or charitable undertakings within the ambit of the TUPE regulations.

Trade unions – under the TUC's umbrella – are also pressing retrospectively the cases of many of their members against the government for having failed to implement EU directives adequately. This followed the precedent of the Francovich case in which the European Court of Justice allowed a claim against the Italian government for failure to implement an EU directive. Health and safety laws in the United Kingdom have had to comply with EC directives.

Early in 1994 legal advances were also made in equal opportunities. By four votes to one the British law Lords ruled that part-time workers were to be covered by the same legal provisions as those working full-time when it came to rights of redundancy and unfair dismissal.

The EU's working time directive – which is being challenged in the European Court by the British government – proposes a maximum average forty-eight hour working week and a minimum three weeks' paid annual holiday a year to workers rising to four weeks by 1999. It also sets minimum daily and weekly rest periods. The TUC explained derogations from the forty-eight hour principle are permitted but only through collective agreements with trade unions. 'Once again the effect is to entrench collective bargaining as a key element in the protection of employees' interests at the workplace,' it added.[27]

The TUC made a formal complaint in 1993 to the European Commission over the British government's decision to abolish the Wages Councils – statutory bodies that established minimum pay rates for those employed in non-unionised low wage sectors of the labour market. It suggested that there was a legal duty under EU law on the British government to provide 'effective means' to ensure the principle of equal pay at work. The TUC argued the ending of statutory minimum wage rates would make it impossible for the United Kingdom to comply with the 1975 equal pay Directive. The majority of workers to suffer from the British government's action are women.

As the TUC explained in its submission to the European Commission: 'Since 1979 the United Kingdom government has removed key elements in the package of protection (for equal pay and equal opportunities), one by one. The ability of trade unions to defend women against exploitation has been severely hampered by the removal of the right to trade union recognition and by numerous restrictions.'[28]

The Importance of European Works Councils

The introduction of European company based works councils by means of an EU directive is seen by many British trade unions as one of the most hopeful of future advances that will help to strengthen their position in large-scale enterprises. Its probable implementation by 1996 in larger European companies with over 1,000 employees in more than one EU country but over 150 in one other could have a profound effect on British industrial relations. As the TUC explained: 'The introduction of European works councils in multinational companies under an EC directive in the next few years will set in place a new structure for trade unions to use.'[29]

The TUC has estimated that even if Britain is not formally covered by the works council directive because of the Maastricht opt-out, around 350 companies operating inside the United Kingdom will be affected by it. As many as 160 of them have their corporate headquarters in other EU states, but have British operations and a further hundred – mainly American and Japanese companies – with their head offices outside the EU also meet the requirements of the directive. A further ninety companies are British owned but with operations in mainland Europe. The TUC points out all of the companies will be obliged to establish information and consultation machinery for their mainland European activities and that this will mean in practice that most of those British employers will include their British workers in the works councils, even if their inclusion is not obligatory under the law because of Britain's Maastricht opt-out.

Towards Global Solidarity

British trade union interests in the outside world are not just confined to the potential opportunities now opening up for them inside the EU. There are also growing signs of a more sustained concern on international labour questions that goes far beyond displaying rhetorical solidarity with embattled trade unionists suffering persecution around the world. Britain's trade unions are also strong supporters of linking the growth in world trade to the extension of workers' rights through the inclusion of 'social clauses' in future international trade agreements. They point out that one of the original objectives of GATT was to raise living standards and maintain full employment through 'a large and steadily growing volume of real income and effective demand', involving 'the achievement and maintenance of fair labour standards related to productivity'. This issue has been raised by President Clinton's administration in the United States and international trade union bodies who do not want to see any direct attack on existing labour standards in western industrialised countries as a result of increasing global competition in the aftermath of the successful conclusion of the Uruguay round. The Brussels based International Confederation of Free Trade Unions (ICFTU) – of which the TUC was a founder member – believe that the introduction of a 'social clause' would help to guarantee minimum labour standards with the right to join and form trade unions, negotiate collectively and prohibit forced and child labour. Many developing countries, particularly around the Asian Pacific rim, remain hostile to such an idea, arguing that it is simply a subtle form of protectionism being introduced by industrialised nations to look after their own interests at their expense as low cost producers.

The trade unions deny this. They want to see a number of the most important Conventions of the International Labour Organisation inserted into trade agreements. These would be supervised by a joint ILO/World Trade Organisation body with some means of redress (including possibly trade sanctions) against those countries that flouted agreed labour standards. This looks likely to become one of the most difficult and important issues to face the future of international labour. However, now the Cold War is over, the bitter ideological conflicts that used to divide trade unions and workers from each other have gone and there is an increasing possibility of much more effective cooperation between organised labour around the world. This has led already to the emergence of a fundamental public debate inside the ILO on the role of trade unions and worker rights in the global economy. In combating the power and influence of the transnational corporations we can expect to see much a greater coordination between workers and trade unions across the boundaries of nation states. While it would be premature to proclaim the arrival of a more coherent and effective international labour movement, at least the possibility now exists of a much closer relationship between workers and unions despite the formidable barriers to cooperation that persist of language, different levels of social and economic development, cultural and organisational divisions as well as the enormous divisive and destructive powers of race, ethnicity and nationalism.

'Workers of the world unite' remains as much a utopian slogan as it did in 1848 with the publication of the Communist Manifesto, but there are important signs that talk of international labour solidarity may become much more than just rhetoric. Britain's trade unions are showing a practical interest in working together with their colleagues in other countries. The positive influences coming from involvement with mainland European trade unionism have already begun to broaden their horizons. Tentatively and pragmatically, we can see signs of trade union unity. The enormous power of the transnationals has begun to encourage a collective counter-voice from the trade unions. This may still be limited, hesitant and weak. But at least a start has been made and Britain's trade unions through their international labour connections promise to play an important part in the gradual emergence of a more coherent and distinctive trade union view on the future of the global economy.

NOTES

1 British Journal of Industrial Relations, June 1993, p 230.
2 TUC 1992 Congress Report, p 284.
3 ibid, p 282.
4 TUC 1993 Congress Report, p 245.
5 AEEU written evidence.
6 TUC written evidence.
7 TUC 1988 Congress Report, pp 568–570.
8 ibid, p 572.
9 ibid, p 567.
10 ibid, p 570–571.
11 Maximising the Benefits, Minimising the Costs, TUC 1988, p 1.
12 ibid, p 6.
13 TUC 1992 Congress Report, p 276.
14 AEEU written evidence, p 70.
15 TUC written evidence, p 4.
16 ibid, supplementary evidence p 1.
17 European Union Green Paper on Social Affairs, December 1993
18 TUC Supplementary Evidence, p 2.
19 EU White Paper on Jobs, Growth and Competitiveness, December 1993
20 Brittan, *The Europe We Need*, Hamish Hamilton 1994, p 151.
21 TUC written evidence, p 2.
22 TUC ibid, p 4.
23 USDAW written evidence, p 80.
24 CBI written evidence pp 319–320.
25 K Ewing, Industrial Law Journal, Vol. 22. No.3, 1993 p 165.
26 TUC internal memorandum on TUPE, September 1993.
27 TUC Supplementary Evidence, p 1.
28 TUC Complaint to the European Commission 1993, p 9.
29 TUC Written Evidence, p 10.

CHAPTER NINE

The New Trade Union Agenda

Britain's trade unions are going through a period of rapid change as they reassess their future role in a more competitive market economy. This has meant not just modernising their internal structures to make them more professional and relevant to the needs of working people but also a radical reappraisal of their fundamental beliefs. It is no exaggeration to suggest – on the evidence of their own submissions in 1994 to the Commons Employment Committee – that the country's trade union leaders are reassessing the traditions and practices of voluntarism that have dominated the Labour Movement for the past hundred years. They may have been reluctant to do this and many of them may still retain a lingering hope that the old system can somehow be revived but increasingly they have begun to think the unthinkable. This has involved the emergence of two distinctive but inter-related concepts for a credible new trade union strategy: the creation of a 'social partnership' with employers and to a lesser extent government and the introduction of positive legal rights of representation for all workers and not just those who are trade union members as well as the legal right to trade union recognition.

The most significant part of the new trade union approach lies in the acceptance of a clearer identity of mutual interest between employers and trade unions over agreed improvements in corporate performance. 'I believe establishing relationships based on long-termism and mutual respect are the best ways to see the economy in better shape than it is at the moment,' said TUC General Secretary John Monks.[1] The TUC wants to develop a 'strategy for the management of change to meet the competitive conditions of the 1990s.' In the new world of open global markets and technological innovation – so the trade union argument now goes –

employers 'need the commitment of their workforce to meet the challenges ahead.'[2] 'It is a truism that in the past the British industrial relations system has focused on conflict resolution rather than consensus building. This must change if our economic performance is to match the best in the world,' declares the TUC which has committed itself to the creation of a 'world class Britain' based on 'the production of competitive, high quality products and services' and a 'real partnership between employers, trade unions and governments.'[3]

The main external influence that is bringing about such a fundamental transformation in British trade union thought is coming from mainland European experiences. As the TUC has pointed out: 'Social partnership is not just rhetoric but a phrase which has a clear meaning and which is applied in practice in continental Europe. Consultation with workers' representatives takes place at almost every level from the European Commission down to a works council in an individual workplace.'[4] 'The consensus among European countries is that unions and employers have legitimate views that should be heard and respected. In the US and Japan where union density is also much lower than in Britain, governments seek a constructive dialogue with the trade unions,' the TUC argued. 'The social partnership approach is delivering results across the developed world.'

The TUC has explained that the term 'social partnership' is no longer envisaged as a euphemism for the revival of a corporatist system of highly centralised industrial relations institutions. Instead, it is concerned with relationships at enterprise level both in the private and public sectors. It is about 'an acceptance by both employers and trade unions of common aims.' These would cover 'a joint commitment to the success of the enterprise', 'a recognition there must be a joint effort to build trust in the workplace' and a 'joint declaration recognising the legitimacy of the role of each party.'

Ideally the union leaders would prefer employers to recognise the value of trade unions as institutions that can help in achieving beneficial workplace change without the need for any resort to the rigours and inflexibilities of state regulation. They argue – and not without sound reason – that the voluntary rather than the regulatory way still remains the most preferable in ensuring successful and relatively painless reforms in workplace organisation through consent. The emphasis on cooperation and flexibility is understood by many enlightened employers who see the value to them of working with the active support of their workforce who belong to recognised trade unions rather than seek to impose change. As the TUC has argued: 'Commitment of workers to their employer is best obtained through the involvement, participation and agreement of the workforce, not by management edict or through the courts. Winning the support of the workforce requires commitment from employers to provide good quality jobs and to consult with the workforce. Unions give people at work a voice and provide the basis for the cooperation needed to secure change. Most big companies recognise the contribution that unions make to a successful enterprise.'[5]

'The British tradition of industrial relations is justly proud of the emphasis on voluntarism,' explained the TUC. 'A valuable contribution could be constructed from British experience in the debate on industrial relations. It should derive from the central role of collective agreements in building on legal standards to meet the needs of individual industries, services and workplaces. That voice is needed in the European Union debate. Yet this position cannot be coherently developed if voluntarism is simply the right for employers to do what they like. Agreement, consensus and the collective bargaining process should be at the heart of the process.'

The emphasis on the mutual identity of interest between employers and trade unions in achieving success in the enterprise marks an important shift in British trade union thinking that has so far failed to attract the kind of public attention it deserves. It reflects the clear-sighted view of a growing number of trade union leaders who want to abandon an adversarial approach and accept the need for cooperation in changing workplace culture in a more consensual direction. Of course, differences of emphasis continue to exist but few voices are being raised nowadays inside the trade unions which question such enlightened pragmatism. Traditionally many trade unions were concerned with job protection and job control or regulation. They tended to operate as defensive, reactive organisations whose primary purpose was to look after the sectionalist interests of their members. Their function was to uphold and extend their organisational strength in the workplace even at the expense of other workers who were not members of their particular trade union. This parochial frame of mind, which was by no means restricted to the craft unions, has been fast disappearing from the British workplace in the past ten years as the self-imposed barriers against the possibilities of cooperation have been coming down.

Voluntarism in Britain used to be dominated by the problems of conflict resolution. It presupposed there was an inherent division of interest between capital and labour, a struggle over the frontiers of control in the workplace. Its emphasis was on the establishment of joint consultation and conciliation to keep those conflicting tendencies under control. Now the new concept of partnership in the workplace has entered the language of British industrial relations and it has done so mainly through the actions as well as the words of an increasing number of trade unions.

Towards an Industrial Partnership

The best example of the new consensual approach can be found in an important initiative that was launched in September 1992 by the independent Involvement and Participation Association (IPA) on the creation of an 'industrial partnership'. The document has emphasised the common goals of management and trade unions. It calls for a 'joint commitment to the success of the enterprise in the interests of customers, suppliers, employees, shareholders and the community' and a 'recognition that there must a joint effort to build trust'. It also backs the idea of a joint declaration which recognises the legitimacy of the role of each party in the enterprise. 'How this is framed will vary, but it must include management's right ultimately to take action in the interests of the organisation and employees' right to see their interests represented.'

The IPA suggested there were a number of 'key areas' where management and trade unions needed to rethink their approach. Firstly, there was the need for employment security coupled with job flexibility. While the manifesto acknowledged no employer could guarantee jobs for life, it also suggested 'a sense of personal security' for the employee had to be at 'the cornerstone of the new approach', though in the long run 'the only guarantee of employment security is a profitable business'. As it argued: 'Trade unions do of course exist to promote the interests and protect the rights of their members. This has often taken the form of defending existing rights through rigid definition of jobs and clear demarcation of responsibilities. Such attitudes are incompatible with the need for job flexibility. Job control hampers an organisation's ability to meet the challenge of competition through rapid change; it also limits the individual from developing his or her full potential by imposing artificial restrictions.' The IPA document seeks to convince managements and employee representatives that there is a vital link between security of employment and genuine flexibility between jobs.

The second area emphasised by the IPA was the need for employees to share in the success of the organisation they work for. This would involve encouragement for a wide range of profit-sharing and employee share-ownership schemes as well as profit-related performance pay and Save-As-You-Earn plans as part of a 'broad approach towards the involvement of the workforce which of itself will achieve this end.' It also called for an expansion by company of educational programmes like that at Ford Motor Company and flexible working arrangements to encourage non-financial employee benefits. The IPA claimed that 'with a philosophy of sharing gains across the entire workforce a business is better able to create non-combative ways of accommodating the results of bad times. For trade unions it points towards a reward structure which includes an element related to the performance of the business and a move away from the traditional pay bargaining agenda of retail price index plus a percentage.'

The 'industrial partnership' project also emphasised the need for much more 'information, consultation and employee involvement'. As it argued:

> Increasingly employees seek to be consulted before decisions are taken and to have their views represented. This requires, in most organisations, a major shift towards a more consultative, teamworking style, which must be set from the top. At the same time, there has to be a degree of understanding and trust that accepts it is neither possible nor desirable to consult on every issue. The key element in consultation is not the machinery by which it happens but the subjects on which managements are prepared to consult with employees or their representatives and the style used.

The IPA suggested trade unions should press management to introduce quality circles, team working or team briefing as ways of improving relations in the workplace. In that way

– it argued – 'trade unions and other employee representative bodies can make genuine progress in changing the atmosphere of the company from one of compliance to one of commitment and thus ensuring a competitive advantage in the marketplace.'

But the IPA also conceded that employee representation remains the most difficult issue on which to reach joint agreement between employers and trade unions. 'Trade unions are having to come to terms with the fact they are no longer the sole channel of representation,' it argued. 'The individual employee is seen by many employers as the new industrial relations entity around whom the fundamental manager-employee relationship will in future be built. Hostility to collective arrangements is not uncommon in many businesses.'

However, the IPA believed employers needed to recognise that there remains 'a very basic justification for representative structures.' As it pointed out: 'Individuals are generally vulnerable when faced with the power of the organisation. Individual contracts are not agreements between equal partners and when problems arise individuals need help when dealing with employers.' In its document the IPA conceded that many trade unions are ready to accept that employee representation can no longer be confined to a single channel through trade union membership. Although accepting it would be a mistake to adhere to only one form of representative structure in a company, the IPA thought at least there had to be one through which workers, could express their views. 'Provided that the new structure is established with care, there is no reason why a universal right to representation should weaken trade union organisation,' it argued. 'On the continent of Europe, management and trade unions operate comfortably within a variety of representative structures and promote trade unionism as the means by which employees can secure full advantage from the basic right to representation which is guaranteed by law.'[6]

At the heart of any new system, however, lies the need for trust, declared the IPA. But this will require a changing role for the trade unions. 'They will need to become facilitators of change together with management,' it said. 'This they will need to do in a market-place which demands even faster technical and organisational responses. Quite clearly too there still exists a place for independent representation of the interests of the workforce, both individually and collectively.'

The list of senior figures in industry and the trade unions who signed up behind the IPA's 'industrial partnership' declaration was impressive. They included Sir John Harvey-Jones, Chairman of Parallax Enterprises; Sir Bob Reid, Chairman of British Railways Board; Mr David Sainsbury of Sainsbury Plc and Mr John Towers, Rover Group's Managing Director. Trade union leaders included Mr Bill Jordan (AEEU), Mr John Edmonds of the GMB, Mr Leif Mills from BIFU and Mr Garfield Davies from USDAW. But the 'industrial partnership' brought no response at all from the government. When asked about it at an Industrial Society lunch in March 1994, Employment Secretary David Hunt made it clear to his audience he had never heard of it. The lack of response from most employers also came as a disappointment to the well-meaning supporters of the industrial partnership project. For others, the negative or indifferent attitude confirmed their belief that no real progress towards implementing such an idea in Britain is possible if the matter is left entirely to voluntary means of persuasion and exhortation. They argue some form of legal regulation will be required if any such ideas are going to gain ground in the workplaces of the future.

The Need for Positive Legal Rights

A growing number of trade union leaders also believe Britain needs fundamental changes in its employment laws to help the trade unions to prosper again. This does not mean a repeal of all the anti-union legislation passed by successive Conservative governments since May 1979 although much of it will have to go. More significantly, it involves a change of position by the trade unions on the value and role of positive legal rights in our industrial relations. Over the past few years a growing convergence of view has taken place among many trade unions behind the demand for a legal right to employee representation and trade union recognition.

The GPMU print union has explained the experience of its own struggle against Reed Elsevier's de-recognition revealed the serious weakness of the present legal position for trade unions: 'This multinational's response to the lack of a legal framework of positive employee's rights to recognition is indicative of the imbalance of provisions covering industrial relations between employers and employees in this country. We consider the government has gone too far in its so-called employment legislation reforms, to the extent that it is allowing employers to deny their employees fundamental liberties established in international law, which are enjoyed everywhere else in Europe, except in this country.'[7]

The GPMU has proposed that 'if workers choose to be represented by a trade union, they should have the right to that choice and if employers are not prepared to recognise this basic right, then it is time to change the law.' 'The relationship between trade unions, on behalf of their members and the law is essential to our existence and our future role and should be based on rights and responsibilities fairly balanced,' the union has argued. 'There must be an established right of membership that includes the right to representation for free trade unions including a legal right to recognition and collective bargaining for trade unions by employers where there is significant support amongst their workforce. Too often employees are faced with their employer saying "You can join but we won't recognise the union" or "you can be in a union and get the sack". Only a new legal framework of positive trade union membership and recognition rights for employees can lay down a fairer system of industrial relations.'

The TGWU, has gone even further down the road to positive rights than the GPMU. As it argued:

> An improved legal framework of employment rights is necessary to give effective protection to people at work. Employment rights should apply as soon as employment commences and should apply equally to full-time and part-time workers and to temporary and contract workers as well as permanent staff. The framework of employment rights should cover a wide range of issues including a statutory minimum wage, protection from unfair dismissal, sex and race equality, maternity and paternity rights, a right to paid holiday, the right to belong to and participate in a trade union without fear of victimisation or discrimination, rights to union recognition, the right to organise and bargain collectively in line with relevant international conventions and the legal right to strike and picket peacefully near or at any place of work concerned in the dispute without fear of dismissal or intimidation.[8]

The TGWU suggested such a framework of legally enforceable rights is necessary 'not just to protect individuals in the workplace but to rebuild a robust and successful national economy'. BIFU, the banking union, also believes there should be 'some legal right for bona fide, independent trade unions to be recognised by employers for collective bargaining purposes where a significant proportion of their workforce wish and a right to represent any of its members on an individual basis over grievance and disciplinary matters.'[9]

As the TUC has explained: 'A legal right is needed because today many working people are denied representation in practice.' Ideally, the TUC would like representation to take the form of a right to trade union recognition. 'It is an absurd anomaly, unknown in the developing world, that it is the employer who chooses whether or not an employee is represented by his or her union for collective bargaining purposes,' it argued.[10]

The AEEU has adopted a broadly similar view, arguing that the eventual success of its own concept of enterprise unionism requires the introduction of a legal right for workers to have representation and trade union recognition. 'The right to employee representation should be embodied in law,' the union argues. The union believes that concept should be established as 'apolitical rather than at the whim of a change of government' and it has pointed out that the present government's approach to individual rights at work was 'meaningless without access to employee representation in order that those rights may be pursued. In the same way the right to join a union is of little use unless union recognition is guaranteed.'[11]

'I think there ought to be an unqualified right to have employee representation in place,' argues Mr Bill Jordan, the AEEU President. 'On the basis of that you would then be able to say that if the union was able to establish itself and its credentials amongst the workforce then they ought to be able to say "We have the right to be represented" but not to have that basic right is (as we have got in the present situation) to give management the right to say, "We have the right not to work together on anything other than on our terms".'[12]

The AEEU President linked the right to worker representation closely to his union's own successful partnership approach to workplace industrial relations. He explained to the how the system might develop without employers feeling something was being imposed on them by statute law that they resented:

> My view is that it would have to come from apolitical rights being given to individuals at work to have representation and that would be the British Parliament basing their recommendations on the experience of best practice around the world where this basic building brick of the right to representation at work is found to be well entrenched in all our main competitors. Once you have got that as a basic building brick you can then put to rights union recognition where the employers have indicated that on top of their ability to be represented they wish to be part of a union. That then flows into a number of other rights. This is Parliament giving a lead where it is thought that good industrial relations were essential to competitiveness and all the evidence is that is the case with those who are beating us in the market-place. At the core of every world-class company is the recognition that without a good partnership arrangement between the management and the workers through representation you are seriously undermining your competitive edge.

The GMB's Mr John Edmonds has argued in a similar vein. When asked bluntly by the Commons Employment Committee how a more mutually supportive industrial relations system might begin to develop between management and trade unions when management felt they had union recognition forced on them, he replied:

> If management do not accept that their employees should be represented, then I think they are in danger of under-valuing their employees and will very likely fail to get the best from their employees because very few employees will give the best of their talent and ingenuity if they do not feel that they have a voice in the important decisions of the company. Management in almost every case that I am familiar with are losing a large part of the most valuable asset they have which is the human talent of their workforce. If you look at it from the other point of view, all the indications are that if management are prepared to accept that representative arrangement then they get the commitment that they need and they get a boost. I think there is a bridge which the management have to cross and that bridge is marked 'the rights of employees' and once they cross that bridge then they find they have a much more committed and productive workforce because the workforce then believe that they have got some stake in the company and they are prepared to devote their whole ingenuity to it. There is a great deal that management have to gain by granting representation rights and recognition.[13]

The TUC would also like to see a change in the balance of the law to enable workers in Britain to exercise the right to freedom of association. It spelt out the reasons why.

> An employer has complete licence whether or not to recognise a trade union for the purposes of collective bargaining. Essentially this means that one party (the employer) can simply refuse to accept the legitimacy of the other (the trade union) even if the workforce have expressed overwhelming support for trade union representation and collective bargaining. Individuals have the right to join a trade union if they wish but they have no right to representation. There are many thousands of good employers in Britain – most of them recognise trade unions – but there are many thousands who are unscrupulous or incompetent. They are encouraged in their negative approach to trade unions by public policy. Faced with such an employer, the individual worker can call upon no countervailing power to represent his or her interests.[14]

This meant – said the TUC – that the United Kingdom was 'out of step with every other member state of the European Union. Even in those countries where there is no legal framework for worker representation (Denmark and Ireland) there is strong public policy support for the collective representation of workers' interests. This is because the logic of collective action is well understood elsewhere in the EU. An employer is by definition a collective body (unless we are considering a one person company) with a good deal of power over the lives of individual employees. The only way in which this imbalance of power can be redressed is for workers to be given rights to representation and consultation, either through trade unions or a body like a works council. To believe otherwise is to accept the fiction that employers and employees enjoy a relationship of equality.'

The Need for Worker, Not Just Trade Union, Rights

The demand for new legal rights for trade unions represents a significant departure from their traditional commitment to voluntarism and the system of legal immunities that has provided the framework for their activities in the past. But the change of trade union attitude has gone much further than this. A growing number of senior trade union leaders have reached the conclusion that they must embrace the cause of individual employment rights in the workplace and not just confine themselves to pressing the rights of workers who happen to belong to a trade union.

Mr Bill Morris, the TGWU's General Secretary, made an important speech on the need for worker, and not just trade union, rights when he spoke in February 1994 to a conference in London held by the Centre for Alternative Industrial and Technological Systems. First of all, he described the radical change that has occurred in the workplace since the 1970s when we had transformed the nature of work under the impact of the global economy. 'We are talking about a different kind of work, low paid, part-time, seasonal, casual,' said Mr Morris. 'New management techniques under the so-called banner of Human Resource Management that has changed the face of modern production.' The 'new challenge', he argued, needs the trade unions to accept 'constructive engagement' and to 'reconnect' not just with their own members but the 'entire workforce'. Mr Morris admitted that the attempts made at industrial democracy twenty years ago had failed because trade union leaders did not carry workers with them. 'We did not consult them. We did not ask them who they wanted to represent them. Whether they wanted the opportunity to choose or whether the representatives were to be imposed,' he said. 'I believe that rightly or wrongly there was a perception within society generally and our movement in particular that what we sought to do was to empower the bureaucracy rather than the democracy. Consequently when the forces of reaction gathered and sought to challenge us we had no constituency to return to, to mobilise a defence.'[15]

Mr Morris went on: 'The fact of the matter is workers on the shop floor in the '60s and '70s were not part – were never part – of that grass-roots understanding about what industrial democracy would mean to them. It was the trade union leaders, it was the bureaucracy, that was the name of the game. No real foundation was built in broad mass collective terms in the workplaces. No real clarity was given and very little conviction and almost no communication.'

In his opinion the trade unions have to 'start again by making some key value statements, the most important being "with whom and for whom"?' 'I believe passionately in 100 per cent trade unionism but I also believe passionately in working people at work,' he argued. 'It seems to me that if we are to turn workers into trade unionists then the first thing we have to do is to be seen to be speaking up for them, giving them a stake, which represents their interests.'

The TGWU General Secretary also emphasised that trade unions had also to make sure they understood 'the importance of their internal democracy'. 'You cannot argue for democracy in the workplace unless you have the mechanisms for democracy in your internal organisation,' he insisted. 'We have come to understand the power of communications. We have come to understand that public opinion does matter. And we have come to understand the impact of our decisions on others as well as the importance in investing in education and training.'

'As trade unionists we must approach the questions in a fundamentally different way. Too often we have been slow and inflexible in our approach. I say and my union says we must move away from one single prescribed model,' he went on. 'If there is one word which sums up the modern workforce that word is flexibility.' Mr Morris linked this to the debate over the creation of European Works Councils. 'We have got to get it right,' he warned. 'We have to build linkages below and around, up and down.' 'Accountability is one of the key value statements,' he said. 'We also need models which can deliver democracy for workers outside the big firms of Europe. We need to develop models which are relevant to part-time workers, temporary workers and the so-called atypical. I am talking about access and representation for all workers,' said Mr Morris. 'All workers need to be protected. We should be looking to talking about workers because trade unions must have concern for workers not just members.'

Mr Roger Lyons, the MSF's General Secretary, has also begun to reassess the vital question of legally enforceable rights for all workers. 'The lack of a legal framework for employment and trade union rights is the biggest single problem we face,' he argued at the February 1994 Centre for Alternative Industrial and Technological Systems conference. In his opinion the case for industrial democracy has to be set 'firmly within the context of the case for greater political democracy', as a 'significant obstacle' to the modernising of the country. Mr Lyons described three 'strands' in that 'wider vision'.[16]

Firstly, he stressed the need to democratise the individual employee/employer relationship. 'The pendulum has swung far too far in the employer's favour,' he argued. 'We need as the first step to restore a sense of balance and fair play at work by providing a legal framework of employment rights.' Mr Lyons believes this should include the right of the individual worker 'to speak out freely where there is fraud, corruption, improper dealing or failure of service or product without fearing for their job.' He insisted trade unions were 'not about rights for trade unions as organisations with a vested interest. What we are about is rights for people who have chosen to join a trade union and who are entitled to have that collective choice acknowledged and respected by their employer.'

'That is what union recognition is all about,' said Mr Lyons. 'That is why it is an abuse of human rights that the UK today is the only country in the European Union where individuals who have chosen to join a union have no right to ensure recognition of that decision by the employer.' But he also argued that industrial democracy be 'about nothing less than bringing the principles of democracy to the operation of every company. It is a new broom to sweep clean the dusty, dark, secretive corners of the corporate world. It also widens the appeal of our message; it is not just about the workers, important though they are. It is about the customers and the public too.'

The TUC itself wants to see a charter of employment rights to protect all people at work and not just trade unionists. This would include:

- A right to work in a healthy and safe environment in the certain knowledge that standards will be enforced.
- Stronger rights to safeguard people against unfair dismissal or unfair redundancy.
- Rights to time off work without loss of pay for education and training.
- The right to fair wages and conditions, including a national minimum wage with legal backing and stronger powers to set legal minimum standards on hours and holidays.
- Effective laws to prevent discrimination in employment on grounds of race and sex.

'These rights should apply to all workers, regardless of the size of their company, hours or contract status,' argued the TUC. But the rights envisaged are not seen as an alternative to collective bargaining. 'The law should underpin and not undermine the role of unions in supporting individuals at work. There must be a clear and effective right to be a trade union member and to take part in trade union activities without victimisation,' it added.[17]

The TUC believes 'social partnership' and new legal rights for workers and trade unions are inter-related objectives that could provide the trade unions with the opportunity to stage a comeback. 'A legal right to trade union recognition cannot be said to be inconsistent with the notion of social partnership,' it wrote to the Commons Employment Committee. 'It is only if this legal right is established that a recalcitrant employer can be made to live up to its obligations as a social partner. Good relationships between employers and trade unions are founded on the notion of 'reciprocal responsibilities'. Both sides have rights and duties. Our current framework of law recognises employers' rights and entrenches managerial prerogatives but does little to recognise that employers have duties.'[18]

Much more detailed work needs to be done by the trade unions on their proposals for legal rights in the workplace. It seems unlikely that Britain can move overnight from voluntarism to regulation over representation and recognition. Some policy-makers in the TUC favour the introduction of what they call 'rungs of representation'. These would start with the right for workers to join a trade union and the trade union's right to recruit them. Workers who joined a trade union that was not recognised by their employer for bargaining purposes should nonetheless expect to secure its representative support in individual complaints. At some point, trade union recruitment would trigger by law a right to hold a workplace ballot for recognition. It would be necessary to have a threshold for this of some percentage figure. This would not have to be 50 per cent plus one but a reasonable proportion like a quarter of the relevant workforce. At that point, the trade union would be entitled to have the right to inform employees and organise meetings for a recognition ballot. Recognition would involve a legal duty on the employer to bargain with the trade unions involved. If recognition was achieved there would then have to be legal guarantees for trade union representatives against dismissal, provision of premises, temporary release from normal duties, opportunities for further training.

In parallel with this works councils or participation bodies would be created by statute in companies above a certain size. In line with European law these would be directly elected through a workplace ballot of the whole workforce and not just trade union members. These institutions would represent the workplace in areas like consultation and communication. They would not be collective bargaining bodies. Trade unions ought to have enough self-confidence to support this development in the knowledge that workers are likely to vote for trade union candidates for workplace councils but they will have to persuade workers through argument to back the trade union. Single-channel trade union representation is not compatible with support for the introduction of universal civil rights for workers. Trade unions will have to point out that those legal rights would be of little use in practice unless workers can secure representation to enforce them with an employer.

The public debate on this crucial question has hardly begun. But if trade unions are serious about the need to move away from voluntarism, they will have to take a more positive view of the value of social regulation. In practice a fruitful way forward would be to establish agreement on a legal framework of rights for workers and trade unions which might include the introduction of legally enforceable collective contracts and the creation of separate labour courts. But in parallel it would make sense to establish the idea of a 'social dialogue' at national and local level on the lines of that now operating in Brussels. In other words, the legal route could remain as an alternative or a complement to an institutionalised voluntarism if cooperation in the workplace was not achieved. This could provide a welcome means of escape for all sides from a too rigid concentration on the use of regulation as the way forward. There is much to be said for an encouragement of flexibility here and not an emphasis on sanctions and punishments. The law might act as long-stop or at most provide a minimalist legal framework for encouraging the laggards to keep pace with everybody else in the establishment of a fair and balanced system of workplace rights and obligations.

An End of Voluntarism?

It is not clear from the current stage in the British debate over legal representation whether many trade union leaders fully realise the logic of the direction in which they are moving rapidly under the pace of events. A commitment to new worker rights and social partnerships will involve making a clean break with the so-called legal immunities tradition of British labour law whose roots lie deep in our trade union history. This is because a growing number of the larger trade unions are saying that their own collective strength alone is not enough to achieve representation and recognition from employers. Historically trade unions – with few exceptions – developed their own competences to pursue their functions free from constraints and they did not look to Parliament or the legal process for help in safeguarding the interests of their members. Of course, statute law was introduced to provide fair labour standards and it was enforced by the state in areas where trade unions found it hard to make much of an impact such as in the low-paid sweated trades, the treatment of women workers and the use of child labour. The Wages Councils (abolished by the government in 1993) and innumerable Factory Acts were created to provide at least some minimum protections to the most vulnerable workers in the labour market. But as the TUC admitted nearly thirty years ago in its written evidence to the Royal Commission on Trade Unions and Employers' Associations such moves – through the positive use of the law – were always seen by the trade unions as a 'second best alternative'.[19] Since the early 1960s, however, statute law has increasingly stepped in to establish and enforce fair workplace labour standards with the support and often with the encouragement of trade unions. But until recently there was still a noticeable reluctance by many trade unions to abandon the voluntarist tradition despite the countless occasions when it had been breached in practice by employers and government. It has taken long and painful experiences for a growing number of trade unions to come around to an acceptance that 'the abstention' and 'formal indifference' of government is no longer a credible attitude to take in a fragmented labour market of small non-union employers and vulnerable, insecure workers.

However, in the abandonment of their traditional outlook many trade unions have perhaps not yet appreciated the legal complexities that they are likely to face if they achieve the changes in the existing labour laws that they seek. As the TUC explained: 'The British industrial relations system has in the past always recognised the trade union channel as the exclusive method of employee representation. The reasons for this are clear enough. Until 1979 the state had displayed a general unwillingness to intervene in trade union – employer relationships. There was also a shared understanding that trade unions were autonomous associations completely independent of the employer and generally representative of the majority of employees.'[20]

But the TUC takes a firm, unsentimental view of that particular issue nowadays. It is realistic enough to understand that the trade unions are unlikely to secure all they really want even if a government was elected to power in Britain with a more sympathetic attitude towards them than the Conservatives. Existing employment law in the larger European Union countries does not provide an exclusive role for trade unions in workplace representation. In Germany worker representatives on the works councils are elected formally through a non-union channel even if it is predominantly trade union activists who are usually elected to serve on those bodies and strong collective bargaining arrangements remain between employer associations and trade unions at national and sectoral level. In Italy legal rights to information and consultation are guaranteed an 'organised presence in the workplace' affiliated to one of the three main national trade union confederations although in practice the workforce in an enterprise can decide to form a works council as the channel for consultation with their employer. In France those trade unions which are recognised as representative at national level have rights to nominate candidates for election as workers' representatives in a particular workplace enterprise committee. Unionisation remains weak in France but trade unions tend to dominate those enterprise committees.

The GMB's John Edmonds has accepted the need to embrace the whole concept of a European based legal framework of rights for individual workers and he does not insist there should be only single channel union representation available for workers on works councils. He admitted in a speech in Washington DC in March 1994 that this position carried a 'significant risk' for the future of the British trade unions. As he explained:

> Traditionally we have insisted that trade unions must be the sole channel for working people. The German works council system breaches that principle. All employees, whether trade union members or not, have the right to elect their representatives and even the elected representatives do not have to be in

> a union. So British unions are gambling that we can match German performance and capture most of the works council seats. If we succeed works councils would become our dream solution to the problem of declining trade union power. But if we fail, we join French trade unionists in a nightmare scenario where non-union representatives dominate the local committees and unions are marginalised. We have made the policy change with our eyes open but success is certainly not guaranteed.[21]

Of course, there are obvious risks for the trade unions in their new policy agenda of worker rights and social partnership. It provides no guarantee of future success. But many union leaders recognise they have no real alternative. Slowly but surely they are moving towards accepting that the well-being of all workers in Britain lies in the full integration of mainland European labour law based on a framework of rights and obligations into our own statutes. No doubt, in practice, the trade unions will not achieve all that they want through this cumulative development. However, enough has happened since May 1979 for them to accept it is no longer possible to return to what even at the best of times were the ambiguities and uncertainties of voluntarism.

Yet talk of 'social partnership' and a charter of legal civil rights for workers will not be sufficient to save the British trade unions from further decline. These ideas provide only some of the necessary means trade unions will need to begin a recovery. In fact, as this book has shown, many of them are responding in a positive and energetic way to the inexorable pressures of global competitiveness and technological innovation; a fragmented labour market and mass unemployment; a hostile state and an unsympathetic legal system. But in the final analysis, the question of the relevance of trade unions will be decided not by the operation of the law or the actions of government, employers or trade union officials but by the response of workers themselves. It is they who after all created trade unions in the first place. As the TUC has declared: 'Throughout the world wherever people work, a need for trade unionism has been found. Wherever trade unions have not existed, people have established them, even in tyrannical societies where the exercise of freedom of association and other basic human rights is suppressed.'[22] Trade unions are democratic institutions and they will survive and prosper only when they carry out the 'function of representation' on behalf of their members. But they also continue to serve an often overlooked social purpose. As Allan Flanders, the Oxford industrial relations academic, once explained:

> Unions and their members are interested in the effect of the rules made by collective bargaining which is to limit the authority of employers and to lessen the dependence of employees on market fluctuations and the arbitrary will of management. Stated in the simplest possible terms these rules provide protection, a shield for their members. And they protect not only their material standards of living, but equally their security, status and self-respect; in short their integrity as human beings.
>
> One can put the same point in another way. The effect of rules is to establish rights, with their corresponding obligations. The rules in collective agreements secure for employees the right to a certain rate of wages; the right not to have to work longer than a certain number of hours; the right not to be dismissed without consultation or compensation and so on. This is surely the most enduring social achievement of trade unionism; its creation of a social order in industry embodied in a code of industrial rights. This, too, is the constant service that unions offer their members; daily protection of their industrial rights.[23]

NOTES

1 House of Commons Employment Committee verbal evidence
2 TUC written evidence, p 13.
3 TUC Negotiators Handbook April 1993, p 3.
4 TUC supplementary evidence, p 3.
5 ibid, p 5.
6 Industrial Partnership, Industrial and Participation Association, November 1992.
7 GPMU written evidence, p 88.
8 TGWU written evidence, p 3.
9 BIFU written evidence, p 82.
10 TUC written evidence, p 13.
11 AEEU written evidence, pp 44–45.
12 Bill Jordan oral evidence, p 56.
13 John Edmonds oral evidence, p 56.
14 TUC written evidence, p 12.
15 Bill Morris speech to CAITS conference.
16 Roger Lyons speech to CAITS conference.
17 TUC Charter of Employment Rights, 1993.
18 TUC supplementary evidence, p 14.
19 Trade Unionism, TUC evidence to the Donovan Commission 1966, p 31.
20 TUC written evidence, p 15.
21 John Edmonds speech in Washington DC, April 1994.
22 TUC written evidence, p 1.
23 A Flanders, *What Are Trade Unions For? Management and Unions*, Faber and Faber 1970, p 41–42.

CONCLUSION

The Trade Unions Have a Future

The future of Britain's trade unions looks more promising in an age of rapid economic and industrial change than many people realise. The conventional view suggests they are locked into a spiral of irreversible decline. Since 1979 the proportion of workers belonging to unions has fallen to around a third from well over half and now only around 48 per cent of workers are covered by collective bargaining agreements. As the TUC's General Secretary John Monks has argued: 'The key question we have to face is whether the decline of trade union membership, organisation and collective bargaining is long-term and irreversible or is a cyclical phenomenon linked to short-term political and economic factors or somewhere between the two.'[1] Despite the formidable problems they must grapple with over the coming years, it is not inevitable that the trade unions face further contraction in their power and influence. They still have the opportunity to renew themselves. They do not have to become the despairing victims of impersonal and hostile pressures over which they can exercise no control. Of course, if they simply sit back, do nothing and play a waiting game in the hope that better times will come in the shape of a majority Labour government, the trade unions can expect to continue declining. It is very much up to them what they do. The trade unions can adapt to meet the challenges posed by global competitive pressures in industry, the structural change in the labour market and the technological innovations that are rapidly transforming the character of the workplace. It would be absurd to underplay the accumulation of legal regulations that have increasingly restricted trade union freedoms in Britain since the Conservatives were elected to government in May 1979. The country's trade unions are now more subjected to the detailed intrusions of the law in their internal affairs than any others in the western industrialised world. The political climate has quite obviously become hostile to the very existence of collective action and organisation in the labour market. The persistence of high unemployment has weakened the security and bargaining strength of many workers and trade unions and this cannot be ignored in any assessment of their future prospects either. The TUC's influence as an Estate of the Realm has clearly diminished since May 1979. The abandonment by both the Thatcher and Major governments of the post-war domestic settlement based on a broad social consensus has also helped to marginalise the trade unions.

It is true most employers have not used the panoply of legal regulations provided for them by government in their dealings with trade unions and their employees but those laws remain in place on the statute book. There can be no doubting the harsher climate within which Britain's trade unions have had to operate throughout the 1980s and in the early 1990s.

Despite the pessimism, however, the trade unions still have a vital and necessary part to play in the achievement of prosperity and social justice. One of the underestimated strengths of Britain's trade unions has been their lack of rigidity and openness to new ideas. Historically they have avoided commitment to any ideology of industrial relations, taking a highly pragmatic view of their strategic position. The powers they were supposed to wield in the so-called days of their industrial and political dominance (roughly from the 1940s to the end of the 1970s) were always more illusory and less substantial than their many enemies liked to suggest. At no time did the trade unions ever establish or enjoy an unquestioned role in the operation of the labour market. Their limited authority stemmed mainly from what organisational collective strength they were able to achieve in the workplace over wage bargaining and job regulation during what turned out to be a limited period of 'full' employment. At no time did that power derive from any agreed legal framework of positive rights for either trade unions or employees. The instinctive desire to keep the law as well as the state at arms-length from their activities has always run deep through the British trade unions who, for understandable historical reasons, were suspicious of institutional regulation and entanglements with governments and the courts. As the CBI has argued:

> The institutions of industrial relations – both trade unions and employer bodies – developed first in the United Kingdom, because of our pre-eminence in the industrial revolution. There has never been a system of union rights in Britain; no right to organise, no right to strike, no right to representation and so on. It is perhaps a reflection of a society in which there is no written constitution. Whatever the reason, the fact is that unions operate by virtue of a series of immunities. The law gives unions and their members certain immunities from prosecution where they would otherwise be caught by the law of conspiracy or contract. In keeping with that approach, collective agreements are non-binding, and neither employers nor unions have shown any wish to change these broadly voluntary arrangements. Unlike their opposite numbers in some other states with different legal and constitutional traditions; the CBI and the TUC have never been in a position to commit and deliver their members to agreements; their members have no apparent wish to see them extend their reach beyond lobbying and advice.[2]

But voluntarism – that honourable and unique tradition – shaped mainly by the pattern of Britain's industrial structure, its always fragmented labour market and the desire to avoid common law threats to trade union freedoms, has reached the end of its useful life. It can no longer provide the trade unions with any obvious means for either their renewal or future legal protection. Fortunately a growing number of trade union leaders have begun to recognise that this is so, which is why so many of them now support the idea of introducing a new legal framework for industrial relations with the legal right for workers to representation and the legal right for trade unions to secure recognition from employers for collective bargaining purposes.

But if voluntarism can no longer ensure the necessary security Britain's trade unions need to survive and prosper, nor is there much hope for a sustained trade union revival through a single-minded concentration on the servicing of workers as if they were merely passive card-holders and regarded belonging to a trade union as an alternative attraction in the mass consumer market to membership of American Express or the Automobile Association. So-called business unionism with its commitment to the gratification of acquisitive instincts has little future for most trade unions. But this does not mean unions can ignore or spurn their servicing function. The trade unions have always sought to service and protect their members through forms of mutual insurance but this cannot be turned into an all-embracing philosophy of trade unionism. A delicate balance always has to be struck between the collective and the individual but the two approaches remain crucially interdependent and by concentrating too much on one at the expense of the other the trade unions would endanger their basic purpose which is to promote and safeguard the interests of their members in the workplace as representative and collective associations free from the control and demands of either the state or employers.

However, it is doubtful whether there is much alternative life to be found in any attempt to restore the kind of industrial relations system that existed before 1979 in Britain and in some countries in mainland Europe. Efforts to create social contract-style national agreements in the corporatist style of the 1970s are of little significance for today's trade unions and their members. The world has moved on and it is simply not possible to bring back the particular historical conditions that enabled trade unions and governments to work together for a limited time in the partial and detailed management of the British economy. It was perhaps a strategic mistake for the state to try and make the trade unions shoulder the burden of wider responsibilities, most notably those involved in trying to maintain national wage restraint through incomes policies over their own members in the so-called public interest when they were neither organisationally nor philosophically equipped to do so. Trade unions cannot be turned, even temporarily, into the willing agents of the state (however benign) and nor should they be expected to play the role of policemen in the workplace, forcing their members to behave in ways that they might question were contrary to their own interests. Unless the trade unions continue to articulate the views and the emotions of the workers they represent in their relations with employers and governments, they will have lost sight of the fundamental reasons for why they exist. They must safeguard at all times not only their own independence and their autonomy but also their internal democratic structures. At no time can they afford to grow out of touch with the views of their own members. In fact, in recent years there have been encouraging internal democratic reforms (stimulated it must be said in some cases by the 1984 Trade Union Act) which have ensured union leaders have become more sensitive and directly accountable to their members, through the introduction of postal ballots for their own elections and before the calling of strikes and other forms of industrial disruption. Further legislation as well as technological improvements have improved the financial efficiency and sheer professionalism of trade union organisation. As a result, the members and the activists have grown much closer together. 'Returning the unions to their members' may have been a misleading populist slogan used by ministers to justify their 1984 legislation but in practice that measure has done much to encourage innovation in organisations that were not all paragons of virtue in the way they used to conduct their own affairs.

But this does not mean trade unions as representative institutions have no role to play at all outside the workplace. They will also need to develop their role as 'social partners', influencing the public policy-makers wherever they are to be found -not just within the limits of the nation state but in the European Union, in the transnational companies and international organisations such as GATT/IWTO, the OECD and the ILO. Britain's trade unions should also continue to try to play an influential part developing macro-economic policy. This can be seen, for example, in their growing belief that a national statutory minimum wage is necessary to protect low paid workers from gross exploitation. Their ideas on how to achieve 'full' employment, to promote higher economic growth, to increase public expenditure without imposing penal taxation rates on workers and their families on average incomes, to encourage public sector infrastructure investments, and to call for more vocational education and training are all important in the wider public policy debate.

The trade unions must also remain crucial institutions in pressing urgently for a radical agenda of social reform. They believe in fairness not only in the workplace but also in society as a whole. They want to see both the creation as well as the redistribution of income and wealth in a more equitable social market economy. Through the forging of wider alliances with other lobbyists and pressure groups they can still provide a powerful collective voice for millions of working people and their families.

There is also welcome evidence that trade unions are much

more sensitive than they used to be to the needs and the feelings of the rest of society. They are now concerned with the wider interests of the citizen. This can be seen in the development of more consumer oriented strategies by the public service unions. The encouragement of a so-called customer culture is of direct relevance to trade union members and everybody else. In backing campaigns against hospital closures, for example, the public service trade unions have shown in recent years they can mobilise sympathetic public opinion on their side. Increasingly trade unions need to network with other organisations at the local level on issues of community concern such as public transport, infrastructure developments, environmental pollution and the provision of schools and hospitals. The trade unions cannot afford to stand aloof from such wider campaigning. They need to show they are not only relevant but vital as associations for change in the locality.

Some inspiration for our trade unions ought to come from the example of the American union local with its multiplicity of activities. Traditionally too much trade union work at branch or district level has been boring, bureaucratic and limited to a narrow range of political and workplace issues. What needs to be done is to revitalise trade unionism in the wider community. Given their limited finances trade unions ought to forge alliances with one another and pool their resources. Instead of going to the Citizens Advice Bureaux workers in need should be able to visit a local trade union centre that can deal with their personal troubles without needing to have a fully paid-up union card. Here inter-union competition should be replaced by trade union solidarity. Workers and their families ought to be able to look to trade unions for help in dealing with their particular demands, for example, with their unemployment problems, training needs and the complexities of the social benefit system. Through a wider bargaining agenda trade unions can also integrate the needs of the workplace with those of the community. In doing so, they might hope to stimulate greater worker interest in their activities and rekindle trade union activism. The 1994 trade union check-off campaign has done much to re-establish lost or decayed links between members, activists and full-time officials. It has helped to stimulate local trade union activity. This newly discovered enthusiasm should not be dissipated but harnessed in a wide range of trade union activities. There are clear lessons to be learned from the experience of mainland European trade unions like those in Sweden and Denmark who have succeeded – at least more than in Britain – to breathe fresh life into local activism.

The trade unions in this country have reached an important crossroads in their history. They need to come off the backfoot and take the initiative. They must grasp the logic of evolving European Union employment law and campaign for its eventual integration into an emerging framework of positive legal rights and obligations based ultimately on the accepted conventions and fair standards of workplace behaviour laid down by the International Labour Organisation. Of course, these are early days. Current legal developments inside the EU are by no means clear cut and much uncertainty still remains. But enough has happened in the past few years to suggest that many of the Social Affairs Directives, emanating from the European Commission in Brussels and perhaps even more importantly their enforcement through the European Court of Justice will come as a welcome relief for the trade unions as they help to restrict the scope of the British government's 'flexible' labour market strategy.

Recourse to the use of more sympathetic pro-worker European employment law by the trade unions will not, however, always prove to be successful. They can expect to suffer setbacks and frustrations in the years ahead. The pace of the EU's economic and social convergence could also prove to be much slower and uneven than the trade unions want to see. But few doubts remain any longer that the EU's regulatory route does provide the trade unions in Britain and elsewhere with the minimum but necessary means to protect and renew their activities.

Of course, much of this promising development will depend on the future behaviour of the employers towards labour questions. The CBI has taken in public a wholly negative attitude to much of the EU's social affairs agenda. In the name of corporate profitability and the containment of unit labour costs, it has opposed most of the EU directives that have begun to establish at least a minimum framework of social regulation for the integrated European market. However, eventually a compromise seems likely to emerge between the demands of European employers for freedom from restrictions to achieve global competitiveness and those of trade unions wanting to re-establish workplace solidarity. The outcome will undoubtedly turn out to be a delicate and complex balance of advantage between capital and labour. However, the future tilt in that balance could be more to the liking of the British trade unions than the country's employers whose commitment to the deregulated labour market model looks much firmer than that of their European mainland counterparts who have a sense of social and ethical responsibility for the wellbeing of their employees.

Confidence that European employment law will ride to the rescue of besieged British trade unions must, however, remain highly qualified. The law alone cannot solve their problems for them. What it may do is provide trade unions with invaluable means which if used effectively can help to promote their interests. The law at best can only be a complement or a back-up not a substitute for the evolution of collective bargaining and individual worker representation. But the very existence on the statute book of fairer laws for workers and trade unions can produce a more conciliatory atmosphere in industrial relations and stimulate a new social consensus that will encourage employers and trade unions to reach agreement on workplace issues without the need to bring in the law.

But the British trade unions cannot simply wait stoically for the eventual arrival of comprehensive European labour law to remove what obstacles they believe block the way to the achievement of a more effective future. What we need is a greater energetic and professional response by the trade unions to their current predicaments. Some British trade unions – notably the MSF, the GMB and the TGWU – have come to look with some success for idealistic inspiration across the Atlantic to the American labour movement. This may, at first sight, seem rather surprising. After all, trade unionists in the United States constitute no more than around 15 per cent of the country's entire labour force, and around 12 per cent in the private corporate sector. But what American trade unions have demonstrated in recent years is that they can make some difference through the aggressive use of modern and sophisticated techniques of persuasion and communication in recruiting workers into trade unions (for example, among janitors of Los Angeles and Harvard University's clerical and technical staff) and perhaps even more importantly, retaining them as long-term members. Corporate campaigning by trade unions in recruitment or industrial conflicts may remain something of a rarity in Britain but it also holds out enormous potential for the future. Indeed, the apparent success of such tactics in the 1993 dispute between the United Mine Workers of America and Peabody Coal Co., part of Lord Hanson's group of companies, suggests this approach can succeed. With the TUC's full backing, the American labour leaders crossed the Atlantic to lobby in London at an extraordinary shareholders meeting of the Hanson company over the dispute. The eventual settlement was to the satisfaction of the United Mineworkers.

A more open style of trade union leadership might also help to stimulate new forms of organising. But this means our trade unions will have to redirect more of their admittedly limited financial resources into becoming much more professional, campaigning organisations. This does not mean they need to create top-heavy bureaucratic structures that insulate them from the needs and demands of their rank and file. But it will require the trade unions to focus more than they have been doing on the provision of a wider range of services of mutual interest to employees in the workplaces like the establishment of wider training facilities for their members, the creation of occupational pensions for all, the spread of employee share ownership schemes and a widening of the range of the collective bargaining agenda. Unions will have to tailor their services in a more focused way to satisfy a diversity of membership workplace needs.

They will also have to become much more concerned with the professional demands of their members and of workers in general. Here, the example of the Royal College of Nursing is of particular relevance. By making itself useful not just as a bargaining body but as an association with an all-embracing interest in the promotion of nursing as a vocation, the RCN has seen its membership rise by leaps and bounds during the 1980s. More traditional and smaller trade unions like ASLEF the train drivers union and the Fire Brigades Union (FBU) as well as medium-sized unions such as the National Communications Union (NCU) have also shown in recent years that it is possible to establish a highly effective membership identity through a blend of the distinctive functions of collective bargaining and professional servicing. So has the First Division Association, the senior civil servants' union, which looks after the well-being of the Whitehall mandarins and also wants to see a code of ethical standards for them as protection against the dangers of a party politicised bureaucracy in a one party state. UNISON is also developing similar approaches while the GMB has been making impressive moves in the same direction. That union wants to develop the concept of trade union membership for life, what would be a portable connection with the trade union that runs throughout an individual's working life whether in or out of employment. Through an increasing range of services open to all working people the trade union would be able to establish a crucial role in the labour market. In a future world of high labour mobility and many new forms of working practice such a flexible approach would energise trade unions and make them much more relevant both inside and outside the workplace to the demands of working people. Technological progress has enabled trade unions to keep a close link with their members through computerised information. It is possible for them to make direct connection with them at home through the mail and not just through a bulletin board in the workplace. This opens up enormous and exciting possibilities for trade unions, making it much easier for them to provide more focused services to meet the particular needs of different kinds of trade union member. Trade unions should be able to offer a range of subscription rates depending on what variety of services individual trade union members require. None of this should downgrade the continuing importance of trade unions as collective bargainers or representative institutions in the workplace. But it does provide a potential area for experimentation in new forms of reviving trade union organisational energies.

Indeed, we need more flexible trade unions in response to the challenge of a flexible labour market. Structural adaptation is required to meet the urgent needs of workers who can no longer count on a job for life with the same employer.

Trade unionism in Britain has been rooted in the workplace. Its increasingly decentralised structure has worked through a loose alliance between local lay activists and full-time officials. But this is much less common than it used to be. As a result, trade unions must find new ways of ensuring they retain close contact with those of their members who change jobs or become redundant. In the new unstable labour market, trade unions must try and develop a wider range of services which will appeal to millions of workers who lack any firm connection with a specific workplace. In the Nordic countries where trade unions remain popular and strong, they perform vital social functions as administrators in the running of the welfare state. This does not look like a realistic option in Britain even if there was a change of government. But it does suggest where there could be some scope for reform. Why cannot unions encourage their members, for instance, to increase the value of their labour by training them in new skills? The portable pension for workers is becoming more relevant. Why should unions – in partnership with financial institutions like the Unity Trust Bank – not establish occupational pension schemes for their members? Why should they not encourage profit sharing and employee share ownership (ESOPs) for their members as part of the development of lifetime financial portfolios for workers? Unions could also – through their own local labour market intelligence networks – start to operate as alternative employment agencies for their members, perhaps through an enhancement of the unemployed worker centres.

However, these developments – using European employment law – emulating American union corporate campaigning styles and becoming both more effective professional bodies and servicing agencies as well as collective bargainers seem unlikely by themselves to reverse the current trend of trade union decline. While the character of Britain's industrial relations in the second half of the 1990s may become more derivative, it would be wrong to suggest the trade unions can or should merely copy the best practices of others in the expectation that this will be enough. As John Monks has argued: 'What seems to be missing is the unique British contribution to the industrial relations of this decade. There is a sense in which we are the recipients of other people's good ideas and often seek to incorporate them but are often not developing our own industrial relations practices in their own right and with their own distinctiveness.'[4]

In fact, the trade unions need to look for guidance and inspiration to their own rich historical traditions. In the nineteenth century they were much more than voluntary institutions, involved in different forms of collective bargaining with employers over pay and employment conditions and ensuring job security for those they represented. Nor were they just friendly societies who protected their members from the cruel vicissitudes of life with a range of insurance benefits. They were also important organisational expressions of worker citizenship, who shared a common concern for the affirmation of human rights. Their trade union roots lay in the radical mythology of the 'free born Englishman', with the self-reliance, probity and independence to be found among the more articulate artisans of pre-industrial Britain. The early trade unions were feared by many employers and the state not just because they were seen as threats to the development of the laissez-faire market economy and absolute property rights but because they articulated democratic principles which enjoyed a universal appeal and challenged the existing political and social order. Trade unions were concerned with the dignity and the self-respect of human beings as workers. Through mutual protection they sought to promote the ideals as well as the interests of those they represented. In their call for the extension of the parliamentary franchise, at least to all working men, the trade unions were determined to exercise a political influence on public life. In doing so they also underlined their commitment to the concept of the worker as a citizen. Robert Applegarth, Secretary of the Amalgamated Society of Carpenters and Joiners, explained it well when he wrote: We do not 'wish to turn our trades societies into political organisations, to divert them from their social objects; but we must not forget that we are citizens, and as such have citizen's rights. Recollect also, that by obtaining these rights we shall be able more effectually to secure our legitimate demands as unionists.'[5]

What Britain's trade unions need to do is look to that important but neglected tradition of free-thinking libertarianism that predates the birth of the Labour Party by more than a hundred years. This is not just a self-conscious appeal to past virtues. It is of direct contemporary relevance. The trade unions should reassert themselves by bringing workplace civil rights to the forefront of their public policy agenda for continued survival and future advance. For too long it has been the Conservatives and the economic neo-liberals who have laid down the narrow parameters of the industrial relations debate in Britain by falsely treating trade unions as the enemies of economic freedom. The time has come to refocus the public debate about the future of the trade unions away 'from neo-classical economic analysis back to its original home of democratic political theory which focuses on voice as a necessary element in the operation of representative democratic processes.'[6]

Britain's trade unions could gain some useful insights from looking at the contemporary debate on employee representation which is going on in the United States, stimulated by President Bill Clinton's labour secretary Mr Robert Reich and the work of the Dunlop Commission on the future of labour-management relations. The promotion of democratic workplace rights needs to take many different forms. But what should be made quite clear at all times is that trade unions are champions of these fundamental rights not merely for the benefit of their own members but all workers whether they are organised in trade unions or not. This may be a difficult argument for some trade union leaders to accept but there can be no future in merely seeking to further exclusive trade union rights for trade unionists. The fact is that trade unions would have nothing to fear from advocating legal workplace rights for all workers. They ought to have the self-confidence to realise that employees in such a situation would turn to them as the only credible representative institutions who would enable their rights to be enforced effectively in the workplace.

The trade unions must also speak out for the return of the politics of economic fairness in what has become an increasingly insecure and socially polarised labour market where fear of losing one's job is widespread and the gap between the level of workers' earnings has grown dramatically. Britain's changing workplace under the pressures of global competition and technological change has undermined older notions of solidarity and stability. In today's fragmented labour market millions of people at work in the service sector as much as in manufacturing, from the management to clerical and manual grades feel in need of forms of protection and the representative strength that trade unions can provide for them. Indeed, trade unions as social institutions have become invaluable to employers as well as workers because they can help to provide the stability enterprises need as they carry through necessary internal change. It is no coincidence in Britain or the United States that many of the most innovative companies are those which recognise and bargain with trade unions. For what modern corporations need from their employees is commitment as well as flexibility at work. They want multi-skilled adaptable workers but they also want the freedom to hire and fire them at will. They want to treat their employees as both human assets and factors of production. Trade unions offer a way out of this apparent contradiction. They can provide workers with a collective voice in the workplace but they also ensure the essential means that companies can use to achieve an effective trade-off between worker security and worker flexibility. Here, in embryo, are the makings of a democratic bargain or social pact that can reconcile the demands of innovative employers with the workplace rights of their employees. A shrewd mixture of Human Resource Management theory and liberal political thought could help in the revival of British trade unionism. The main problem stems from the undoubted fact that too few companies recognise that this is so and continue to pursue arbitrary managerial strategies that seem to be more concerned with the assertion of power for its own sake over their employees rather than the maximising of corporate performance through consensus. However, a growing number of far-sighted collective agreements have been negotiated in recent years in both the private and public sectors that demonstrate the enormous value of trade unionism to the success of the enterprise in meeting the remorseless challenges posed to it by global competition in the open market.

It is no exaggeration to suggest Britain is going through a workplace revolution which involves a decisive transformation of its industrial relations system. The once familiar British labour problems of job demarcation, skills exclusiveness, closed shops and restrictions on training have disappeared from much of industry. Unofficial strikes are all but a memory of a bygone age. Most trade unions have responded positively to the challenges imposed upon them by structural change and technological innovation. The spread of single-table collective bargaining, the long overdue harmonisation of pay and benefits between blue and white-collar workers, the trade-off between Human Resource Management techniques and comprehensive fringe benefits have all been helped by the change in basic trade union attitudes. The fascinating evidence from many large private companies to the Commons Employment Committee suggests collective bargaining remains a highly effective and flexible way of organising workers under modern conditions. What needs to be done now is to see a growing number of trade unions – perhaps in a strategic alliance with more enlightened employers – encouraging the spread of the new employment practices into those companies that believe they do not need an organised workforce in order to succeed. The evidence that a genuine and practical form of social partnership between employers, trade unions and employees can work in Britain is impressive. But the move away from the traditional system of adversarial industrial relations has not so far been overwhelming. Too many companies still pay lip service to working in harmony with trade unions and employees but in practice prefer to act unilaterally under the pressures imposed upon them by change.

There remains another key role the trade unions need to accept more positively in the future. They must reassert themselves as forces for social justice, demanding more security and fairness in the workplace by articulating the fears and aspirations of their members. Trade unions must rediscover their lost sense of ethical purpose. 'Their great theme of the cry for justice' needs to be heard once more in today's deregulated and inequitable labour market.[7]

But this will also depend on the energy and idealism generated by their full-time officials and lay activists. After the long years of retreat it may be difficult for many trade unions to believe they can launch an effective, coordinated counter-offensive in the growing non-unionised part of the workforce. But they have no real choice open to them if they want to survive in reasonable shape outside the public sector of the labour market into the next century.

Fortunately a growing abundance of evidence exists to suggest many trade unions recognise what needs to be done. A new generation of younger full-time union officials is emerging with the vision and the intelligence to map out the difficult way ahead. It is vital they should succeed. It is not only because trade unions as representative institutions of working people – independent of state control or employer influence – remain a vital part of any democratic society. It is also because such bodies are needed in Britain more than at any time since the last century. The harsh and insecure conditions of our fragmented and deregulated labour market suggests the restoration of the power of collective but voluntary organisation is long overdue. In a very real sense, the trade unions need to go back to first principles in their appeal to workers and employers.

But in doing so, they also need as a matter of urgency

to convince young workers – known to many union officials as Mrs Thatcher's children – coming onto the labour market who have little knowledge or experience of organised labour that trade unions are neither obsolete nor irrelevant, but on the contrary, provide the necessary organisational strength that all workers still need to counter the power of capital.

The American labour movement slogan: 'Solidarity forever: For the union makes us strong' has not lost its meaning. It needs, however, to be translated into a modern idiomatic language that resonates with the new workforce in the new workplaces. This will require imagination and effort and it will never be easy. But there is no reason to abandon hope. Indeed, if British society is to see a renewal of its democratic values and the growth of new forms of democratic expression, the trade unions must be a part of that development. Their functions may have to be modified under the pressure of events but their historical mission is far from over. In many important ways it has only just begun. Indeed, trade unions can become part of a wider coalition of associations dedicated to the revival of an ethically based civic culture. In a system of workplace rights based on the principles of democratic political thought, they can integrate once again into a wider civil community. The concept of the citizen worker is no longer a figment of the romantic imagination but a crucial force in a revival of the trade unions, as voluntary institutions dedicated to the protection and promotion of democratic rights for all working people in Britain.

In the past trade unions were resilient because they performed a variety of functions in response to a range of different needs. The same is true today. They are primarily collective bargainers. But they also act as mutual insurance societies. They are democratic political institutions concerned with social justice and public policy-makers seeking to influence governments and employers. They can be job regulators. They are now allies of management in the negotiation of workplace change.

It has become fashionable in recent years to suggest trade unions have become obsolete in the deregulated flexible labour market because they are essentially collectivist bodies and in the new workplace individualism is the dominant force. But this is a profound mistake.

In fact, it is a false dichotomy which is sometimes posed between collectivism and individualism. The two concepts are indeed interdependent in the new workplace where consensus is much more vital than competition in the achievement of corporate success.

But this debate in an important sense misses the main point. The future of the trade unions will be shaped by a balanced or twin track strategy. On the one hand there is the continuing need for strong trade union organisation and recognition in the traditional sense and on the other hand the need for a statutory framework of representation, in particular to support the millions of workers who would otherwise enjoy no representational rights at all in our labour market. In many sectors these two tracks will merge, as trade unions succeed in winning the confidence and support of employees that this is the way that they can best be represented.

Most of the time our trade unions have had to function in adverse circumstances. They rose to maturity in response to a polarised and deregulated labour market very much like that which exists in Britain in the 1990s. Today they should draw comfort both from their past and from the current opportunities that are opening up for them. Britain's trade unions remain adaptable and pragmatic enough to shape the agenda and grow once more into the next century.

NOTES

1 J Monks, A Trade Union View of WIRS 3, British Journal of Industrial Relations Vol 31 No 2, June 1993, p 228.
2 CBI written evidence, p 3.
3 CBI, ibid, p 2.
4 J Monks, Human Resource Management Journal Vol 3 No 3, Autumn 1992, p 37.
5 H Pelling, *The History of British Trade Unionism*, Penguin 1987 edition, p 51.
6 P A Greenfield and R J Pleasance, essay in Employee Representation: Alternatives and Future Directions, Industrial Relations Research Association 1993, p 173.
7 A Flanders, *Management and Trade Unions*, Allen and Unwin 1970, p 67.

INDEX